THE
PIRATE
DICTIONARY

Terry Breverton

PELICAN PUBLISHING COMPANY
Gretna 2006

First printing, July 2004
Second printing, November 2005
Third printing, June 2006

ISBN-13: 978-1-58980-243-8

Printed in Canada

Published by Pelican Publishing Company, Inc.
1000 Burmaster Street, Gretna, Louisiana 70053

THE PIRATE DICTIONARY

We hear the terms, *steer clear of*, *hit the deck*, *don't rock the boat*, *to harbour a grudge* and the like, and give little thought to their nautical origin. This alphabetical 'handbook' is written to be entertaining as well as informative, to give a flavour of these interesting times from the 15th to the 18th centuries, when pirates controlled many sea lanes.

Just in the A-B section following, the reader will find the origin of country *'bumpkin'*, a *'brace of shakes'*, *'born with a silver spoon'*, *'booby prize'*, *'to take on board'*, *'above board'*, *'bombed'* (in the sense of being drunk), the *'blues'*, *'blind-side'*, *'blind drunk'*, *'the pot calling the kettle black'*, *'reach the bitter end'*, *'wasters'* (in the sense of people being useless), *'ahoy'*, *'all at sea'*, *'to keep aloof'*, *'piss-artist'*, *'taken aback'*, *'barbecue"* and *'bamboozle'*. Other colourful terms which have passed out of common usage, such a *'bring one's arse to anchor'* (sit down), *'belly timber'* (food) and *'bog orange'* (potato) are also included, as well as important pirate haunts and technical terms.

ABACK
When sails face into a head-on wind, the ship stops going forward. Today's phrase **'taken aback'** comes from this nautical term, when one struggles to make progress and goes backwards. Many nautical terms begin with '*a*' such *as abaft, aboard, about, abreast, adrift, afloat, afore, aground, ahead, ahoy, ahull, alee, aloft, aloof, amain, amidships, apeek, ashore, astern, athwart, atrip, avast,* and *aweigh.*

ABAFT, AFT
From a situation in the forepart of the ship, this refers to the stern, e.g. *'the mast hangs abaft'* means that the mast points towards the stern.

ABOVE A MARK
To pass above a mark it to pass on its windward or weather side; to pass below a mark is to pass on its lee, or leeward, or downwind side.

ABOVE BOARD
One origin of this phrase is that pirates hid **'below board'** if they were sneaking up on an unsuspecting merchantman. Pirate ships had up to 12 times the crew of an equivalent trading ship. If all the crew were above board, all was fair and square.

ACT OF GRACE, or ACT OF PARDON
A general amnesty given to a pirate who promised to reform his ways. The November 1698 proclamation offered a free pardon to all pirates operating east of the Cape of Good Hope, except for Captain Kidd. However, nine of his crew that surrendered under this Act of Grace were hung with him, in Execution Dock, off

Wapping Old Stairs. Captain John Bowen and his crew would not surrender because they did not trust the authorities.

ACT FOR THE MORE EFFECTUAL SUPPRESSION OF PIRACY 1700
An English law, which allowed severe punishment without recourse to a jury. If captured upon the ocean, pirates could be immediately hung at the yardarm, as no legal judgment can be made on a sea voyage. Pirates who attacked a ship belonging to the British Empire could be executed without any legal procedures or access to a man of religion to repent their sins.

ADAM'S WILL
The nickname given to the Treaty of Tordesillas, when Pope Alexander VI confirmed Spanish 'ownership' of the New World.

ADMIRAL
Highest ranking naval officer, in charge of a squadron or fleet at sea. The buccaneer Henry Morgan was Jamaica's 'admiral' in charge of dozens of privateering vessels.

ADVANCE NOTE
This piece of paper, worth a month's pay, was given to a sailor when he signed on for a voyage, and could be cashed by his wife or relatives after his ship had sailed. However, many sailors would cash it in advance, usually at a very poor rate with a ship's chandler or the like, to spend on women and alcohol.

ADRIFT
The modern word *'drifter'* comes from this nautical term. A ship is adrift when she has no mooring and her direction is at the mercy of the tides, winds and currents, drifting along.

AFT
The shortening of *'afterward'*, the rear of the vessel.

AHOY
This naval term seems, to this author, to stem from the *'hoy'*, a common 16th century coastal vessel (q.v.), although no dictionary attributes this derivation. One index states that 'ahoy' was a Viking battle cry, however. However, according to Smith in 1691, a ship was hailed thus *'Hoa the ship?'* or just *Hoa!*, asking where it was bound. The answer was *Hoa!*

ALBATROSS
It was unlucky to kill one, as they were supposed to carry the souls of dead sailors. Coleridge's *'The Rime of the Ancient Mariner'* was inspired by the shooting of a black albatross, described in Captain Shelvocke's *'A Voyage Round the World.'* Nowadays, anything cumbersome, that makes life very difficult for one, *'hangs round your neck like an albatross'*.

ALCATRICE
The offspring of an African slave and a native Indian.

ALL AT SEA
The Viking term was 'all at sea' when they could not see land. If absolutely unsure of their whereabouts, they released a raven (which came to be their emblem), which soared into the sky until it could see land. The Vikings then followed its direction. See 'straight as the crow flies'.

ALL HANDS HOAY
An order for 'all hands on deck'.

ALL IN A DAY'S WORK
In 'The Universal Dictionary of the Marine' by William Falconer, published in 1789, we read that a 'day's work' was defined as 'the reckoning or account of the ship's course during the 24-hour period between noon and noon.'

ALL WASHED UP
A nautical term for shipwrecked, used today referring to someone with no hope.

ALMIRANTA
The ship which carried the Almirante, the second-in-command of a Spanish fleet. They were documented as carrying 40 cannon in 1677.

ALPHABET
The following sea shanty is called 'The Sailor's Alphabet':
A is the anchor that holds a brave ship,
B is the bowsprit that often does dip,
C is the capstan on which we do wind, and
D is the davits on which the jolly boat hangs.
Chorus:
O hi derry, hey derry, ho derry dwon,
Give sailors their grog and there's nothing goes wrong,
So merry, so merry, so merry are we,
No matter who's laughing at sailors at sea.
E is the ensign, the red, white and blue,
F is the fo'c'sle, holds the ship's crew,
G is the gangway on which the mate takes his stand,
H is the hawser that seldom does strand.
Chorus
I is the irons where the stuns'l boom sits,
J is the jib-boom that often does dip,
K are the keelsons of which you've told, and
L and the lanyards that always will hold.
Chorus

M *is the main mast, so stout and so strong,*
N *is the north point that never points wrong,*
O *and the orders of which we must be 'ware,*
P *are the pumps that cause sailors to swear.*
Chorus
Q *is the quadrant, the sun for to take,*
R *is the riggin' that always does shake,*
S *is the starboard side of our bold ship, and*
T *are the topmasts that often do split.*
Chorus
U *is the ugliest old Captain of all,*
V *are the vapours that come with the squall,*
W *is the windlass on which we do wind, and*
X, Y *and* Z, *well, I can't put in rhyme!*
Chorus

ALOOF

On a lee shore, the order *'keep aloof'* meant to keep the ship's head nearer to the wind to prevent the vessel being driven to the shore. Hence the modern expression to *'keep aloof'*, means to *'keep away from'*, or *'keep your distance'*. Sir Henry Mainwaring wrote *'If the ship go by a wind, or quarter winds, they say aloof, or keep your loof, or fall not off, wear no more, keep to her, touch the wind, have a care of the lee-latch; all these do imply the same in manner, and are to bid him at the helm to keep her near to the wind.'* (quoted in John Harland, *'Seamanship in the Age of Sail'*, 1984). The term comes from the Dutch *'loef'* meaning windward.

AMAIN!

The word shouted by a Man-of-War to its enemy, asking it to yield. It comes from *'Strike amain!'* i.e. to lower the Main Topsails and make escape impossible.

ANCHOR, TO BRING ONE'S ARSE TO AN

To sit down

ANGRIA DYNASTY

A Black African Muslim family, powerful Indian pirate kings from c.1704, which in the 1720's repelled three British fleets, until finally defeated in 1756.

ANTILLES

The larger Antilles islands in the Caribbean, Cuba, Hispaniola, Porto Rico and Jamaica were those first taken by the Spanish from before 1500. From there, they moved on to Mexico and the rest of South America. This left the chain of *'Lesser Antilles'*, that is the Leeward and Windward Isles, open to other European powers to colonise. The Dutch were trading in the West Indies from 1542, and had a toehold in mainland Guiana by 1580. Between 1609 and 1619, various French English and Dutch missions moved onto islands in between the mouth of the Orinoco River and that of the Amazon. The English settled in St Kitts from 1623, and Barbados in 1624-25. In 1628, St Kitts settlers moved on to Nevis and Barbuda, then in 1632 to Antigua and Montserrat. In 1625 the Dutch and English jointly took possession of Santa Cruz. The French took Guadeloupe, Martinique and other Windward Islands from 1635 onwards. Between 1632 and 1634 the Dutch established trading stations on St Eustatius, Tobago and Curacao.

ANY PORT IN A STORM
A term used for a ship needing refuge from the elements, first recorded my Captain Frederick Marryat in 1836 in 'The Pirate'.

APOSTLES
17th century term for the charges carried in a bandolier, slung across a pirate's chest when operating on land, because there were usually about a dozen cartridges.

ARQUEBUS
An early handgun, called by Esquemiling in 1684 a 'harquebus', and also spelt in early sources as: arkbusshe, hacquebute, hargubush, harquebuz, herquebuze and hagabus. Its name was possibly derived from the Spanish 'acrabuz', but this was a cannon, three feet to six feet long, mounted on a wooden shaft that has been reinforced in the back to support the weight of gunpowder. This overcame the danger of overheating or bursting. Another origin was probably the German 'hakenbuhse'. This was literally, a 'hook gun' as a hook near the muzzle was fastened to a wall to soften the recoil.

ARMADA
Spanish for a fleet of warships. 'The Armada of the Ocean Sea' was organised in 1522 to protect the West Indies trade, and a tax called the 'averia' was levied to pay for the fleet. It originally escorted the merchant fleet to the Azores, and met the homecoming fleet also at the Azores, to protect it from privateers. Later, protection had to be extended across the Atlantic. 'The Armada of the South Seas' escorted loot from Peru to the Pacific coast at Panama. The Armada de Barlovento attacked pirates in the Caribbean; the Armada del Mar Oceano defended the Spanish coast; the Armado del Mar del Sur safeguarded traffic between Peru and Panama; and the Armada de la Guarda de la Carrera de Indias guarded ships sailing from South America.

ARMADILLO
A Spanish term for a smaller fleet, or flotilla of warships. The term could apply to just two Spanish men-of-war.

ARRACK
Very potent liquor brewed from rice, sugar and coconuts juice. The home-made hooch made from coconuts in the West Indies was particularly strong. In modern Lebanon, the strong alcohol Arak has an aniseed taste.

ARTICLES

The rules of the ship, that every pirate had to sign, or put his thumb-print to. These simple rules helped stop arguments and fights developing. There had to be a form of discipline upon ship, and they were arrived at by a democratic process of agreement, among the ship's crew. The Welsh Captains Black Bart Roberts and John Phillips had their articles transcribed by Daniel Defoe (alias Captain Charles Johnson) after speaking to captured and forced men, and condemned pirates.

After Walter Kennedy's 'desertion', the despondent *Black Captain* drew up his famous *'articles'* to be kept by the crew, and signed by all new members. Each pirate signed the articles, as Black Bart commented *'for the greatest security it is in everyone's interest to observe these articles if he is minded to keep up so abominable a combination (profession)'* According to Charles Johnston (Daniel Defoe), writing just four years later, in 1724, *'The following, is the Substance of the Articles, as taken from the Pyrates' own Informations.*

THE ARTICLES OF CAPTAIN ROBERTS

I

Every Man has a Vote in Affairs of Moment; has equal Title to the fresh Provisions, or strong Liquors, at any Time seized, and may use them at Pleasure, unless a Scarcity make it necessary, for the Good of all, to vote a Retrenchment.

II

Every Man to be called fairly in Turn, by List, on board of Prizes, because, (over and above their proper Share) they were on these occasions allowed a shift of Cloathes (change of clothes): But if the defrauded the Company to the Value of a Dollar, in Plate, Jewels or Money, MAROONING was their punishment. This was a barbarous Custom of putting the Offender on Shore, on some desolate or uninhabited Cape or Island, with a Gun, a few Shot, a Bottle of Water, and a Bottle of Powder, to subsist with, or starve. *If the Robbery was only betwixt one another, they contented themselves with slitting the Ears and Nose of Him that was Guilty, and set him on Shore, not in an uninhabited Place, but somewhere, where he was sure to encounter Hardships.'*

III

No Person to Game at Cards or Dice for Money

IV

The Lights and Candles to be put out at eight a-Clock at Night: If any of the Crew, after that Hour, still remained inclined for Drinking, they were to do it on the open Deck; which Roberts believed would give a Check to their Debauches, for he was a sober Man himself, but found at length, that all his Endeavours to put an End to this Debauch, proved ineffectual.

V

To keep their Piece (firearm), Pistols, and Cutlass clean, and fit for Service: In this they were extravagantly nice, endeavouring to outdo one another, in the Beauty and Richness of their Arms, giving sometimes at an Auction (at the Mast) 30 or 40 pounds a pair, for Pistols. These were slung in Time of Service, with different coloured Ribbands, over their Shoulders, in a Way peculiar to these Fellows, in which they took great Delight.

VI

No Boy or Woman to be allowed amongst them. If any Man were found seducing any of the latter Sex, and carried her to Sea, disguised, he was to suffer Death; so that when any fell into their Hands, as it chanced in the *Onslow,* they put a Sentinel immediately over her to prevent ill Consequences from so dangerous an Instrument of Division and Quarrel; but here lyes the Roguery; they contend who shall be Sentinel, which happens generally to be one of the greatest Bullies, who, to secure the Lady's Virtue, will let none lie with her but himself.

VI
To Desert the Ship, or their Quarters in Battle, was punished with Death or Marooning

VIII
No striking one another on board, but every Man's Quarrels to be ended on Shore, at Sword and Pistol, thus: The Quarter-Master of the Ship, when the Parties will not come to any Reconciliation, accompanies them to Shore with what Assistance he thinks proper, and turns the Disputants Back to back, at so many Paces Distant: At the Word of Command they turn and fire immediately, (or else the Piece is knocked out of their Hands:) If both miss, they come to their Cutlashes (cutlasses), and then he is declared Victor who draws the first Blood.

IX
No man to talk of breaking up their Way of Living, till each had shares a 1000 pounds. If in order to this, any Man should lose a Limb, or become a Cripple in their Service, he was to have 800 Dollars, out of the publick Stock, and for lesser Hurts, proportionately.

X
The Captain and Quarter-Master to receive two Shares of a Prize; the Master, Boatswain, and Gunner, one Share and a half, and other Officers one and a Quarter.

XI
The Musicians to have Rest on the Sabbath Day, but the other six Days and Nights, none without special Favour.

These, we are assured, were some of Roberts' Articles, but as they had taken Care to throw over-board the Original they had signed and sworn to, there is a great deal of Room to suspect, the Remainder contained something too horrid to be disclosed to any, except such as were willing to be Sharers in the Iniquity of them; let them be what they will, they were together the Test of all new Comers, who were initiated by an oath taken on a Bible, reserved for that Purpose only, and were subscribed to in the Presence of the worshipful Mr Roberts.'

ARTIST
A skilled man such as a surgeon, carpenter or navigator. Sometimes these, like musicians, were '*forced*' to join the pirates to cover gaps in the crew. Pirate captains then issued them with a notification that they had been '*forced*', in order to use at any possible trial by the Crown. While most pirates at trial would say that they had been '*forced*', usually only skilled men, '*artists*', would be acquitted. All of Black Bart's surgeons were acquitted, except Scudamore who seemed to revel in telling the truth of the matter, that he joined up voluntarily. The term '*piss-artist*', meaning

someone whose trade is drinking, comes from the use of *'artists'* as a skilled tradesmen.

ASIENTO, TREATY OF
A part of the peace settlement when Britain defeated Spain in the War of Spanish Succession (1702-1713). Britain was given the monopoly on supplying Negro slaves to the Spanish West Indies for thirty years, at 4,800 slaves a year. Many more slaves than this were smuggled into the Spanish colonies, along with smuggled English goods. By 1739 continued conflict between British merchant ships and the Spanish *'garda costa'* led to another war, *The War of Jenkins' Ear* in 1739. An *'asiento'* meant any contract to supply Spain and its dependencies, although by the 17th century the British came to understand it to refer exclusively to the provision of African slaves to Spanish-America.

AS RICH AS A WEST INDIAN PLANTER
With sugar and rum coming from the plantations to supply an insatiable European demand, this phrase supplanted *'as rich as Croesus'* from the 1660's onwards. The more successful buccaneers like Captain Morgan (after whom the best-selling rum is named) bought plantations to retire.

ASTROLABE
A navigational instrument to measure the altitude of the sun (Spanish *'astrolabio'*).

ATHWART
Across, or transversely.

AT LOOSE ENDS
We are *'at loose ends'* if there is little to be done. The ends of rigging ropes at sea became easily unravelled, forming *'loose ends'*. They had to be tightly bound to keep them unravelling, so when there was little work, the captain might order the crew to **check for loose ends** – to check the ropes and repair any with loose ends.

ATTACK
Buccaneers were superb marksmen, and their favoured method of attack was to sail in fast sloops into musket range of heavy, home-ward bound merchant ships. Most of the crew lay prone on the deck to avoid terrible injuries caused by grapeshot, while the musketeers picked off the helmsman and any sailors in the ship's rigging. As soon as the merchant was unable to manoeuvre, the pirates made for the stern, often in a pinnace, to jam the rudder and swarm up the side of the boat. Homebound ships were preferred as they carried silver, jewels and easily traded loot, rather than slaves, wine and wheat. Night attacks were also popular, especially off Tortuga.

AVAST YE!
Be quiet, or stop! Possibly from the Italian *'basta'*! (enough!), or from the Old Dutch words *'houd vast'* meaning to hold fast.

AVERIA
The convoy tax on goods carried to and from the Americas, to pay for the protection of Spanish galleons.

AVISO
A small, very fast boat carrying dispatches between Spain and its warships and colonies.

AWASH
The term when a ship is at the sea's mercy, with the waves washing over her, now used when a person has no control and is sinking, as in *awash with debts*.

AWEIGH
Order to raise the anchor. Also the state of a ship's anchor as soon as it leaves the bottom. The saying *anchor's aweigh* is often mis-spelt as *anchor's away*.

AWNINGS
These were pieces of sails supported like canopies on deck, to give pirates shade in hot climates.

AYE AYE SIR!
The answer on board ship upon receipt of an order.

BACKSTAFF (see Quadrant)
Navigational aid to measure the apparent height of a landmark, of which the true height is known, e.g. a lighthouse. From this information, the distance of the ship to the landmark can be calculated.

BAD NAME
A ship acquired a 'bad name' if she was inefficient compared to the rest of the fleet. (See Give a Dog a Bad Name)

BAGGYWRINKLE
The name given to old ropes used as 'chafing gear', which prevents damage to the ship from rubbing against other ships or moorings.

BAGNO, BAGNIO
North African slave prisons used by the Barbary Corsairs to hold prisoners for ransom, mine workers or slaves to man the galleys. Algiers' state bagnio held 3000 prisoners, and Tunis in the 17th century had 8 prisons.

BAIL OUT
This modern term had a nautical origin, in that one had to bail out water from a sinking ship or boat to ensure survival.

BALLAST

This is from the Old German, and meant *'belly load.'* Weight has to be carried in the belly, or hold of the ship to give her stability and keep her *'trim and shipshape'* in the water.

BAMBOOZLE

Dating from the 17th century, this was the Spanish custom of flying false flags to disguise your nationality.

BANDANNA, BANDANA

It is unknown whether pirates used these brightly coloured headbands, popularised in pirate films, but in cold weather they wore leather or cloth tight-fitting caps. The privateer William Williams in the 18th century wore a Scotch Bonnet, similar to today's beret, which protected from the Caribbean sun and was unlikely to blow away. The Scotch Bonnet chilli pepper (Habanero) is named after its similarity to this pirate headgear. The word comes from the Hindi *bandhnu* or *badnu*, a dyeing technique.

BANK

A rising ground in the sea, differing from a shoal, because it was not rocky (like a shoal) but formed from sand, mud or gravel.

BANYAN DAYS

Queen Elizabeth I introduced this cost-saving measure in her navy, meatless days where fish or cheese were served instead. The name came from the custom of Hindu seamen refusing to eat meat.

BAR

Shallow water caused by wave and tide action, usually parallel to the shore, where the mud or sand is higher than usual.

BARBADOS

Until the taking of Jamaica in 1655, this tiny island and St Kitts were England's only possession in the West Indies. It was a lawless, brawling place, and used by Cromwell to send defeated Irish and Welsh prisoners in the Civil War as indentured servants (slaves). Henry Whistler described it thus: *'This island is the Dunghill whereine England doth cast forth its rubidge (rubbish): Rodgs (rogues) and hors (whores) and such like people are those who are generally Broght (brought) heare. A rodge in England will hardly make a cheatere here; a Baud (bawd, harlot) broght over puts on a demuor (demure) comportment, a whore if hansum makes a wife for sume rich planter.'* It was full of deported Irish and Welsh, Royalist prisoners, beggars, exiled Huguenots, Quakers and political dissidents such as *'Perrot, the bearded ranter who refused to doff his hat to the Almighty, ended up in Barbadoes'.* A description of Barabados' inhabitants in 1665 is *'convict gaol birds or riotous persons, rotten before they are sent forth, and at best idle and only fit for the mines.'* Its escaped bondsmen, transported criminals and unemployed seamen made a happy breeding-ground for piracy, especially at the end of Queen Anne's War in 1713.

BARBAROSSA

This was the name given to Khair-ed-Din (1466-1546), the Barbary pirate who with his brother ravaged Christian Mediterranean shipping.

BARBARY WARS (see Corsairs)

By the Treaty of Paris in 1783, the USA gained independence, and British troops had left America. However, American merchant ships were now no longer protected by the Royal Navy, and became easy targets for pirate attacks. The Muslim corsairs from North Africa systematically seized and looted any American ship in the Mediterranean, and held crews for ransom. In 1795, Congress decided to pay tribute to the Barbary States to protect US shipping, as the infant nation was too involved in Indian Wars and war with France to spare the resources. A treaty was concluded with Algeria, Morocco, Tunisia and Tripolitania (modern Libya). US merchant captains were given a special passport that guaranteed no corsair attacks, and their voyages could now be insured again. The USA paid over $2,000,000 in tribute and ransom, only a fifth of what was expected, so soon the corsairs began their attacks again. In 1801, upset by the poor payments, the Pasha of Tripolitania, Yusuf Karamanli, ordered the flag-staff of the US consulate to be cut down. Thomas Jefferson halted the tribute in 1801, as the naval war with France had ended, and took the Pasha's attack on the 'stars and stripes' as a declaration of war. By 1804, the Pasha's fleet was virtually restricted to Tripoli harbour. This was the *First Barbary War*, 1801-1805. It was ended by the US Marines attacking Derna after a six-week march through the searing Libyan desert. Their success is commemorated in the Marine Corps hymn *'to the shores of Tripoli.'*

The *Second Barbary War* involved Algiers and the USA, and lasted from 1812-1815. When the war with Britain ended in 1815, President James Madison asked the navy to attack Algerian shipping. Stephen Decatur's squadron reached Algiers in that year, and the Dey of Algiers sued for peace. The British, French and Spanish were also at war with the Barbary States, generally between 1518 and 1830

BARBARY COAST

From the 14th century, this was the name for the coastal regions ruled from Tripoli, Tunis and Algers. These were the Barbary States, city-states on the edge of desert. Later, Morocco was included, although its rulers did not live by piracy. It was a pirate haven from around 1520-1830, *'barbary'* being derived from the original Berber inhabitants. In 1538, Andrea Doria led a combined Christian fleet against Barbarossa, off the Albanian coast, and was defeated by a smaller force, despite leading 80 Venetian, 30 Spanish and 36 papal galleys with 60,000 men and 2,500 guns. In 1541, the Islamic corsairs won a great battle off Algiers, against the 500 ships of a Christian European fleet, led again by the Italian Andrea Doria. Thousands were taken as slaves, and 8,300 men were killed or drowned. In the late 16th century, Elizabethan pirates and captains such as Callice began joining up with the Barbary pirates, teaching them sailing skills. In 1622, English towns raised £70,000 to ransom English captives held on the Barbary Coast.

BARBECU

The Carib Indian term for a wooden grate or hurdle (*grille de bois*), placed at a distance from a slow fire. The meat cured this way was called '*boucan*' as was the place where it was cooked. The flesh of cattle was usually dried in the smoke rather than salted first, and it dried a red colour. Wild hogs were salted first. '*Barbacoa*' or '*arjoupa*' was the Indian name given to the rough house of leaves and skins used by the '*boucaniers*'.

BARCO DE AVIFO

A Spanish '*packet-boat*', or mail-ship, sent every year between the King of Spain and his '*flota*' or '*treasure fleet*' captains. It usually held vital intelligence upon the movements and timings of the treasure galleons. The captains of these packet boats '*navios de avifo*' swore to the King to destroy or sink any letters rather than let them fall into pirate hands.

BARE POLES

A ship with no sail set, because of bad weather, is '*under bare poles.*'

BARNACLE

These stuck in huge numbers to the hull of wooden sailing ships, slowing them down and attracting weed. Until around 1800, they were generally thought to turn into Barnacle Geese.

BARQUE or BARK

A smallish, fast-sailing ship with three masts. The foremast and following mast are rigged square and the aftermast (mizzen mast) is rigged fore and aft. It could hold 90 men, and was a fast ship with a shallow draft. Before the 1700's, the term was applied to any small vessel.

BARQUENTINE

A small three-masted ship, square-rigged on the fore-mast only, and fore-and-aft rigged on the other two masts.

BAR SHOT

Large iron bars, fired by cannon from short range as their trajectory was unpredictable, to smash the ship's rigging and shrouds.

BATH TOWN, NORTH CAROLINA, 'THE HOME OF BLACKBEARD'

Founded in 1705, North Carolina's oldest town, on the Pamlico River, 50 miles inland from the Atlantic. Pirates were made welcome here, the shallow waters lending themselves to smuggling and the hiding of shallow-draft pirate ships. Governor Charles Eden even offered Stede Bonnet and Blackbeard (q.v.) pardons, and with his officials accepted bribes for turning a blind eye to the great trade in illegal goods. In 1718, Blackbeard made Bath Town his home, as his activities around Ocracoke in the Outer Banks has made him and Captain Charles Vane targets for Governor Spottiswood of Virginia. After Blackbeard was killed, Captain Maynard took the captured crew, along with those rounded up in Bath Town, to Williamsburg. 13 of the crew were tried and hung in March 1719. (see Charles Town)

BATTEN DOWN THE HATCHES
The hatches in the deck allowed crew and cargo to be transported below board. A batten is the wooden strip which secures tarpaulins over the wooden boards which cover the hatches, to prevent and rain and seawater getting in when bad weather approaches. Thus we 'batten down the hatches' when we expect an adverse situation.

BAWDY HOUSE BOTTLE
A term for a very small sized bottle of alcohol. This probably derives from the brothels making excessive money on selling alcohol, similar to modern strip-joints and sleaze-parlours.

BAYAMO
A violent storm of heavy rain and lightning that occurs around southern Cuba, especially in the Bight of Bayamo.

BEAM ENDS
'Nearly on one's beam ends' means that the ship is lying over and about to sink. The deck beams are almost perpendicular to the sea's surface. Now 'to be on one's beam ends' means to be without money, a job or prospects, i.e. in a hopeless position.

BEAR
To bear with the wind is to sail towards it; to bear in is to fall with a wind into a harbour or channel; to bear up is an order to sail more with the wind; and to bear up round is to put the ship right before the wind. To bear down is to sail downwind rapidly towards another ship.

BEAT
Sail against the wind, usually on alternate tacks.

BECALMED
'We say a calm sea, or becalmed, when it is so smooth the Ship moves a little, and the men leap overboard to swim.' – Smith 1691

BEFORE THE MAST
In most ships, the crew's quarters were in the forecastle, the section of the ship forward of the mainmast, so 'before the mast' indicated someone low-born, or a seaman rather than an officer. The phrase 'he sailed before the mast' comes from this origin.

BELAY (BELAGE)
Similar to 'avast', belay meant stop doing something, or else something nasty would happen to you. In knotting, belaying is looping the line around the base, under the arms of a cleat, bringing it up and over diagonally, around and over one arm, then

over, around and under the other, in a continuous figure eight, securing the bitter end by tucking it under the last crossover. To '*belage*' was to make fast any running rope.

BELAYING PINS
These thick wooden movable posts held ropes in place, and were also useful in an emergency for hitting someone, if a pirate was '*out of arms*' (his pistols had fired) or his sabre was stuck between someone's ribs.

BELLY TIMBER
Food, especially meat. '*There can be no adventure without belly timber*' was a saying of the 18th century. The ready availability of green turtles in the West Indies in effect helped the spread of piracy, and the were kept for weeks on deck until ready to be eaten. The leatherback turtle was inedible, and the hawksbill, or tortoise-shell, turtle unpleasant to taste. Greet turtles were the only vegetarian turtle, and made superb soup when laced with sherry.

BENT ON A SPLICE
Splicing is the art of bringing two ends of two ropes together by intertwining the individual strands. A seaman who is '*bent on a splice*' is one who is about to be united with his fair lady in the bonds of matrimony.

BERMUDA TRIANGLE (DEVIL'S TRIANGLE)
The 500,000 square miles of sea between Bermuda, San Juan in Puerto Rico and Miami, where we find '*hurricane alley*'. Millions of pounds of treasure lies in sunken Spanish and Portuguese galleons in this area. The term comes from as recently as an article in 1964 about the disappearance of Flight 19. The currents in this area are strongly affected by the Gulf Stream, which flows north-easterly from the tip of Florida. Seamen unfamiliar with the area can easily pushed off-course either to the north or north-east by the Triangle's swift currents. One cannot assume that one is travelling east, as there is one would probably be travelling east-north-east. Navigational errors, compounded by sudden freak storms make this a dangerous area for shipping. Huge amounts of warm water press through the Florida Straits into the Gulf Stream. Because of evaporation, they are extremely saline, and their sinking, with lighter water rising, causes whirlpools and heavy turbulence in the sea. Another problem may be that earth tremors release vast pockets of methane gas, which can cause sea conditions that cause a ship to sink. In 1963, the Marine Sulphur West, an 11,000-ton tanker with 39 crew, disappeared 200 miles off Key West.

BETWEEN WIND AND WATER
The few feet around the waterline on a sailing ship are alternately exposed to the air or water, as the ships rolls through the sea. It was the area aimed at by gunners, as the seas would gush in as the target rolled. It now means that one has suffered damage that can be repaired.

BIGHT (1)
A *bight* is a usually a narrow inlet of the sea.

BIGHT (2)
Any part of a rope between its ends.

BIGHT OF BENIN
It was said that the Royal Africa Company had three governors for each of its Guinea Coast trading forts. There was one who had just died, one in post, and one on his way to replace him.
'Beware and take care of the Bight o' Benin
For one that comes out there were forty went in'

BIGWIG

Centuries ago, wearing wigs was high fashion. Just as in the early years of the 20th century, all men wore hats, so all men, whether they were bald or not, wore wigs. The richer the person, the more wigs he had. France's Louis XIV started the practice of wearing really long and tall wigs, and soon all of Europe's royalty began to copy him. In England, the length of the wig that a man wore depended on his importance. The more important you thought you were, the longer and bigger the wig, so soon a lot of people began to wear these full-length wigs, such as naval captains and admirals. Smyth in his *'The Sailor's Handbook'* described *bigwigs* as *'the term applying to high-ranking naval officers.'* Sir Henry Morgan (q.v.) wore a full-length black wig, and Captain Chaloner Ogle, who killed Black Bart, wore a white one. As a result, a law was passed in England declaring that only nobility, judges, and bishops could wear full-length wigs — they became the *'big wigs'*. Incidentally, *'to pull the wool over the eyes'* refers to the wool on these wigs. Street robbers would pull the wig down over the victim's eyes to confuse him and make their getaway.

BILBOES
Long iron bars fastened onto prisoners' legs stretching them apart and making it difficult to escape. The sliding shackles meant that usually prisoners could only sit and not stand. Bilboes were also humorously known as *'garters'*. They were almost equivalent to the village stocks, and the word derives from Bilboa, which was supposed to make the best steel for fine swords in Europe. A *'bilbo'* was a rapier bought from the Bilboa region.

BILGE
'The breadth of the place the ship rests on when she is aground' – Smith 1691. Also, the bilge was the filthy, dirty, stagnant lowest part of the ship, where rats could always be found. Rats were despised both for their urine smell, and for fouling precious food. However, in bad times, they were the only source of fresh meat on a vessel. Bilge-water stank as it lay on the floor of the flat bottom of the ship, so could not be pumped out. Rubbish and waste gathered in it, in the *'waist'* or centre of the bottom of the boat, creating difficulties in steering. **'Waisters'** were older, unfit or

forced seamen who were given the unpleasant job of trying to clear up the mess, and prevent the bilge-water becoming too much of a problem. There were useless sailors who could not be trusted in the rigging, and were given other menial tasks like *'swinging the lead'*, casting around to sound out the depth. Spelling over time changed to today's *'wasters'*, people who are a target for derision.

BILGE RAT
Common term of abuse, as in *'you scurvy bilge rat!'*

BILGE WATER
Because bilge water was so offensive, giving off noxious fumes, and full of all sorts of waste, to say someone was *'talking bilge water'*, became *'talking bilge'* and meant spouting rubbish.

BILGED
If a ship is bilged, it has struck some of its timbers on a rock, shoal or even anchor, and has sprung a leak.

BILLIARDS
Several taverns such as the George and the Feathers in 17th century Port Royal had billiard rooms, which were usually situated in the yard, or away from the main bars, to prevent fights occurring.

BINNACLE LIST
In the 18th century, this was the list given to the officer of the watch, indicating which men were unfit for duty. It was kept at the binnacle, the stand on which the ship's compass was mounted.

BITE THE BULLET
Men suffering the cat-o-nine-tails were given a bullet to bite on to stop them screaming. If they did 'sing out', they were cruelly called a *'nightingale'*.

BITTER
A turn of a cable about the *bits*. The *bits* are the two huge square pieces of timber, to which the cables are fastened when the ship lies at anchor.

BITTER END
The last part of the anchor cable that remains within the ship when the ship is at anchor. The anchor rope (now called a line) on old sailing ships was secured to an oak post called the *'bitt'*, which was fastened by *'partners'* to the deck. Securing turns were held around the bitt, as the anchor was paid out into the sea. The bitter end was the last part of the rope, nearest the bitt. Thus to let a chain or rope out **'to reach the bitter end'** means that has all been paid out and there is nothing left to be let go. It was hard work paying out the anchor. You are literally **'at the end of your rope'** when you have reached the bitter end. If one came to the end of one's rope without the anchor securing purchase on the sea bed, you were **'in deep**

water', and at the end of your rope because there was no possible solution to the problem.

BLACKAMOOR'S TEETH
Cowrie shells.

BLACK ARSE
A kettle, this was the origin of the more polite term used today, *'the pot calling the kettle black (arse)'*.

'BLACK' BART ROBERTS (d. 1722)
This most famous pirate in history was born John Roberts, and was a lifelong teetotaller. It is interesting that in the 19th century, doing *'a John Roberts'* in Wales, was to drink enough to keep drunk from Saturday morning until Sunday night. He was also known as *'The Great Pyrate'*, *'The Black Captain'*, and is generally regarded as the *'last and most lethal pirate'*. He took over 400 recorded prizes from the coast of Africa to the Caribbean, and wa sby far the most successful and most feared pirate of all time (see the author's book, published 2004, *'Black Bart Roberts – The Most Famous Pirate of All Time.'*)

Black Bart Roberts

Black Bart's personal flags

BLACKBEARD

Edward Teach, also known as Thatch Drummond, was a giant of a man from Bristol. First sailing under the pirate captain Hornigold, by 1718 he was in charge of the forty-gun *Queen Ann's Revenge*. He dressed al in black, had a beard to his waist, and tied coloured ribbons in his pigtails. One of the more foul-mouthed of the pirate captains, he set fire to slow-burning fuses on his hat in battle, to make himself appear more frightening. For a joke, he shot Israel Hands under his captain's table, crippling him for life. (For these probably fictional events, we are indebted to Defoe.) Blackbeard blockaded Charleston, South Carolina, and a reward of £100 was on offer for his head. The Governor of Virginia sent Lieutenant Robert Maynard with two slops to Ocracoke in the Outer Banks. On November 21, 1718, Blackbeard was killed and beheaded. It took twenty-five separate wounds to kill him in his fierce battle with the Royal Navy. (Israel Hands appears in R.L. Stevenson's *'Treasure Island'*). The sailing master Israel Hands was also known as 'Basilica' Hands, and was sentenced for piracy in Virginia, September 1718, but pardoned. He was last heard of begging in London. The Welshman Owen Roberts was Blackbeard's ship's carpenter, and was killed with Edward Teach in *Queen Ann's Revenge* off North Carolina on November 22nd, 1718. Blackbeard took 23 ships in 7 months, all in the West Indies, which puts Black Bart Roberts' total of over 400 in two years, on both sides of the Atlantic, into perspective.

BLACK BIRDERS

Slave ships. Crews were difficult to get for these, as the mortality amongst them probably rivalled that amongst the *'blackbirds'* or slaves. This evil trade was known as *'blackbirding'*, and many merchants made fortunes from it after the Treaty of Asiento.

BLACK BOOK

Acquitaine's *'Laws of Oleron'*, a series of maritime laws, were adopted by England's French kings in the 12th century and codified in 1359. They included the duties of the captain in enforcing disciple, and were bound in black leather, and so the documentation came to be known as *'The Black Book of the Admiralty'*. Punishments included marooning, starvation and drowning, for offences such as pilfering. For repeatedly sleeping on watch, the culprit was hung over the side of the ship in a basket with a knife. He either starved to death, or cut the rope and drowned. For robbery, the punishment was tarring, feathering and marooning. For murder, the sailor was tied to the corpse of his victim and thrown overboard. Thus *'to be in someone's black book'* now means that you have incurred their displeasure, and can expect some kind of unpleasant sanction.

BLACK BOY

A vicar, or man of God, from his clothing. Also called a *'black coat'*. Later in the 18th century, a *'black fly'* came to mean a clergyman, because farmers had to pay church tithes and looked upon the clergy as the worst of land pests. A *'black box'* was a lawyer, from the colour of the case where he kept his papers. A *'black gown'* was a learned gentleman.

THE BLACK CAPTAIN, THE BLACK PYRATE

Bartholomew Roberts, a very tall man, with a *'swarthy'* demeanour, and therefore a *'black look'* about him. This may have come from the fact that this Welshman first went to sea aged 13, so his skin would have been extremely weathered and tanned. His pirate flags were the most feared of all.

BLACK DOG

Between 1705 and 1730, a counterfeit silver coin. The bad mood associated with this term became a colloquialism in the 19th century. To *'blush like a black dog'*, or a *'blue dog'* meant that a pirate never blushed at all, i.e. he was absolutely shameless.

BLACK GENTLEMAN

The devil. The term *'blackguard'*, meaning scoundrel, comes from someone evil who guards the devil. *'Black Spy'* also meant the devil.

BLACK IVORY

Dealing in *'black ivory'* was a euphemism for the slave trade. Pope Alexander VI gave Spain all new lands west of Brazil in 1494, and gave Portugal all new lands east of it. Spain was therefore unable to get slaves from the Guinea Coast of Africa. The English merchant marine (and the reigning sovereign) found great profits here, especially the Royal Africa Company (see Asiento Treaty, Black Birders, Middle Passage).

BLACK JACK (1)

Another name for the pirate flag, The Jolly Roger. Also the slang given to a sailor who suffered from the bubonic plague, as he was supposed to turn black. A *'black jack'* was also a leathern drinking-jug.

BLACK JACK (2)

A large leather tankard made stiff with a coating of tar, used in dockside taverns for beer or wine.

BLACK-MOUTHING

Slandering.

BLACK PIRATES

Black Bart Roberts employed at one time around 140 blacks, mainly former slaves, and Samuel Bellamy's Whydah had between 30 and 40 aboard. Black pirates had equal shares as white pirates, and some became quartermasters and boatswains the *Golden Age of Piracy*. A black, Diego Grillo, commanded a ship in Henry Morgan's sack of Panama in 1671. A pirate ship was the very essence of social democracy in these times of slavery.

THE BLACK PYRATE

Black Bart Roberts, the most successful pirate of all time, who almost halted transatlantic shipping.

BLACK RENT
Herring had to be salted within 24 hours to retain its flavour, so lords who owned ports grew rich on the dues (*black rent*) paid to them by fishermen for the use of their harbours for refitting, re-victualling and landing a catch. Because of its quickness in going 'off', herring was the only fish (with mackerel) allowed to be sold on a Sunday. (See Holy Mackerel!)

'BLACK' SAM BELLAMY
This pirate captain died in the wreck of the Whydah (q.v.), and Daniel Defoe (Charles Johnson) made up a terrific ranting speech for him, with Bellamy shouting at one captured merchant captain: '*They vilify us, the scoundrels do, where there is only the difference (that) they rob the poor under cover of law, forsooth, and we plunder the rich under the protection of our own courage; had you not better make one of us, (rather) than sneak after the arses of those villains for employment?*'

BLACK SHIP
An East-India Company trading ship, built from teak.

BLACK SPOT
In '*Treasure Island*' this was a death threat given by Blind Pew to a pirate, a piece of paper with a black mark on one side signifying death, and a more explicit message on the other side. It seemed to have been a fictional device, but the intimidation symbol (after the skull and crossbones) of pirates was the Ace of Spades with its single black spot. This card was intentionally shown to a traitor or informer warning that his life was in danger. Anyone sent an Ace of Spades was '***on the spot***'.

BLACK SQUALL
A sudden and violent storm in the West Indies, responsible for the unexplained loss of many a privateer and pirate. The differential between very warm air near land and the onset of colder air off the sea sometimes generates spectacular electrical storms.

BLACK'S THE WHITE OF MY EYE
A sailor's way of vehemently protesting that he has told the truth, when accused of wrongdoing.

BLACK STRAP
A lethal combination of rum, molasses and chowder beer, the favourite tipple of Black Bart's crew. Later in the 18th century it was the pejorative term for thick, sweet port, also known as '*black stripe*'.

BLACK VELVET
The term given by Black Bart Roberts' and Howell Davis' pirate crews to the accommodating native women in the Gambia and Sierra Leone. It seems that a child who was a '*picanniny*' (little one, from the Spanish *picayune*) with a paler skin was a mark of prestige with some women.

BLADDER
A chattering, talkative fellow who irritates.

BLAZER
In the Royal Navy, captains were permitted to deck their crews out in uniforms of their choosing, if they bought the garments. The crew did not have uniforms, but on ceremonial occasions, some captains tried to better the others with the smartness of their crews. The boat's crew of the HMS Harlequin were dressed in Harlequin costumes, and the HMS Caledonia's in tartan. However, the poor crew of HMS Tulip were forced to dress in green suits with a flower in their caps. By common consent, the most admired of these uniforms were those of HMS Blazer, with navy blue jackets and blue and white striped jerseys. The blazer is now a semi-formal casual jacket.

BLIND
Extremely drunk. *'Liquored'* had the same meaning. A *'blind man's holiday'* was the night-time. The *'blind-side'* was the weakest part to attack, the origin of the rugby union position *'blind-side wing forward'*. *'When the devil is blind'* meant *'never'*, as in *'I'll win the National Lottery when the devil is blind'*.

BLOODING AND SWEATING
The pirate Captain Francis Spriggs carried out this torture on one of his captives, and later ended up marooned by his crew amongst the Miskito Indians of Nicaragua. In 1718, Captain George Shelvoke made a captured merchant captain, hated by his crew, run the gauntlet of pirates while naked, while they stuck sail needles into him. The vicious Shelvoke added a new refinement: *'Thus bleeding, they put him into a sugar cask swarming with cockroaches, covered him with a blanket, and there left him to glut the vermin with his blood.'*

BLOODY FLAG
Naval warships used to raise this large flag upon going into battle. When pirates hoisted the red flag, it meant that they would give no quarter, after exhausting negotiations to take a ship peaceably.

BLOOD IS THICKER THAN WATER
Not a pirate term, but first used by Commander Josiah Tatnall of the US Navy in 1859. In the Second China War, he rescued several boatloads of the defeated British after their land attack on Peiho forts. This violated American neutrality and Tatnall could have been court-martialled, but he justified his actions with this statement.

BLOOD MONEY (1)
This was the *'bounty money'* paid to the crew in the Royal Navy for sinking an enemy vessel, and was based upon the number of enemy killed.

BLOOD MONEY (2)
The fee given by the ship's master to the *'crimp'* (q.v.) for procuring seamen.

BLOWING MARLINSPIKES

Marlinspikes (marling spikes) were metal spikes used for repairing and joining ropes. If there was a heavy storm where the skin was made to sting, the weather was *'blowing marlinspikes'*.

BLOW ME DOWN

A *'blow'* is a short but intense gale, which springs up quickly, and can knock one off one's feet, so the phrase came to mean a surprise.

(TO COME OFF) BLUELY

To have bad luck, to miss a prize.

BLUE MONDAY

Traditionally the day for handing out the brutal punishments of the Royal Navy. There was a superstition that evil would befall the ship if the treatment was not delivered on Mondays - see *'gunner's daughter'*. Boteler noted in 1685 that *'the idleness of ships' boys is paid out by the boatswain with a rod – and commonly this execution is done on Monday mornings.'* One might dread *'the blues'*, and slave music on plantations evolved into *'blues'* music. *'Blue Monday'* is the title of a wonderful record by New Order. (See Liar)

BLUE-SKIN

The offspring of a white man and black woman in the West Indies. Also the term for a Presbyterian. A *'bluenose'* was the name given to a sailor from Nova Scotia, or the ship he sailed in, as it was so cold there.

BLUE WATER

Deep or offshore waters, usually over 100 fathoms. Those ships suited to rivers and coastal waters are called *'brown water'* vessels as opposed to *'blue water'* ocean-going vessels. *'Green water'* is the phenomenon when so much water is awash on the deck of a ship that it appears to be green.

BLUNDERBUSS

The *blunderbuss* was a close range, devastating weapon, a large shot rifle, superseded by the *musketoon* of 1758. This so-called *'thunder gun'* was a huge shotgun with the firepower of a small cannon. There was a 2-inch bore which fanned out to a funnel shape at the end of the barrel, which was supposed to help spread the pellets over a wider area. This long hand-gun, about half the length of a musket, was so powerful that it had to be held away from the body - the recoil would knock a pirate over. Alternatively, it was held against the hip, and used for boarding-parties and personal defence.

BOARD

If anything at sea went overboard it was 'by the board', with no chance of being recovered. To **'take aboard'** was to put all useful things on the deck, ready for immediate use. **'All above board'** meant that the planks, or boards, which make up the deck are visible to everyone, nothing can be hidden. Above board meant having one's hands above the card table when gambling. Similarly, *'under board'* meant acting deviously. Thus today, when we take instructions **'on board'**, we will not forget anything.

BOARD AND BOARD
Smith (1691) describes this when two ships are alongside each other after a chase: *'when two Ships lie together side by side, but he that knoweth how to defend himself, and work well, will so run his ship, as to force you to enter upon his quarter, which is the highest part of the Ship, and only the Mizzen Shrouds to enter by, from whence he may do you much hurt with little danger, except you set fire to him, which a pirate will never do, neither sink you, if he can choose, unless you force him to defend himself.'*

BOARDING
Smith follows on: *'In a Sea-fight we call Boarding, in Boarding where we can, the greatest advantage for your Ordnance, is to board him athwart the Hawse, because you may use all the ordnance you have on one side, and she only them in her Prow; but the best and safest Boarding for Entering a Ship, is on the Bow, but you must be careful to clear the Decks with burning Granadoes, Fire-pots, Pouches of Powder, to which give fire by a Gunpowder-Match, to prevent Trains to the Powder-chest, which are long Boards joined like a Triangle, with divers broad ledges on either side, wherein lieth many Pebble stones as there can lie; those being fired, will make all clear before them.'*
When pirates *'boarded'* or went aboard a victim's ship, the *'boarding party'* was usually chosen by ballot. Everyone had an equal share of the booty, but being on the *'boarding party'* against a ship which had not struck its colours was obviously dangerous. *'Sea-artists'* like carpenters and surgeons were never risked. Some pirates volunteered to board, and made up for those on the list who did not wish to board.

BOARDING HOOKS and AXES
Hooks were used with lines to haul ships together, and the rails were lashed together for easy boarding. Axes with two or three feet handles, had a sharp blade on one end of the head and a blunt hammer on the other. The blade was used to cut the ropes of boarding hooks and the other ship's rigging and spars, and the hammer was used to break down doors and bulkheads in the melee of boarding. The axe could also be used in fire-fighting to chisel out hot cannon balls which might ignite the timbers of a ship.

BOAT (TO HAVE AN OAR IN EVERY BOAT)
To meddle in other people's business.

BOATSWAIN
The *bo'sun* was in charge of the rigging, sails, cables and anchors, making sure they all work efficiently. He was also usually in charge of stores, and replacement of provisions. In charge of all the work on deck, he translated the captain's orders into operations by the crew. Interestingly, the lower ranks on board, boatswain, coxswain and seaman are all derived from the people's language, Anglo-Saxon. The names of

the officers, admiral, captain and lieutenant are all derived from the language of the court in medieval times, French.

Incidentally, so many West Countrymen went to sea that they influenced our pronunciation of words like boatswain, which became *'bo'sun'*. Similarly, coxswain is pronounced *'cox'n'*, bowline is pronounced *'bo'lin'*; gunwale is pronounced *'gunnel'*; leeward is *'loo-wud'*; forward is *'forrud'*, forecastle is *'focs'l'*, foresail is 'fors'l' and main sail is *'mains'l'*. The Spanish equivalent of the boatswain was the *'contramaestre'*, superior in rank to all sailors except the *'piloto'*. The *piloto* was the equivalent of the British ship's master.

BOG-ORANGE

Potato – so many came from Ireland. A *'Bog-lander'*, later *'bog-trotter'*, was an Irishman, the nationality despised by Black Bart because of the supposed desertion of the Ulsterman, Walter Kennedy.

BOMBED

This used to be a fashionable slang for being drunk. A *'bombard'* was a leather jug or pitcher which held 4 or 8 pints of ale. We must remember that ale was far stronger in past centuries, until beer was taxed on its strength in the Fist World War to stop munitions workers becoming slapdash. Thus anyone who drank a full container was definitely *'bombarded'* or *'bombed'*. The phrase **'tanked up'** has a similar derivation, from tankard.

BONE IN HER TEETH

When the ship is sailing so well that spray is thrown out at the stem of the boat. *'Bone'* is the foam at the front of a vessel when it is underway.

BONNET

This is an addition to another sail, and the order to fasten it on is *'lace on the bonnet'*. To take it off is to *'shake off the bonnet'*. Bonnets were used only on the mizzen, main, fore and sprit sails, and if they were in place, each sail was called a *course*. Thus it was a *main-course and bonnet*, not *main-sail and bonnet*. Bonnets were put to the sail in moderate winter to hold more wind.

CAPTAIN STEDE BONNET

One of the more unusual pirates, a middle-aged Barbadan plantation-owner, who took to piracy to escape a nagging wife. After some success, he sailed with Blackbeard against his will as a 'guest', and was later captured and hanged with 29 of his crew at Charleston.

BOOBY

The brown gannet, *'sula cyanops'*, eaten when no other meat at all was available. **'Booby prize'** came to mean something that no-one particularly wanted, but had to have. The word comes from the Spanish *'bobo'* meaning foolish or slow-witted, as the birds were easily caught, perceiving no danger from man.

BOOBY HATCH

A sliding cover or hatch, has to be pushed away to allow access below decks. The modern connotation of *booby hatch* with a mental institution may come from the punishment of sailors by imprisoning them in the booby hatch. This was a small, hooded compartment near the ship's bow. However it may have come from the times when sailor captured the poor dim boobies for food, and kept them alive in improvised hutches.

BOOMS

Fenders to which sails are fixed to control its position.

BOOT-TOPPING

For pirates, this was a hurried and partial cleaning of the ship's hull. Only the upper part of the ship's bottom was cleaned. It was also the name for a resinous mixture of tallow and sulphur or lime used to coat the bottoms of ships, to deter barnacles and weeds, and reduce friction when sailing.

BOMBS

As well as cast-iron shot, cannon could fire bombs, hollow balls filled with powder and topped with a fuse. The intention was that they exploded on impact, which was timed by the length of the fuse and when it was lit. They could be fired from 50 to 500 yards, whereas a standard cannon ball might reach 1000 yards.

BONGO (BOMBO)

Small vessel used in Central American ports to load and unload larger ships.

BORN UNDER A THREEPENNY-HALFPENNY BLANKET

That is, not even *worth a groat*, a pirate or buccaneer who was thought to be very unsuccessful, and therefore unlucky to sail with.

BORN WITH A SILVER SPOON

This term was applied to those officers in the Royal Navy who entered the service without examinations and because of family connections. They were said to have joined the navy *through the cabin windows*. Those *born with a wooden ladle* were officers who attained their posts by merit, and entered the navy *through the hawseholes*, the holes through which the anchor passes.

BOSTON

Like New York and the Rhode Island ports, Boston welcomed pirate trade in the 17th century, and even gave pardons to certain pirates. In 1703, Captain Daniel Plowman was sent out to privateer against the Spanish and French, but his crew imprisoned him and voted John Quelch as captain. The 80-ton *Charles* took many Portuguese prizes off Brazil, but on its return to Boston the crew were investigated and arrested. Quelch and other ring-leaders were hung outside Boston in June 1704. The despicable Captain Edward Low was hung in chains at Nick's Mate Island in July 1724.

BOTTLE-HEAD
Idiot or fool.

BOW
From the Old English *'bog'*, meaning bough, the front of the ship. (Boat is derived from the Middle English *'boot'* and the Old Norse *'beit'*. The stern, or rear of a ship, comes from the Old Norse *'stjorn'*, the steering oar in the back of the older ships.

BOWSPRIT (SPREET)
The spar sticking forward over the bows of the ship, above any figurehead, carrying the headstay as far forward as possible.

BRACE OF SHAKES
A phrase still used today – brace means a pair, as in *'bagging a brace of pheasant'*. *'I'll be with you in a brace of shakes'* literally means 'I'll be with you before the sail has time to shake twice,' that is almost *'straight away'*.

BRACE UP
Tighten the rigging, for better sailing efficiency. The braces are two opposing sets of lines controlling the swing of the yards. A sail is said to be 'braced up' when it is drawn to sail very close to the wind, so tensed in expectation of a fair wind.

BREADFRUIT
A tropical fruit in the Pacific Islands. The pulp is starchy and edible, which may possibly be mistaken for the taste of bread.

BRETHREN OF THE COAST, LES FRERES DE LA COTE
From the 1530's onwards, Europeans had formed small settlements on the coasts of Jamaica, Cuba and especially Hispaniola. The surviving Indians, those not wiped out by the Spanish, showed them how to cure long strips of meat on a barbecue over a slow fire, in a hut called a *'boucan'*. They caught wild cattle and pigs, and exchanged the hides, meat and tallow for guns, clothes, provisions and alcohol. These butchers evolved a system of living where the past was not mentioned, and were only known to each other by Christian names. Excellent sharpshooters, their favourite food was the warm marrow from the bones of newly slaughtered animals. In retaliation against Spanish attacks on their settlements, they attacked Spanish shipping in *'pirogues'* or *'piraguas'*, hollowed-out tree-trunks that served as canoes. The Spanish tried to massacre their herds, and this turned the 'Brethren of the Coast' even more to piracy and buccaneering, and from 1630 the island of Tortuga became their unofficial headquarters. They evolved a strict code, the *'Custom of the Coast'* whereby they shared booty on an even basis, and did not know each other's pasts or surnames. Crossing the Tropic of Cancer *'drowned'* their former lives, according to their superstition. A *'buccaneer council'* of equals decided where they would get provisions, and where they would attack under an elected captain. Esquemeling records these negotiations from the point of view of a former buccaneer: *'In the first place, therefore, they mention how much the Captain ought to have for his ship.*

Next the salary of the carpenter, or shipwright, who careened, mended and rigged the vessel.... Afterwards for provisions and victualling they draw out of the same common stock....Also, a competent salary for the surgeon and his chest of medicaments.... Lastly, they stipulate in writing what recompense or reward each one ought to have, that is either wounded or maimed in his body, suffering the loss of any limb, by that voyage. Thus they order for the loss of a right arm 600 pieces of eight, or six slaves; for the loss of a left arm 500 pieces of eight, or five slaves; for a right leg 500 pieces of eight, or five slaves; for the left leg 400 pieces of eight, or four slaves; for an eye 100 pieces of eight, or one slave; for a finger of the hand, the same reward as for the eye.' The above was paid out before any booty was shared, with the captain receiving five or six times the reward of an ordinary sailor, and officers three or four times. Stealing or hiding of plunder was forbidden. Anyone stealing from a brother had his nose sliced off, and a second offence led to marooning with just a jug of water, a musket and some shot.

BRIG
From about 1700, a popular two-masted sailing ship. Both masts are square-rigged, and on the main-mast (the stern mast) these is also a gaff-rigged sail. It was formerly an abbreviation of brigantine, but came to mean a brigantine with greater sail-power. (Also naval slang for the ship's prison).

BRIGANTINE (Italian *Brigantino*, Brigands' Ship, Spanish *bregantin*, *bergantin*)
A twin-masted workhorse of a ship, favoured by pirates for its manoeuvrability. Both masts are usually fully square rigged, with a fore and aft sail on the lower part of the mainmast. The choice of many pirates, they could hold 100 crew and many cannon. A standard ship might be 100 tons, 80 feet long and mounting 10 cannon. The availability of various combinations of square or fore and aft sails made her extremely versatile in different sea conditions, so it was the choice for battle or combat, rather than quick, *hit and run* piracy.

BRIGHTWORK
This originally applied to polished metal objects, and came to then refer to bright painted woodwork which was kept scrubbed on the topside of a boat. There is an old saying *'Bright it should be, and work it is.'* (See Gilt)

BROACH
To spike or pierce a cask of rum, brandy or wine for drinking. Also to incline suddenly to windward of the ship's course against the helm, so as to present her side to the wind, and to endanger her losing her masts.

BROACH THE ADMIRAL
An old story tells of an admiral dying in the West Indies, and his body being put in a coffin filled with rum to preserve it on the way home. A sailor left to guard the coffin was often seen to be drunk. *'To broach the admiral'* came to mean stealing drink from a cask.

BROADSIDE

Firing a broadside meant that every cannon on one side of the ship could be fired at once. Some would aim for the waterline, others for the men on decks, others for the gundecks and others for the rigging, depending upon their purpose and how they were loaded. A standard *culverin* could fire one cannon ball a minute, but soon became too hot too operate. The powder charge and its wad were rammed firmly home and set under the touch-hole, the 18-pound cannon ball tamped hard, right down the barrel, the priming powder was ignited by a slow-burning match, and everyone stood clear. The 3-ton culverin would recoil, held fast by its breech-rope, and the ship would shake. The modern saying **'deliver a broadside'** means to give someone a real and unpleasant shock.

BROUGHT UP SHORT

After a '*warning shot across the bows*' the intended prize hopefully would immediately drop anchor and '*be brought up short*', or '*brought up all standing*'.

BRULOT

French for fireship, a ship loaded with explosives and set alight to drift into the enemy's fleet, especially successful if the fleet was anchored in port. (see Fireship)

BUCCANEERS

These '*boucaniers*' attacked ships, but not usually those of their own homeland. They were named after a French term '*boucan*' (from the Indian '*bukan*') – a hut in which a slow grill of animal dung and green twigs over which meat was smoked or cooked. See '*Brethren of the Coast.*' Their favoured form of attack was in long canoes or small single-masted barques. They packed the boat with sharpshooters to fire at anyone trying to fire a cannon at them, and came from astern of the prize ship, giving a minimal target to aim at. They then jammed the rudder and climbed up the stern of the ship, under cover of a fusillade of musket-fire. Although they called themselves '*privateers*', they rarely had letters of commission or marque. Sometimes they carried expired commissions, and sometimes forgeries.

A Hispaniola Buccaneer

BUCKO

A bullying officer.

BULLY BEEF

Meat such as pork and beef was packed into barrels and covered with salt to preserve it at sea. Salt beef was sometimes boiled to make it edible, and the French '*boeuf bouille*' became '*bully beef*'. Sometimes the meat was too tough to eat, and the pirates made snuff boxes or ornaments out of it to pass the time. It was in the interest of the ship's cook to boil meat extremely well, as all the fat and grease could be used by the cook to make tallow or candles, a perk of the job.

BULK-HEAD
'A bulks-head is like a feeling or a wall of boards thwart the ship, as the gun-room, the great cabin, the bread room, the quarter-deck, or any such division; but them which doth make the fore-castle, and the half-deck, which mariners call the cubbridge-heads, wherein are placed murtherers (murderers, guns), and abaft falcons, falconers or robinits to clear t he decks fore and aft so well as upon the ship's sides, to defend the ship and offend an enemy.' (Smith 1691) It is a transverse, or fore and aft partition in a vessel, which gives rigidity of structure, creates compartments for rooms and storage spaces, and helps control the spread of fire. They were often knocked out by pirates to lighten the ship.

BUM BOAT
Derived from the Dutch boom-boat, a broad-beamed small boat which carried provisions to ships, and also to remove their rubbish.

BUMBOO, BOMBO
Along with *rumfustian*, the favoured alcoholic beverage on New Providence, a mix of rum, water, nutmeg and sugar. Because all the ingredients were readily available, it was quick to make, and undeniably effective, it was the common drink of sailors

BUMPKIN
A nautical terms for wooden vessel for carrying water. The term 'country bumpkin' came to refer to a non-seafarer, with only water in his 'wooden' head, i.e. an idiot.

BUNDLE SHOT
Packs of short metal bars fired from a cannon as anti-personnel devices, to *clear the deck*.

BUOYED UP
The use of a buoy to raise the bight of an anchor, to stop it chafing on a rough ocean bed. Buoy comes from the French *boyer* (to fetter) and/or the Spanish *boyar* (to float). As buoys will always rise to the surface, and float freely on the surface, being '*buoyed up*' has come to mean uplifted.

BURGOO
Oatmeal, boiled and seasoned with butter, sugar and salt – a gruel similar to porridge. It was easy for anyone to prepare this in the ship's galley, even in the roughest seas, and it had enough sustenance to help with the hard work aboard ship. Pirates uniformly hated it. First mentioned in 1656 by Edward Cox in '*Adventures by Sea*'. *Burgoo* could also be hard tack and molasses.

BURIED TREASURE
Very few buccaneers or pirates ever buried plunder. They shared it out and usually spent it within days on women, gambling and alcohol. One buccaneer is known to have paid a hundred guineas just for the sight of a naked prostitute. The Dutchman Roche Brasiliano was known to the English as '*Rock the Brasilian*', and was noted for his extreme cruelty, roasting Spanish prisoners on wooded spits until they told him where they had hidden their valuables. Captured by the Spanish, he was tortured by the Inquisition at Campeche, and told them of his treasure buried on the Isla de Pinos, off Cuba. Spanish soldiers retrieved over a hundred thousand pieces of eight, upon which the Spanish put '*Rock*' out of his misery. Legend persists that Black Bart hid treasure inside a cave on Little Cayman Island, after his pillaging of the Portuguese fleet at Bahia.

BURNING ONE'S BOATS
The first recorded instance was Cortez, whose men did not want to head through the Yucatan to invade Mexico. The men thus had no option but to start their terrible conquest.

BURTHEN
A ship's tonnage or carrying capacity, based on the number of *tuns* of wine that could be carried in the holds, the total number giving the burthen (burden).

BUTCHER'S BILL
Slang for the dead and wounded littering the deck after a battle.

BUTTOCKS
The breadth of a ship, which *has a narrow or broad buttock*, according to Smith (1691)

BY AND LARGE
Meaning 'for the most part', this term comes from the nautical '*by*', into the wind, and '*large*' with the wind. So '*by and large the ship handled well*', means that it steered well with the wind, or against it. In general, it was a reasonable ship. Sailing *large* meant that one could use the large or square sails.

BY GUESS AND BY GOD
Navigation which relied on intuition, guesswork, experience and the Lord Almighty.

BY THE BOARD
The board is the side of the ship, so if you (or anything) fall off the ship, you '**go by the board**' and the chances of rescue are extremely remote.

CABLE
Nautical unit of distance, a tenth of a nautical mile, rounded to 200 yards for practical purposes.

CABOOSE
In 1789, Falconer referred to this as a sort of box, and it was a very small galley for cooking, on the open deck of naval ships.

CACAFUEGO
A bully, braggart or *'spitfire'*, meaning literally to defecate fire. *Nuestra Senora de la Concepcion* was pursued by Francis Drake for several days before he took it on March 1st, St David's Day, 1579. She was the greatest prize in history, being valued at around 1.5 million ducats at the time, or around half a billion pounds in today's money. She had been given the vulgar name of the Cacafuego by the chasing privateers, *'shitfire'*, because she was one of the few Spanish ships of the time to have cannon on the Pacific Coast of South America. Queen Elizabeth took most of the booty. A Spanish youth on the captured vessel said that his ship *'shall no longer be called the Cacafuego, but the Cacaplata (shit-silver)'*, and that Drake's Hind should be renamed the Cacafuego.

CACKLING FART, CACKLE FRUIT
An egg. A *'cackling cheat'* was any type of fowl. A *'cackler'* was a blabber who gave away secrets.

CALICO JACK
The nickname of the pirate John Rackham, who wore clothes made of coarse white 'calico' cotton from Calcutta – he was hung in Jamaica in 1720..

CANKY
A standard native meal for the men serving on the Guinea Coast. Indian meal and water or palm-wine, baked to make bread and cakes, or boiled to make cakes.

CANVAS
All sails and hammocks were made from strong-fibred hemp, the Greek *'kannabis'*. Although modern sails are made of oil-derived materials, they are still named after a semi-legal drug.

CAPE HORN FEVER
Term for a fake illness claimed by a sailor wanting to be excused duties.

CAPITANA
Flag-ship of a Spanish fleet, *'almiranta'* being a vice-flagship, the inverse of the British admiral - captain relationship. By the end of the 18th century, both the capitana and almiranta were carrying up to 80 cannon.

CAPSTAN
'The capstan' was a punishment whereby the arms the outstretched on a capstan bar and a heavy weight suspended from the neck, popular in the navy through the 17th century until the early 18th century.

CAPTAIN

A pirate captain had remarkably few rights or benefits, only being in charge when the crew was fighting, chasing or being pursued. In such action, he was allowed to strike, stab or shoot any man who disobeyed his orders. He also had power over prisoners and whether they were ill-used or freed, but no power over the captured vessel or its cargo. He was usually chosen for being 'pistol-proof', having a dominating and daring character. He had the right to sole use of the great cabin, but no privacy there. Any man could enter his cabin, drink from his punch bowl, swear at him and take his food with little come-back. He was usually deposed by popular vote, just as he was elected. Most of the day-to-day tasks were delegated to the quartermaster.

THE CAPTAIN IS NOT AT HOME

To have run out of money. ('The captain is at home' came to mean menstruation in the late 18th century, perhaps a pun on catamenia.)

CAPTAIN GRAND

A haughty, or 'hoity-toity' individual.

CAPTAIN OF THE SEA

The name given to the admiral who commanded the corsairs of Algiers, Tunis and Triploi (Libya), and who dealt with Christian governments in peace-time.

CAPTAIN SHARP

Bartholomew Sharp was a famous pirate, but possibly not the origin of this term from the late 17th to early 19th centuries. It means that someone is a cheating, sneaking, cowardly bully. In the same period, 'captain Tom' was the leader of a mob.

CAPTAINS' NAMES

There is a rich seam of humour here, with known privateering and pirate captains known as Bull, Best, Boggs, Catro, Cocke, Crosse, Cooke, Cooke, Cotton, Crosse, Crane, Fly, White, Rose, Browne, Green, Yellowes, Shivers, Danne, Diego the Mulatto (Diego Grillo), 'Long Ben' Every, Newport, Lancaster, Essex, England, Holland, Irish, Francke, Funnell, Gasparilla, Geare, Graves, 'Bully' Hays, Hankyn, Hassan 'Il Marabutto' (The Holy Man) Reis, Diabolito, Higgenberte, Hore, Hoorn, Hussey, Kidd, Kyd, Knight, La Buze (The Buzzard), Le Basque, Le Clerc, Le Pain, Le Picard, Le Sage, L'Hermite, L'Olonnais 'Fleau des Espagnols' (Flail of the Spanish), Low, Lucifer, Maggott, 'The Great Moor', Murat 'The Great' Reis, Myngs, Noble, Prince, Gentleman, Nutt, Porco, Pain, Sores, Pay, Bartholomew Portugues, 'Jolly Jack' Rackham, Reneger, Sir Rolando of Thessalonika, Seelander, Sherley, Stout, Swan, Teach ('Blackbeard'), Valentine, Vane, Weak, Wall, Want, Winter, and Yankee.

But alas, no Captains Hook or Blood, but Emperor VIII Palaeologus of Constantinople (reigned 1259-1282) was a noted pirate patron, as was Mithridates VI 'The Great' (reigned 121-63 BC) on the Black Sea. Sion Simonson, the Dutch Barbary Corsair in the early 17th century, was known variously as 'der Tantzer' (the

Dancer), and *Delli Reis* (Captain Devil). The German pirate Stortebecher, who was executed in 1402, was named '*the gulper of glasses*'. He made captives drink a whole pitcher of alcohol or they were executed. The pitcher held an amount equivalent to 4 bottles of wine. His motto was '*Friends of God, Enemies of the World*'.

CARAVEL
Portuguese and Spanish (*carabela*) ships used for ocean voyages as well as coastal trade, with two or three masts. They were large and narrow, with no lookout stations on their masts. With a single deck, a pointed prow and a flat stern, it had lateen sails.

CARDS
With dice, the most important way of passing the time when pirates were on board ship, or holed up hiding somewhere. Many men lost all their booty this way, and were thus condemned to a life of perpetual piracy. Arguments were very common, and arguments were settled by a duel or by the ship's quartermaster. ames of '*Pontoon*' and '*Blackjack*'.

CAREEN
A ship was taken to a quiet and isolated place ('*careenage*') and hauled over ('*heaved to*') on its side to clean or repair the wooden hull. It was a time when the pirate was most vulnerable, for example Bannister's 36-gun Golden Fleece was destroyed by the Royal Navy when he was careening in Hispaniola in 1686. The masts had to be pulled to the ground, in order to present the ship's bottom for inspection. Marine borers and weed made vessels not only slow, but awkward to steer, fatal for a pirate ship. The worst borer was a mollusc known as the teredos, with saw-shaped teeth. (See *Teredos*) Careening had to take place in warm waters at least every two or three months. Guns were set up to guard the bay, and provisions taken off the boat. The hull was scraped of barnacles, patched, and if time allowed coated with tallow and pitch to try and keep out the teredos worm. Incidentally, late in the 18th century it was noted that copper sheathing upon hulls deterred the barnacles and seaweed which clung to ships, necessitating their '*careening*' every six months or so. (See Copper)

CARPENTERS
These were vital for not only ship repairs and careening, but for stripping prizes to be used as pirate ships. Also, because of their great saws, they used to amputate limbs, rather than the ship's surgeon. Often he would have separate quarters combined with a workshop. He repaired battle damage to masts, yards, hatches and the hull, and also kept leaks out with wooden plugs and oakum fibres.

CARRACK
The precursor of the galleon, a huge ship weighing up to 1200 tons, used by the Spanish and Portuguese for trading with Indian, China and the Americas. With high fore and aft castles and enormous fire-power, pirates could only take them by stealth. They were three-masted, with square sails on the fore and main masts, and lateen-rigged on the mizzen.

CARTAGENA, CARTHAGENA

This was the treasure port between Panama and Venezuela, now part of Colombia. It was one of only three treasure ports visited by the annual Spanish *flota*. Pearls were shipped from Margarita Island, as well as precious woods, gold, silver and emeralds. Founded in 1533, it was heavily defended and the only major Spanish port never taken by the buccaneers, although Henry Morgan had wanted to attack it. The French took it in 1689.

CARTRAGE (CARTRIDGE)

A bag of canvas, made upon a frame or a round piece of wood smaller than the bore of the gun, also made of paper or metal, with a little gunpowder within, which must be kept dry.

CASE SHOT, CANISTER SHOT – See Langrace

CAST AWAY

To be forced away from a ship by disaster - *The Mariner's Dictionary*

CASTING AROUND

In fog or mist, a ship will cast its sounding line into the water to ascertain the depth (se Sounding Out).

CAST OFF

To let go mooring ropes and lashings. Some were left on land – the '*cast-offs.*'

CATGUT SCRAPER

Any of the ship's band's fiddlers.

THE CAT HAS KITTENED IN MY MOUTH

I have a foul taste after drinking too much.

CAT O' NINE TAILS

A short stick with nine knotted ropes used to flog seamen. One lash could take the skin off the back, and six would make the back raw. Punishments of over a hundred lashes meant that the miscreant died in agony. From this implement of torture, we get today's phrase '*there's no room to swing a cat*' – the deck was sometimes too full of on-lookers and cannons etc. to draw back the arm properly to inflict the '*cat o' nine tails*' (see '*gunner's daughter*'). As the gun decks had only 4 feet 6 inches headroom, the punishment had to be carried out on the main deck, where there was hopefully plenty of room to use the '*cat*'.

The punisher '*combed the cat*' after each lash, drawing each of the bloody 18 inch ropes apart. If this was not done, the coagulated tails would stick together, and give permanent damage to the victim. In the Royal Navy, the prisoner was forced to make the '*cat*', and tie knots in the each of the nine tails. It largely replaced keel-hauling as a method of punishment in the Royal Navy, where there was a theoretical maximum of 12 lashes that could be given. Vicious captains ignored this, and it was only ended as a form on punishment in 1879. For theft in the army and navy, a special 'thieves' cat' was used, which had three knots in each of the nine tails. Originally made by the victim, they were later standard ready-made issue at military stores. (See 'let the cat out of the bag').

In the Newgate Calendar, we see the former Governor of Goree (Senegambia) being hung, after being convicted of ordering a soldier to be flogged to death nearly twenty years previously. Benjamin Armstrong had been sentenced to 800 lashes by Governor Wall, and died 5 days later, on July 15th, 1782. The blameless Armstrong, who had not been tried on any offence, had been strapped to a gun-carriage, and whipped by black men brought in for the purpose, instead of the drummers, as was usual. 32 men each gave Armstrong 25 lashes, not with the normal cat o' nine tails, but with a thicker rope, which inflicted more punishment. Wall encourage the men to whip harder, urging 'Cut him to the heart and the liver.' The Board of the Admiralty put out a reward for Wall's arrest, but he lived on the Continent and under assumed names. Wall was hung on January 28th, 1802, and the calendar states: *'Without waiting for any signal, the platform dropped, and he was launched into eternity. From the knot of the rope turning round to the back of his neck, and his legs not being pulled, at his particular request, he was suspended in convulsive agony for more than a quarter of an hour.'* His body was taken for dissection.

CAT'S PAW, CAT'S SKIN
A warm and light wind on the surface of the sea. Also a certain type of hitch on a shroud lanyard.

CATTING
Chasing harlots.

CAULK
An unpleasant job, often given as a punishment, driving strands of old rope or oakum, into the ship's seams (between planking), then sealing with pitch or resin to prevent leaking, or the oakum rotting from contact with salt-water. Before this a shipwright used a 'beetle' (heavy mallet) to drive 'reeming-irons' (iron wedges) into the sides and decks, to open a gap between the planks. The oakum was 'chinched' in by pressing it with a knife or chisel into the seam, as a temporary measure if there was no time for proper caulking. The narrow seam between planks, which is sealed with oakum and pitch, is necessary as wood expands in water. As the planks 'take up' the water, they compress the oakum and make the boat more water-tight.

CAY, KEY
Small islands, often coral formations, in the West Indies, with sparse vegetation and usually no water. From the word 'cayos' (Spanish for rocks), the Florida Keys are examples. In these hundreds of islets, e.g. off Florida (the Florida Keys), pirates could lay low, carouse or clean (careen their ships. Sometimes men were marooned on them.

CAYMAN ISLANDS
Grand Cayman and Little Cayman were discovered by Columbus in 1503, and he named them *Las Tortugas*, because they resembled turtles. Francis Drake in 1585

noted that there were *'great serpents, large like lizards, which are edible'*, as well as turtles there, and the existence of caiman on the isles was doubted, until archaeological digs in 1993 and 1996 proved that they had been native to the islands. The islands came under Britain's control when captured from Spain, along with Jamaica, by Cromwell's expeditionary force. They were officially ceded to England in 1670 by the Treaty of Madrid. They were a popular stop-over for Sir Henry Morgan, and the Owen Roberts Airfield was opened in 1935.

CELESTIAL NAVIGATION
Calculating the position of the ship using time, the position of the stars and mathematical tables.

CERVANTES (1547-1616)
The author of *Don Quixote de la Mancha* fought at the great naval battle of Lepanto in 1571, and was captured by the Barbary Corsairs in 1575. The experience influenced his writing. As he carried documents that exaggerated his importance, he had a huge ransom set, which his family could not afford. Although he was a slave of three successive owners, his perceived value meant that he was not mistreated unduly. Over the years, two European orders of the Redemptionist Fathers ransomed around 140,000 captured Europeans from the bagnios (q.v.), helping Cervantes' family raise 500 gold escudos for his release in 1580.

CHAIN SHOT, KNIPPLE SHOT
A pair of small iron balls joined with a chain or bar, fired from a cannon from medium range. As it rotated through the air, it would destroy rigging and sails, and mangle seamen, but not do much damage to the intended prize.

CHANNEL
Water deep enough for navigation, today usually indicated by buoys. Also the deepest part of a strait or bay, through which the main current flows.

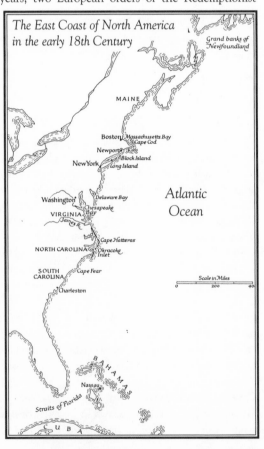

The East Coast of North America in the early 18th Century

Grand banks of Newfoundland

MAINE

Boston / Massachusetts Bay
Cape Cod
Newport
Block Island
New York
Long Island

Washington
Delaware Bay
Chesapeake Bay
VIRGINIA
James R.

Cape Hatteras
NORTH CAROLINA
Okracoke Inlet

SOUTH CAROLINA
Cape Fear

Charleston

Atlantic Ocean

Scale in Miles
0   200   400

BAHAMAS
Nassau
Straits of Florida

CUBA

CHARLES TOWN, CHARLESTON

One of the most attractive cities that this author has visited, Charleston owes its ante-bellum attractiveness to not being sacked in the Civil War. After the war, the town was too poor to rebuild, so existing buildings were renovated and exist today. It was founded on the banks of the Cooper and Ashley Rivers in South Carolina in the 1600's, and named in honour of Charles II. Pirates like William Lewis raided the port, and Blackbeard blockaded the town in May 1718. The pirate Charles Vane became such a nuisance that Governor Robert Johnson sent Colonel William Rhett commanding the *Henry* and *Sea Nymph* to capture him. Rhett just missed Vane, but instead caught Stede Bonnet up the Cae fear River in September 1718. Bonnet and 30 crew were hanging in November at Charles Town. (see Bath Town)

CHASE

'Now being at sea, the Topmasts are seldom without one or another to look out for the Purchase, because he that first descries a Sail, if she prove to be a Prize, is to have a good Suit of Apparel, or so much money as is set down by order, for his Reward; as also he that doth first enter a Ship, there is a certain reward allowed him.

When we see a Ship alter her course, and uses all the means she can to fetch you up, you are the Chase, and she the Chaser. In giving Chase, or Chasing, or to escape being Chased, there is required an infinite Judgment and Experience, there being no Rule for it; but the shortest way to fetch up with your Chase is the best. If you be too leeward, get all your Tacks aboard, and shape your course as he doth, to meet him at the nearest angle you can, then he must either alter his Course, and Tack as you Tack as near the wind as he can lie, to keep his own (distance) till night, and then Strike a Hull, so you may not descry him from his sails. Or do his best to lose you in the dark; for look how much he falls to leeward, he falls so much in your way.

If he be right ahead of you, that is called a Stern-chase, if you weather him, for every man in chasing doth seek to get the Weather, because you cannot board him, unless you weather him, he will lask, or go large (see go large), if you gather on him that way, he will try you before the wind; then if your Ordnance (cannon) cannot reach him, if he can outstrip you, he is gone. But suppose you are to Windward, if he clap close by a wind, and there goes a head-sea, and yours a Leeward Ship, if you do the like your Ship will bear against the Sea, she will make no way; therefore you must go a little more large, though you chase under his Lee till you can run ahead.' – Smith, 1691

CHASE GUNS

Cannons in the bows of the ship, used when 'chasing' another ship.

CHEW THE FAT

Meat was preserved in brine in wooden casks, and a chemical reaction meant that salt-hardened fat became attached to the walls of the barrel. The cook might scrape this and give it to the crew while they were waiting to eat - they would 'chew the fat' and make small talk before their meal. However, the cook generally tried to secrete some of this fat in his 'slush fund'. The fat was used for greasing masts, preserving leather, cooking and making candles, and he could sell it when he reached port. Pirate cooks generally shared their slush fund with the crew.

CHICKCHARNIES
In the Bahamas, mysterious little monkey-like creatures that are almost never seen.

CHOCK-A-BLOCK
When two tackle blocks are so close that there can be no movement in the sails. The sails could be pulled in tight so that the ship sailed '*as close to the wind*' as possible. To '*chock*' is to secure goods tightly on deck, when the vessel is rolling in high seas. Also known as '*two blocks*'. Them modern term '*the room is chockers*' meaning full, comes from chock-a-block.

CHOCK-FULL
A chock is a wooden wedge used to stabilise cargo in the hold, and chock-full meant that the hold was filled to capacity. It is probably a corruption of choke, as one can choke off movement.

CHOCOLATE GALE
A brisk North-Westerly wind common in the Spanish Main and West Indies.

CLAP IN IRONS
To chain up a prisoner.

CLEAN BILL OF HEALTH
Merchant ships were issued with a '*Bill of Health*' document to notify that they had suffered from no epidemic or infection at time of departure.

CLEAN SLATE
Courses, distances and tacks were recorded on a log slate. If there had been no problems, the new watch would disregard the old record and '*start a clean slate*'.

CLEAN SWEEP
The term when a huge sea knocks everything off the deck.

CLEAR THE DECK
Get ready for battle by getting rid of all coils or rope etc., which might hinder movement.

CLEAR THE YARDARM
To swing the yards inboard so they did not obstruct other ships or buildings when berthed.

CLOSE QUARTERS
A small wooden fortress or barricade erected on the deck of a merchant when attacks by pirates were expected. Small openings, loop-holes, enabled sailors to fire weapons with some protection. Wooden partitions in the quarters below decks also had loopholes pierced in them to allow defenders to thrust pikes and cutlasses through, and fight off boarders.

CLOSE-HAULED
The sails and boom are pulled in tightly, allowing the boat to point as near as possible to the direction the wind is coming from.

THE COAST IS CLEAR
Possibly from the days of smuggling, when it was safe to land.

COB DOLLARS
Shapeless gold doubloons, hammered rather than minted, often with the end clipped.

COCK UP
In port, the merchant ship's 'cock up crew' had to slew the (horizontal) yard arms inboard, and neatly brace them so that they did not interfere with another ship's rigging or any dock equipment, before the crew was allowed ashore. The yards are neatly turned up (cocked up or cockbilled) so that they lie at an angle to the masts (vertical spars).Today, 'cock up' has come to mean making a mess of something, the opposite of its original meaning. However, yards are said to be scandalised (Latin scandalum, a cause of offence) when they are cocked up. Yards were cocked up in a mark of respect to a dead crew member, but if the yards were accidentally cocked-up, this might have been the origin of today's dismissive expression. (See Ship Shape and Bristol fashion)

COLOURS 'TIED TO THE MAST'
This meant that a ship would not surrender, and that a fight could be expected - there was no going-back.

CONFEDERACY OF THE BUCCANEERS OF AMERICA
The grandiose name the 'Brethren of the Coast' gave themselves when they banded in their ships under Henry Morgan to go privateering.

COOK
The ship's cook was often a disabled pirate.

COOPER
These travelled on some ships, as at sea everything not in a canvas bag was in a wooden cask. He made casks to keep gunpowder dry, food pest-free, and to stop spirits leaking. With imperfect storage, the casks needed constant maintenance to keep them intact.

COPPER
The Royal Navy 'copper-bottomed' its extensive fleet, at huge expense to the public purse, and consequently out-sailed Napoleon's fleet at the Battle of the Nile and elsewhere. The term **'a copper-bottomed guarantee'** stems from this time. (See Careen) Most British copper came from Parys Mountain in Anglesey, Wales and the British supremacy of the seas dates from this sheathing of the hulls of its naval

warships and (later) merchant ships. With supremacy of the seas, Britain took over world mastery from the Spanish and French, and consolidated the greatest Empire the world has ever seen. It was this event, more than anything else, which led to the virtual end of piracy across the world.

COPPER-BOTTOMED INVESTMENT
Merchantmen followed the 1761 innovation of the Royal Navy in copper sheathing the hull to prevent the ravages of the teredos worm. It was expensive, but was an investment that was sure to pay off.

CORSAIRES
French for pirates, like the Spanish 'corsarios', and associated with the Mediterranean. The Barbary corsairs operated from North African states, and were often 'hired' by Islamic nations to attack Christian ships. In return, the Christian corsairs were known as the Maltese corsairs and followed the orders of the Knights of St John to attack the Turks.

COSTA GARDA see Garda Costa

COURSE
The point of a compass on which the ship sails, bur also in some circumstances a sail (see Bonnet).

COXSWAIN, COCKSWAIN
Originally the 'swain' or boy in charge of the cockboat. The cockboat was used to row the ship's captain ashore. In time the coxswain became the helmsman of any boat, regardless of size. The term dates from at least 1463.

CRACKING A BOTTLE
This familiar modern slang, as in 'let's crack a bottle of wine' stems from the days when pirates captured ships containing alcohol. In their eagerness to drink, corkscrews were not necessary as the heads of the bottles were cracked off against the nearest hard surface, or with a cutlass.

CRACK ON
A common term nowadays, for 'let's get on with it' – the former meaning was to carry sail to the full limit of the ship's masts, yards and tackles. When the ship was 'cracking on,' the straining sails and sheets would make cracking noises.

CRAMP ONE'S STYLE
This was originally 'crab one's style', where if a rower 'caught a crab' (missed a stroke and fell backwards) it would ruin the style of the rowing.

CRANK
A ship that was difficult to sail, and unstable. The modern adjective 'cranky', meaning eccentric, awkward or difficult to understand, comes from the saying that

'this ship's too cranky'. Possibly from the Dutch *'krengd'*, a sailing vessel which was quite unstable.

CRIMP
A person who swindled or press-ganged sailors. The abusive term derives from the owner of a port boarding house, or a shoreside agent who supplied sailors to captains in need of crew. They virtually controlled the seamen, by extending them board or loans so they were always in their debt. A verse from a song called *'The Sailor's Prayer'* reminds us of their sharp practices:
When the crimp comes round
I'll take his pound
And his hand I'll be shaking;
Tomorrow morn
Sail for the Horn,
Just as the dawn is breaking.
Oh Lord above; send down a dove,
With beak as sharp as razors,
To cut the throat of them there blokes
Who sells bad beer to sailors.

CROMSTER, CROMPSTER, CRUMSTER
Most of Harry Morgan's buccaneering fleets were *cromsters*, a merchant ship which looked like a small galleon, quite fast, but not as manoeuvrable as a sloop. It had a foremast, a mainmast and also a third mast to the rear supporting a lateen (triangular) sail (or sometimes a gaff sail). Its advantages over the sloop was that it could carry more treasure, place more cannons and hold three or four times as many crew. Perhaps 16 guns could be carried on a gun deck, with more guns lashed to the top deck.

CROSS HIS BOWS
Henry VIII passed a law that no junior officer should cross the bows of his admiral. This would put his ship to windward, 'taking the wind' out of the senior ship. It is international law that no ship must cross the bows of another.

CROW'S NEST
A resting platform on a mast for sailors working the yard-arms. Also used as a look-out point. (see *'straight as the crow flies'*)

CRUELTY
Captain Edward Low was a byword in evil. A Portuguese captain dropped a large bag of gold moidores overboard rather than let the pirates take it. Low had the poor man's lips cut off and boiled in front of him, forced the mate to eat them and then slaughtered the whole crew. He also strapped a French cook to a mast of a ship, which he then set on fire as he would fry well *'being a greasy fellow.'* Captain Lowther, who sailed with Low, used to put slow-burning fuses between a captive's fingers, letting them burn through to the bone to find out where valuables had been

hidden. He cut off a New England whaling captain's ears and made him eat them with pepper and salt.

The sadism of some pirates had been embedded in them in their days in the merchant and royal navies. William Richardson served under a slave-ship captain and recorded in his diary that he *'would flog a man as soon as look at him'* The same captain *'flogged a good seaman for only losing an oar out of the boat, and the poor fellow soon after died.'* One officer forced his men to swallow live cockroaches and others took delight in rubbing beef-brine onto the wounds of flogged sailors. An old tar complained about water rations and had his front teeth knocked out and an iron pump-bolt* fixed into his mouth.

His Majesty's Royal Navy was even worse. In 1704 Captain Staines of the Rochester used a tarred one-inch diameter rope to give six hundred lashes to one of his crew. Any sailor caught swearing or blaspheming was forced to hold a heavy marlin-spike in his mouth until his tongue was bloody, then the tongue was often scrubbed with sand and canvas. If a man drew a weapon his right hand was cut off. The concluding verse of the famous shanty *'The Flash Frigate'* reminds us of cruelty at sea:

'Now, all your bold seamen who sail the salt sea,
Beware this frigate wherever she be,
For they'll beat you and bang you till you ain't worth a damn,
And send you an invalid to your own native land.'

CULVERIN
A standard 3-ton cannon, taking 18-pound cannon balls.

CUN, COND
From Smith's 1691 work, we read: *'To cond or cun is to direct or guide, and to cun a ship is to direct the person at the helm how to steer her. If the ship goes before the wind, then he who cuns the ship uses these terms to him at the helm: Starboard, Leeward, Port, Helm a Midships. Starboard is to put the helm to the starboard (or right) side, to make the ship go to the larboard (or left) side, for the ship always sails contrary to he helm.*

In keeping the ship near the wind, these terms are used: Loof, Keep your Loof, Fall not off, Veer no more, Keep her to, Touch the wind, Have a care of the lee-latch. To make her go more large, they say, Keep the helm, no near, bear up. To keep her upon the same point, they use Steady, or as you go, and the like. The ship goes Lasking, Quartering, Veering or Large are terms of the same signification, viz. that she neither goes by a wind nor before the wind, but betwixt both. The word **'cunning'** comes from this source, the art of directing the helmsman to guide the ship in her proper course.

CUT A FEATHER
'Against the bow is the first breach of the sea, if the bow be too broad, she will seldom carry a bone in her mouth, or cut a feather, that is to make a foam before her: where a well-bowed ship so swiftly presseth the water, as that it foameth, and in the dark night sparkleth like fire. If the bow be too narrow, as before is said, she picketh her head into the sea…' – Sea-Man's Grammar, 1691

CUT AND RUN

This term comes to us from the days of sail. A hemp cable was cut with an axe, leaving the anchor embedded, to make an emergency getaway. It was also applied to the fact that square rigged ships were sometimes anchored in an open '*road*', with the sails furled and held by ropeyarns. Again, in an emergency, the ropeyarns would be slashed and the sails dropped ready for action. Other terms from this action are '**cut loose,**' '**cut the ties** *(that bind)*' and 'break out.' The '*ties*' are thin lines holding the sails furled. Unfettered sails are said to have been '*broken out.*'

CUT OF HIS JIB

French and Spanish ships which frequented the notoriously stormy Bay of Biscay, had their foresails cut thin, so that they could not be blown off the wind when pointing. A British ship might see a large three-decker, and if it had a thin foresail, '*not like the cut of his jib*', knowing it to be an enemy ship. The French often had two jibs when other ships only had one, and French jibs were cut much shorter on the luff than English jibs, showing a more acute angle. The British ship might then decide to '**cut and run**', cutting the lashings on all sails to run off before the wind at speed. The crew would then '**look around for loose ends**' or rope and lash the sails when the enemy had been '*left in its wake.*' Many warships also had the foresails or jib sails cut thinly, to enable them to maintain point and not be blown off course, so for a pirate ship this indicated a potential problem.

CUT THE SAIL

Unfurl it, let it fall down. 'A *sail is well cut*' means that it is well-fashioned.

CUT YOUR LEG

To become drunk. Billy Connolly does an excellent impression of a drunk trying to walk when one leg stays rooted to the ground, so any progress is circular.

CUT OF HIS (HER) JIB

The ability to recognise the nationality of a ship from afar, by the shape and position of the job, the sail on the stays of the foremast. It now refers to the characteristics of a person.

CUTLASS, CUTLASH

A short curved sword, ideal for close range fighting on deck. One lashes out to cut the opponent, hence the name. Rapiers and '*small swords*' had long thin blades to slide between an opponent's ribs to puncture the heart of lungs. The cutlass was shorter, thicker and wider, used like a machete for hacking at limbs. A 'basket-guard' covered the handle to protect the hand. However, some Caribbean cutlasses could be up to 3 feet in length. As the curve was slight and the tip was sharpened, a pirate with strong arms could also use it as a rapier when needed. Another origin of the name is the Medieval French '*coutelace*' or knife. The handles were usually cushioned with leather, strapped on a bone or ivory stock. There was also a straight cutlass called a '*shortsword*' or '*stabbing dagger.*'

CUTTER
A one-masted ship favoured by smugglers. Galleons were too slow, and were useless after they had been ransacked. They kept any gaff cutters, fast sloops, and often redesigned the sails to get a better airflow and increase speed.

CUT THE PAINTER
To make a silent departure, when the boat drifts away. The painter is the rope which attaches a boat to a pier or buoy or ship. It has come to mean a sneaky getaway, but was used by sailors as a term for permanent retirement from the sea.

DAGGERS, DIRKS
A pirate's dagger was used for eating and killing. Its straight blade was meant to thrust and puncture, not slash like a cutlass (q.v.) Its cross-bar or hilt meant that the hand could not slip onto the blade, and also deflected the strike of an enemy's cutlass, allowing the pirate to use his own cutlass on his undefended foe in a split second. The dirk was a small sharp knife used for throwing. Pirates usually carried daggers and dirks on their person at all times.

DANCE AT THE GRATINGS
To be flogged with the cat-o-nine-tails.

DANCE THE HEMPEN JIG
To hang. The rope was usually made of hemp fibres.

HOWELL DAVIS, 'THE CAVALIER PRINCE OF PIRATES'
A notable Welsh pirate, renowned for his bravery and cunning, who captured Bart Roberts from a slaver. Roberts succeeded him as captain when Davis was killed in an ambush in 1719.

DAVY JONES'S LOCKER
The first clear reference is in Tobias Smollet's 'The Adventures of Peregrine Pickle' in 1751: 'I'll be damned if it was not Davy Jones himself. I know him by his saucer eyes, his three rows of teeth, and tail, and the blue smoke that came out of his nostrils. This same Davy Jones, according to the mythology of sailors, is the fiend that presides over all the evil spirits of the deep, and is often seen in various shapes, perching among the rigging on the eve of hurricanes, ship-wrecks, and other disasters to which sea-faring life is exposed, warning the devoted wretch of death and woe.' Davy Jones was a spirit, or sea-devil who lived on the ocean floor. Sending someone to Davy Jones's Locker meant despatching them to the ocean's depths. The 'locker' was the bottom of the sea, the last resting place for sunken ships and bones.

How this Welsh name is attached to a sea-devil is unknown in dictionaries, but the author believes that it probably refers to a Welsh pirate in the Indian Ocean called David Jones. Serving under Captain William Cobb, then under Captain William Ayres, Jones was in charge of a lightly manned, recently taken prize ship, filled with loot, accompanying Ayres in the 'Roebuck'. The East India Company ship 'Swan' under Captain John Proud took Ayres' ship in 1636 off the Comoros Islands. Jones knew he could not escape with his heavily laden ship, so he scuttled it with all its incriminating evidence. 'Old Davy' was also known as the devil from the 18th century. Another source tells us that David Jones ran a London tavern, with his own press gang who drugged his unwary patrons and stored them in the ale lockers at the back of the inn until they could be taken aboard some departing ship.

Phrases from these times include the following: 'I'll see you in Davy Jones's' (a threat to kill someone); 'He's in Davy's grip' (he is scared, or close to death); and 'he has the Davys' or 'he has the Joneseys' (he is frightened).

DEAD AS BILGE WATER

The current phrase 'dead as dish water' comes from this expression. The foul, stinking water in the bilges in the bottom of the ship gave out noxious gases, and could asphyxiate pirates.

DEAD CATS DON'T MEW

The South American pirate Pedro Gibert said this in 1832, after he captured the American brig Mexican. After stripping the ship, he told his crew to lock the prisoners below decks, slash the rigging and set the ship on fire, making the above comment. However, the crew managed to free themselves, and let the fire burn until Gibert had vanished, then extinguished it. He was captured by the English navy off West Africa in the next year and hanged.

DEADHEAD

Not a Grateful Dead aficionado, but a floating log.

DEADMAN

'Deadman - an "Irish Pennant" - a loose end hanging about the sails or rigging' - 'The Mariner's Dictionary

DEAD MAN'S CHEST

Edward Teach, 'Blackbeard' (died November 22, 1718), marooned some of his crew that he considered 'mutinous' upon a tiny island off Tortola in the British Virgin Islands. It is now called Dead Chest Island. The rock was known to sailors as 'The Dead Man's Chest' as nothing could live there except lizards, snakes and mosquitoes. Each mutineer was handed a cutlass and a bottle of rum, in the hope that they would kill each other, but a month later when he visited, fifteen were all still alive. The incident sparked the verse in Stevenson's 'Treasure Island':

> Fifteen men on the dead man's chest,
> Yo ho ho and a bottle of rum!
> Drink and the Devil had done for the rest,
> Yo ho ho and a bottle of rum!

DEAD MARINE

Also known as a dead soldier, this was an empty wine bottle. It seems that sailors use to imply that an empty bottle was 'as useless as a dead marine'.

DEAD RECKONING

Until the 18th century, captains relied on a system of 'dead reckoning' to gauge their distance east or west of a home port. *Dead* seems to be an abbreviation, like many sailing terms, of which the origin was 'deduced'. The captain or navigator threw a log overboard and observed how quickly it moved away from the ship. This crude speedometer reading was noted in the log-book, along with the direction of travel, taken from the stars or a compass, plus the length of time on this particular course, reckoned by a sand-glass or pocket-watch. Intuitively reckoning the effects of currents, winds and errors of judgement, the captain could guess his longitude. Sometimes he missed his destination altogether, as did Black Bart. Other times not enough food and drink was aboard, as the voyage lengthened through navigational errors, and the crew contracted scurvy or dehydrated to death.

DEAD WATER

The eddy water that follows the stern of the ship, not passing away as quickly as the water on the ship's sides.

DEADWOOD

Heavy longitudinal timbers fastened over the keelson, to which are attached the timbers of the bow and stern. The term now is used for people who are 'along for the ride' in the terms of being a waste of space, and dragging everyone else down.

DECLARATION OF PARIS 1856

Nations agreed to officially abolish privateering, but Spain, the USA, Mexico and Venezuela did not support the declaration.

DEEP SIX

This term has come to mean to discard or throw out something. It comes from the custom of ensuring that any body was only committed to the deep if the water was 6 fathoms deep or more.

DEFOE, DANIEL (c.1660-1731)

Captain Charles Johnson, the most reliable authority on pirates (much like Esquemeling on buccaneers) wrote 'A General History of the Robberies and Murders of the Most Notorious Pyrates', which was first published in 1724. Many editions followed, and much information came from the transcripts of pirate

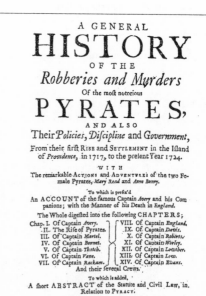

A GENERAL

HISTORY

OF THE

Robberies and Murders

Of the moſt notorious

PYRATES,

AND ALSO

Their *Policies, Diſcipline* and *Government*,

From their firſt Riſe and Settlement in the Iſland of *Providence*, in 1717, to the preſent Year 1724.

WITH

The remarkable Actions and Adventures of the two Female Pyrates, *Mary Read* and *Anne Bonny*.

To which is prefix'd

An ACCOUNT of the famous Captain *Avery* and his Companions; with the Manner of his Death in *England*.

The Whole digeſted into the following CHAPTERS;

Chap. I. Of Captain *Avery*.
II. The Riſe of Pyrates.
III. Of Captain *Martel*.
IV. Of Captain *Bonnet*.
V. Of Captain *Thatch*.
VI. Of Captain *Vane*.
VII. Of Captain *Rackam*.
VIII. Of Captain *England*.
IX. Of Captain *Davis*.
X. Of Captain *Roberts*.
XI. Of Captain *Worley*.
XII. Of Captain *Lowther*.
XIII. Of Captain *Low*.
XIV. Of Captain *Evans*.
And their ſeveral Crews.

To which is added,

A ſhort ABSTRACT of the Statute and Civil Law, in Relation to Pyracy.

By Captain CHARLES JOHNSON.

LONDON, Printed for *Ch. Rivington* at the *Bible* and *Crown* in St. Paul's-Church-Yard, *J. Lacy* at the *Ship* near the *Temple-Gate*, and *J. Stone* next the *Crown* Coffee-houſe the back of *Greys-Inn*, 1724.

Frontiſpiece of the General History

trials of the time and accounts published in the Daily Post and London Gazette. In 1732 it was claimed that this was none other than Daniel Defoe, who had also published pirate fiction (Robinson Crusoe and Captain Singleton) and pirate non-fiction (on Captain Avery and John Gow). P. Furbank and W. Owens rebutted this argument in 1988 ('The Canonisation of Daniel Defoe'), and David Cordingley at least among pirate experts, believes that the book can no longer be attributed to Defoe.

DERELICT
A ship that has been abandoned at sea, from the Latin *derelinquere*, to forsake, it has come to mean a tramp or vagrant.

DERROTERRO
Sailing directions used by the Spanish. The equivalent Portuguese 'roteiro' became the French 'routier', and the English 'rutter'. These were of incomparable value in the New World and East Indies. A captain could see views of the coast taken from seaward, with instructions added. Captain Bartholomew Sharp captured one in the South Pacific from the Spanish ship Rosario in 1680. This was most unusual, because they were usually thrown weighted overboard in the face of pirate attack. When the pirate Captain Bartholomew Sharp was tried for piracy, he gave Charles II the translation of a priceless derroterro he had captured from the Rosario in 1681. He was acquitted, and made a captain in the Royal Navy.
English *rutters* held details of anchorages, harbours, courses etc., and were continually updated by their owners, often being passed down from father to son. Famous Spanish derroteros were of the Americas and Spain (1575), and Florida, the Carribean and Veracruz (1583).

DEVIL TO PAY (also see Caulk)
The first plank on the outer keel of a wooden ship was called the *garboard*, but known universally by seamen as the '*devil*', because it was the most awkward to get at during careening. It was the longest seam in the vessel. It was almost impossible to keep the devil above water, to '*pay*' oakum into its seam, hammer home and cover with hot pitch to seal it. '*The devil to pay, and no hot pitch*' was a desperate situation where seamen could see no means of solving a problem. '**Between the Devil and the deep blue sea**' also comes from a ship's devil, meaning that there was only the thickness of the ship's hull plank between the garboard seam and the ocean depths. The use of '*devil bolts*' was a corrupt practice used by ship-builders to save money. The 64-gun warship York foundered in the North Sea because copper bolts were not used to hold the ship's timbers together at key points. Instead, the bolts had been faked by inserting copper heads and tails in appropriate positions, connected only by hidden wooden dowels.

DINGBAT
Slang for a small rope swab used for drying decks in the navy.

DINGHY
A small ship's boat with no sail.

DIRK
A ling thin knife favoured by pirates for fighting, throwing and cutting rope.

DISEMBOGUE
To sail out of the mouth or strait of a gulf.

DISMANTLE
Originally a nautical term, to unrig a vessel and discharge all its stores.

THE DOCTOR
The name given by West Indians to the cooling trade wind. The '*Harmattan*', a cooling easterly wind from December to February (the dry season) on the west coast of Africa, is also known as the 'doctor'. Perhaps slavers or slaves took the terminology across the Atlantic with them.

DOGSBODY
Sea biscuits, or hard tack, soaked in water to a pulp, with added sugar. Somehow the term came to mean a general factotum.

DOGWATCH
In the navy, half-watches of two hours each, from 4 to 6 and 6 to 8 pm. The term dates at least from 1700. Dogwatch may be a corruption of '*dodge watch*' as it is only two hours long. Another reason may be that it enabled sailors to dodge having the same watch every night, as the dog watch permits a shift in the order of the watch. It could also be a reference to the fitful sleep known to sailors as '*dog sleep*', because it is a stressful watch, as dusk falls. The watches aboard ships are:

Noon – 4pm	Afternoon Watch
4 – 6 pm	First Dogwatch
6 – 8 pm	Second Dogwatch
8 – Midnight	First Night Watch
Midnight – 4am	Middle or Mid Watch
4 – 8 am	Morning Watch
8 – Noon	Forenoon Watch.

Pirates kept the same watches as their naval and merchant counterparts. One watch was on duty, the second *at ease*, and the third sleeping. The ship's bell was struck on the half-hour as the watch-glass was turned.

DOLDRUMS (See Trade Winds)

DONKEY'S BREAKFAST
Naval slang for a seaman's bed or mattress, formerly stuffed with straw.

DON'T SPOIL THE SHIP FOR A HA'PORTH OF TAR
Leaving a job half-done by not properly using hot tar to fill in the planks when careening. Ships would leak if too little was applied, so a minimal extra effort would be worth it. '*Ha'porth*' is the old abbreviations for '*half-penny's worth*'.

DOWN THE HATCH

We say this as regards drinking alcohol, but again its origins are naval, as the ship appears to consume cargo as it travels down the hatch into the hold.

DOUBLOONS

The largest of Spanish gold coins, derived from '*doblon*'. The '*ducado*' was worth less, about 10 '*reales*', and known to the British seaman as a ducat. The '*escudo*' was worth 10 reales. Silver pesos were known as '*pieces of eight*' (q.v.) A doubloon was worth about 7 weeks wages to a sailor. The doubloon weighed slightly less than an ounce of gold, and originates from the Latin *duplus*, or double.

DOUGHBOYS

Hard dumplings made of a quarter pound of flour and boiled in sea-water, described in Dampier's '*Voyages*' of 1697. They were still standard fare in the Royal Navy in 1897. The use of the word in the early twentieth century, describing an American private in the army, was because the shape of the buttons on his tunic resembles '*doughboys*'.

DRESSING DOWN

Canvas sails could easily become waterlogged, which made the ship hard to handle and caused rot and tears. Thus they had to be treated with heated preservatives and oils to repel water. This could only be done when the sails were rigged, rather than rolled up. Thus to '*dress down*' both sides of a sail, hanging off ropes, while the sail was flapping and snapping in one's face, was an unpleasant but necessary experience, the origin of today's term.

"Roberts' crew carousing at old Calabar River".

DRINK LIKE A FISH

A term from the 1640's on, meaning to constantly drink alcohol. Pirates drank to while away the boredom between prizes.

DRINK TILL YOU GIVE UP YOUR HALFPENNY

To drink until one vomits.

DROGER

A coastal trade ship in the West Indies.

DROGUE

Francis Drake used an improvised drogue to slow his ship down when chasing the Nostra Senora de la Concepcion. It was a conically shaped bag which trailed behind the ship, its mouth open to the water. The Spaniard was racing away as night fell, and thought themselves secure. However, Drake cut the drogue and quickly caught up and surprised the Spanish prize. The Space Shuttle uses a drogue chute to slow down its momentum on returning to earth.

DROPSY
Old naval term for Oedema, internally swelling with water retention.

DRUNK WITH A CONTINUANDO
Plastered, in a drunken condition for days at a time.

DRY GRIPES
Pirates referred to this as a peculiarly West Indian disease. It was poisoning caused by drinking large quantities of rum, which had been distilled in lead pipes as glass was not readily available.

DRY TORTUGAS
A shoal of islands used by British pirates, at the western end of the Florida Keys. Turtling was important to pirate diets, and they wee possibly called this to distinguish them from Tortuga (Ile de la Tortue) off Hispaniola, and Salt Tortuga off Venzuela. Turtles caught at Sale Tortuga were cured using salt from the nearby salt-pans of the Araya Peninsula. Perhaps turtles caught at the Dry Tortugas were dry-cured.

DUCAT
The Spanish *'ducado'* was a monetary value equivalent to 11 *'reales'*. The *real* was a silver coin weighing 3.43 grammes, and there were 8 reales to a peso, hence the term *'pieces of eight'* for pesos.

DUCKING AT THE YARD ARM
For a punishment in the Royal Navy, a seaman was tied under his arms, around his waist and under his groin, hauled up on a rope to a spar and dropped violently into the sea several times. (See *Keel-Hauling*). Some pirates amended the ducking so that the victim was dropped onto the deck, to encourage others to divulge the whereabouts of loot, before it was their turn for a *'ducking'*. Other punishments favoured at sea were being forced to eat live cockroaches, filling up someone's mouth with iron bolts, and knocking out teeth with metal bolts.

DUFFLE, DUFFEL
This was the name given to a sailor's personal effects. It referred to his main clothing, as well as to be bag in which he stowed it and carried ashore. Duffel is a town near Antwerp, which made the rough woollen cloth which made the duffel bag.

DUNGAREES
Worn by sailors since the 18th century, from the Hindi *'dungri'*, a type of cotton cloth.

DUTCH
Slang for good beer. A *'Dutch bargain'* was a one-sided transaction. A *'Dutch caper'* was a small privateering ship. The *'Dutch pump'* was a punishment involving vigorous exercise pumping out bilge-water. A *'Dutch widow'* was another term for a prostitute, or bawd.

DUTCH COURAGE
There seem to have been fewer Dutch pirates, although it was a great seafaring nation, because Holland had fisheries where men could find work, whereas in England and Wales men had to beg for a living. Pirates were also wary about attacking Dutch ships because of their reputation for bravery and prolonged resistance. Thus the alliance of *'Dutch courage'* with the effects of alcohol giving bravado seems to be a demeaning, and later use of the phrase. In the 17th century the Dutch were hated commercial and military enemies, and other derogatory meanings of Dutch are **'Dutch auction'** (where everything is backwards); **'double Dutch'** (gibberish); **'to go Dutch'** (to pay for yourself, a variation of **'Dutch treat'**, and **'I'm a Dutchman'**.) It seems to have stemmed from the Anglo-Dutch Wars in the 1660's, when British captains propagandised their crews by saying that the Dutch could only fight when fortified with schnapps. A historical account of the time reads *'the (Dutch) captain of the Hollander man-of-war, when about to engage with our ships, usually set a hogshead of brandy before the mast, and bid the men drink … and our men felt the force of the brandy to their cost.'* However, it may be that the origin was the ability of Dutch gin to give an Englishman courage. Until its sale was restricted to licensed premises, Dutch gin was the cheapest and most powerful alcohol freely available in Britain, as Hogarth's brilliant *'Gin Street'* etchings show its effect upon the general population. One last possible origin of the term is when Dutch traders sailed up the Thames in the time of the Great Plague to carry on business, although all other commerce had stopped.

DUTCHMAN'S BREECHES
A patch of blue sky gave optimism that a storm would end soon. The Dutch were note for their thrift, and even a small piece of sky would be *'enough to patch a Dutchman's breeches.'*

EARRINGS
These may have been popular in pirate companies, as some believed that they improved eyesight. Early blindness was common for lookout men, perhaps squinting into the sun for hours at a time. However, it seems that the real reason for the wearing of an earring by nautical men was that it would pay for their funeral if they died on land.

THE HONOURABLE EAST INDIA COMPANY
One of 8 companies set up in the late 16th century to exploit trade in India, the East Indies and the Far East. Others were set up by Scotland, Holland, France, Denmark, Spain, Austria and Sweden, but only the Dutch company was significant competition. It was given a charter by Elizabeth 1 on December 31, 1600, with 215

shareholders, and by 1612 friendly relations were established with the Shogun of Japan, thanks to John Adams. By 1630, it had a practical monopoly of the India trade. There is a remarkable description of torture carried out on East India Company men by Dutch officials, relating to the 'Amboyna Massacre' in the wonderful 'Nathaniel's Nutmeg' by Giles Milton. To relate these practices, carried out to protect the spice monopoly, would sicken the reader.

EAST INDIAMAN
A magnificent armed merchant ship, owned and operated by the East India companies for trading with India and the East. A 'Guineaman' traded with the Guinea coast of Africa. These were the largest ships built, and the captain, passengers and officers had relatively excellent accommodation. About 300 tons and 160 feet long, there was a maximum crew of 300, but the top gun capacity of 54 cannon was often undercut to make more room for cargo.

EDWARDS FAMILY CLAIM ON MANHATTAN
Probably the most intriguing court-case in the world is the one involving the heirs of the Welsh privateer Robert Edwards, and the ownership of a large chunk of Manhattan real estate. He was given 77 acres of what is now the heart of Manhattan, by Queen Anne, for his services in disrupting Spanish shipping. His will gave the area to the Cruger brothers, on a 99-year lease, with the understanding that it would revert back to his heirs after that. Somehow the land has ended up in the hands of Trinity Church, one of New York's biggest landowners. The land is valued at $680 billion. It includes 'ground-zero' (the site of the World trade Centre), Broadway and Wall Street). Legal proceedings have meandered on for a period of over 75 years.

EGAD, MATELOT!
According to W. Adolphe Roberts, a traditional buccaneer greeting, but far more likely, fiction.

END FOR END
When a rope runs all out of its block, so that it is unreeved. When a cable or hawser runs all out at the hawse, 'the cable at the hawse is run out end to end.'

ESCUDO
A gold coin worth 16 silver pesos, each of which was worth 8 reales. 8 escudos make a 'doblon' (Anglicised to **doubloon**).

ESQUEMELING, JOHN (c.1645-c.1707)
This French Huguenot, often described as a 'Dutchman', wrote the definitive history of the buccaneers, 'The Bucaniers of America'. He tells us that he went voluntarily to the West Indies, to Tortuga, in the service of the French West India Company. They sold him on to a cruel landowner, who fell ill, and sold Esquemeling to a surgeon for seventy pieces of eight. The surgeon treated him humanely, supplying reasonable food and decent clothes, and after a year offered Esquemeling his

freedom for indenture, for just one hundred pieces of eight, that should be repaid when the Dutchman was *'in a capacity to do so.'* Being an honourable man, he resolved to repay this debt and joined the buccaneers as the quickest way of doing so. He voyaged during these years in the fleet under Henry Morgan. As he had assisted a surgeon, he travelled as a ship's surgeon until he returned home in 1674, some time after the great assault on Panama. See Sea Rovers. The first edition, in Dutch, was printed in 1678. The 1684 English version was translated from the anti-English Spanish version and was therefore libellous to Sir Henry Morgan. The first edition of the book was principally entitled *'De Americaensche Zee-Roovers'* and published in 1678 in Amsterdam. It was followed by a 1679 Nuremburg edition called *'Americanische Seerauber'* and the 1681 Spanish edition *'Piratas de la America.'*

Buccaneers taking a Spanish ship, from Juhn Exquemelin's *Bucaniers of America*, Amsterdam, 1700.

EXECUTION DOCK

This is still pointed out by the guides on river trips on the Thames in London. Pirates were executed here at Wapping Old Stairs, usually by hanging, but in former years by tying them to poles in the mud, and waiting for the tide to come in and cover them. Usually the pirates were left on tall gallows, hung in chains as an example to others.

EYE OF THE WIND

The direction from which the wind is blowing.

EYE-PATCH

The most common cause for this amongst *'sea-dogs'* was not sword-play but staring into the sun. Before John Davis invented the *'backstaff'* in 1595, navigators had to use *'sighting-sticks'* to measure the sun's height above the horizon by looking directly into its glare to find latitude. In a few years, the sight of the eye was ruined.

EYE TO THE MAIN CHANCE

It may be that this phrase originated in the possibility of making cast sums of money operating in the Spanish Main. More likely it came from the dice game of *Hazzard*, in which players throw twice. The first throw is the main throw, and the second is the 'chance' throw.

FACE (OR BRAG) IT OUT WITH A CARD OF TEN

To set upon the enemy with none too sure an opinion of the outcome. In a card game, a card of ten spots is useful, but not sure to win. This assumption of a bold front would be better with a 'sure card', another saying of the time.

FACK, FAKE

A circle of rope or cable, coiled around. It is unknown whether the expletive 'fack!' comes from the fact that one could trip over a coil or rope on deck, or whether it is an attempt to sanitise another, similar swear-word.

FAG END

The frayed end of a rope on ship, possibly corrupted from fatigued, now meaning a cigarette butt.

FAGGED OUT

A rope that has not been maintained and has a 'fag end' was said to be fagged out. The current meaning of being fatigued comes from this nautical term.

FAIRWAY

The origin of this golfing term was the channel of a narrow bay, river or haven, in which ships usually navigate up or down.

FALL FOUL OF

When one ship impedes the progress of another. A foul anchor is when a ship's own rope gets entangled.

FATHOM

A depth of six feet, the origin of which was the Anglo-Saxon 'faethm', meaning to embrace. Measurements were based on the human body, such as the foot or hand, which is why horses are still measures in 'hands' of height. As a man stretched his arms to embrace his sweetheart, it was decided that this measure was to be the unit of measure. We also use it when we are trying 'to fathom something out', i.e. trying to figure something out. Our problem is that this good old measures translates to 1.8256 metres in this sadly decimalised world.

The Spanish used the same measurement, the 'braza' as a measurement of depth, with the sounding lead on a line bein g measured by the seaman pulling in the line. However, the width of his arms from finger-tip to finger-tip could vary from 5 feet 6 inches to 6 feet 6 inches, depending upon his build.

FEELING BLUE

This may refer to the dread of 'Blue Monday' with its harsh punishments. It is more likely to have come from the fact that any sailing ship that lost its captain or any officer at sea, flew a blue flag, or painted a blue band across the hull, when returning to port.

FELONY

In these times, all felonies were capital offences (see Punishment and Pillory). However, for very minor offences, if a thief could prove he could read he might plead *'benefit of clergy'* and escape with being branded 'T' for thief on his cheek. This punishment lasted until 1829. Some pirates managed to get away with the brand of 'P'.

FEMALE PIRATES

In 1720, Ann Bonney and Mary Read were captured in Jamaica by Captain 'Calico' Jack Rackham. When Rackham and his crew were taken, the women were tried separately. They had taken part in battle and were convicted to be executed, like the rest of the crew. The judge asked if there was any reason why they should not be hanged, and both answered *'My Lord, we plead our bellies'*, the traditional plea of pregnant women. As it was illegal to kill an unborn child, they were reprieved until they had given birth, and they seem to have escaped execution.

FEND OFF

To push a boat away from the harbour wall or pier or another vessel and prevent damage, by using a boat-hook, spar or fender.

FID

A wooden pointed tool used to separate strands of rope for splicing. If made of metal, it was called a marlinspike (q.v.)

FIELD DAY

Originally a nautical expression, in the US Navy a day set aside for cleaning and clearing up all parts of the ship.

FIGHTS

In Mainwaring's *'Seaman's Dictionary'* of 1644, these are *'the waist cloths which hang around the ship to hide men from being seen in fight. Also any bulkhead or small shot (compartment) wherein men may cover themselves and yet use their arms are called close fights.'* *'Top armours are the cloths which are tied around the top of the masts for show, and also for men to hide in fight which lie there and throw firepots, use small shot, or the like.'*

FIGUREHEAD

There is no practical purpose to the figureheads on sailing ships – they just are ornamental devices to show the owner's wealth or taste, and to inspire the crew in sailing in a good-looking ship. Thus we have today's term for a person who lends credibility to an organisation, but contributes nothing. The fashion for topless ladies as figureheads came from the belief that bare-bosomed ladies could calm the stormy seas.

FILIBUSTIERS

Another French term for buccaneer, in Spanish *'filibusteros'* and in English it became *'filibusterers'* and freebooters. The origin is the Dutch *'vrijbuiter'*. Other sources say that the French could not pronounce vrijbuiter or freebooter, and their attempt, *'filibustier'* returned into the English language as filibuster in the nineteenth century. A more recent theory is that the origin was the Dutch *'vliebooter'*, the small flyboat used so successfully in the fight for independence from Spain in the 16th century. By the end of that century, the term had come to mean a fast sailing vessel used for piracy or discovery, and by the late 17th century had come to mean sea borne raiders.

An American politician described his opponent's tactics in obstructing legislation as *'filibustering against the United States'* so it has come to be synonymous with this activity, such as making an endless speech to prevent a vote on a bill.

FIRE ARROW, FIRE DART
Captain Smith tells us to: *'Provide a long staff, and join it to an iron head, and about the middle of that head of iron, having first made a bag of strong canvas, in the form of an egg, leaving open at the end a hole to fill the bag with the composition following Take a pound of salt-peter, half a pound of gun-powder, and as much brimstone in powder, mix all these together in oil of petrol; with this composition fill the bag, round the arrow-head, and bound all about with annealed wire. For the priming of these darts or arrows, dip cotton-wick into gun-powder wet with water, and let the cotton be well-fried before you use it.'* Also *'fire-wheels'* were made to attack shipping.

FIRESHIP
As used against the Spanish Armada, and by Henry Morgan. The preferred option was to use grappling irons to attach the fireship against an enemy vessel, whereupon the attacking crew would light a slow match and escape in a small boat. Smith in 1691 describes their use: *'Now between two Navies they use often, especially in a Harbour or Road where they lie at Anchor, to fill old Barks with Pitch, tar, Train-oyl, Lynseed-oyl, Brimstone, Rozin, Reeds, with dry Wood, and such Combustible things. Sometimes they link three or four together in the night, and put them adrift as they find occasion. To pass a Fort some will make both Ships and Sails all black, but if the Fort keep but a Fire on the other side, and all the pieces point blank with the fire, if they discharge what is betwixt them and the fire, the shot will hit, if the Rule be truly observed; for when a Ship is betwixt the fire and you, she doth keep you from seeing it till she be past it.'*

FIREWORKS
Devices used to set alight enemy ships, such as fire-balls, which were cannon heated red-hot in a brazier before being fired. Fire-pikes were boarding pikes with burning twine or cloth attached, thrown like javelins at the sails and decks. From Smith's 1691 'The Sea-man's Grammar' we read: *'Fireworks are divers, and of many compositions, as Arrows trimmed with Wild-fire to stick in the sails or ship's side, burning. Pikes of Wild-fire to strike, burning into a ship's side to fire her. There is also divers sorts of Granadoes, some to break and fly in abundance in pieces every way, as will your Brass Balls, and Earthen-pots, which when they are covered with quartered bullets stuck in Pitch, and the Pots filled with good Powder, in a crowd of people will make an incredible*

slaughter.; some will burn underwater, and never extinguish until the stuff be consumed; some will only burn and fume out a most stinking poisonous smoke, some, being only an oil anointed on any thing made of dry wood, will take fire by the heat of the Sun when the Sun shines hot. There is also a Powder, which being laid in like manner upon anything subject to burn, will take fire if either any rain or water lights upon it; but those inventions are bad on shore, but much worse at sea, and are naught because so dangerous, and not easy to be quenched, and their practice worse, because they may do as much mischief to a friend as to an enemy, therefore I will leave them as they are.'

FIRST MATE
In some pirate ships, this was the captain's right-hand man, who would take over if the captain was killed or incapacitated in battle. As it was the equivalent of the hated lieutenant's role in the Royal Navy, most pirate ships chose a quartermaster rather than a first mate.

FIRST RATE
Implying excellence. Naval ships of the line, until the age of steam, were rated by the amount of cannon they carried, from 1 to 6. A ship of 100 or more guns was a First Rate line-of-battle ship. The modern terms of derision **second rate** and **third rate** come from these ratings. (See Rate)

FISH
A large piece of wood attached to the mast to strengthen it.

FISH BROTH
Salt water, the sea.

FISHMONGER
'*Fishmonger*' meant whore, probably derived from '*fleshmonger*', and '*fishmonger's daughter*' also came to mean a harlot, from the late 16th century.

FIT THE BILL
A bill of lading (loading) itemised the items of cargo carried on board a ship. As the ship was unloaded at its destination, the items were checked to see if they exactly matched what was on the bill of lading, i.e. to see it they '*fitted the bill*'.

FLAGSHIP
The ship that carries the admiral, or in a merchant fleet, its most important ship. It has passed into the language as being the best store in a chain, the best car in a range and so on.

FLAKE OUT
It was important to keep the anchor chain in good condition, and it was regularly laid out along the deck - '*flaked*' - to check for weak links. The anchor was also often '*flaked out*' on deck in preparation for anchoring, laid out in such a way so that it does not '*foul up*' when the anchor is dropped. Lying down in the sun on deck

became known as *'flaking out'*. The term flake also applied to ropes. A rope was coiled so that each coil, on two opposite sides, lay on deck along the previous coil, allowing the rope to run freely.

FLASH IN THE PAN
In flintlock rifles and muskets, sometimes only the powder in the ignition pan would light. The propelling charge would not light, so the gun would not fire – there was merely a *flash in the pan*.

FLAW
A sudden and unexpected gust of wind. The modern word *flaw*, in the sense of an unexpected defect, may have the same origin.

FLIP
A strong, and favourite pirate *'cocktail''* of *'small beer'*, brandy and sugar, heated with a red-hot iron, popular from the 17th century onwards. *'Small beer'* was a light or watered beer, and *flip* seems to have been derived from the name Philip. The pirate captain, Henry Every, was described as *'lolling at Madagascar with some drunken sunburnt whore, over a can of flip.'* This sounds a very appealing description of piracy to those tolling under the most onerous taxation burden in Europe in the present day.

FLOGGING (1)
Sails do not flap, they 'flog', so flogging sails are not being used correctly.

FLOGGING (2)
Carried out with a cat-o-nine-tails, even officers could be flogged in the Royal and American navies when they were reduced to the ranks. The victim was spread-eagled to a hurdle or ladder, or sometimes across a gun on deck (over a barrel). Under 'The Articles of War' Act of 1653, English captains were limited to a flogging of 48 lashes, with a court-martial being required for more than 12, but very few captains observed the limit. The practice was finally stopped in 1850 by the United States and 1879 by the Royal Navy.

FLOGGING A DEAD HORSE
The *'Horse Latitudes'* are an area around the Atlantic's Canary Islands, named after the Spanish *'Golfo de las Yeguas'* (*Golf of the Mares*) Sailors were paid a month in advance, and usually spent it straight away or gave it to their families. It took around a month to cross the Atlantic from the Americas and reach the horse latitudes, and it was known as the *'dead horse month'* because the seamen had no pay. To mark its end, crews stuffed a canvas likeness of a horse with straw and marched it a around the deck. It was then strung up from the yardarm and cut adrift to float away in the sea, as the crew chanted to the captain, *'Old man, your horse must die.'* Admiral William Smyth commented that it was difficult to get crews to work properly when they were not being paid in that first much, about as much use as trying *'to flog a dead horse into activity'*.

FLOGGING THE MONKEY

Small casks of rum were known as *monkeys*, and a thirsty sailor would obtain an illicit drink by rinsing it out with water to get some alcohol into his system.

FLOGGING ROUND THE FLEET

Yet another device used by the Royal Navy to encourage men to desert or become pirates. A court-martialled man was strapped across a grating on a boat and rowed alongside the ships of the fleet lying in harbour. He was given 12 strokes of the cat o' nine tails at the first ship by the boatswain's mate, twelve at the second and so on, up to his quota of lashes, sometimes up to 300 or 500, which meant certain and agonising death. The crew of each ship was paraded on deck to watch the punishment.

FLORIDA

In the 16th century this meant any portion of the coast of North America, north and east of Mexico, and was only limited to its current location in the 19th century. Banco Florida was the Florida keys and coast.

FLORIDA STRAITS

Probably the best place for pirates and privateers to wait for Spanish treasure fleets leaving America. Passing through these, the Spanish could then pick up strong Westerly winds to get back to Spain.

FLOTA

The Spanish treasure fleet that usually made its way once a year towards Spain from the gold and silver mines of South and Central America. Its captains took an oath to burn, sink or destroy their ships rather than let them fall into enemy hands and enrich their resources. Thus pirates tried to take such ships by stealth, or extremely quickly. Swinburne, in 'Travels in Spain', 1779, wrote *'The flota is a fleet of large ships which carry the goods of Europe to the ports of America, and bring back the produce of Mexico, Peru, and other kingdoms of the New World.'* A flotilla was a small fleet.

The convoy of treasure ships would use the strongest ships to carry the most treasure. The flota would shun contact and run rather than fight, but could be caught by sloops. However, the galleons' tremendous firepower deterred most pirates and buccaneers. If a ship came in close enough to attempt to board a Spanish galleon, there were razor-sharp crescent blades attached to the edges of its outermost masts, which would cut the boarder's sails to shreds. The galleons also had fighting platforms halfway up the mainmast and foremast, from where archers would release showers of arrows and crossbow bolts. They could not use firearms for fear of sparks setting the oiled sails on fire. The annual fleets heading for Veracruz in Mexico were known as flotas, and to avoid confusion, the fleets sailing to Cartagena (Colombia) and Panama were known as 'Galeones'.

The Flota de Nueva Espana was the convoy, with warships, which brought precious metals from Mexico to Spain via Havana. The Flota de Terra Firme came to Spain via Havana from South America, guarded by the Armada de la Guarda de la Carrera de Indias.

FLOTSAM AND JETSAM

Flotsam is lost off a ship by accident and found as floating debris. Jetsam is a ship's goods and equipment that has been jettisoned (thrown overboard) to make the ship more stable in heavy seas, or to lighten it if being chased. 'Waveson' is goods floating on the surface after a wreck.

FLUKE (1)

The end of the anchor which digs into the seabed.

FLUKE (2)

A wind irregularity, and *fluky* described such a variable wind. This has come to mean a chance happening, lucky or unlucky in its consequences.

DUTCH FLUTE, FLUTE, FLEUT

Early 17th century ship, cheap to build, with a large hold, and easy prey for pirates. She was about 300 tons and 80 feet long, and needed only a dozen seamen to man her. With a flat bottom, broad beams and a round stern, it became a favourite cargo carrier, with about 150% of the capacity of similar ships. However they were slower and less wieldy than the normal merchant ship (q.v.) so were more easily taken. A German Flute was a transverse 8-key musical instrument, not suitable for sailing.

FLYBOAT

From the Spanish *'filibote'* – a vessel with a capacity of around 100 tons. Used for passenger and cargo traffic in fairly sheltered waters.

FLY BY NIGHT

When sailing downwind at night, a large, single, *'fly-by-night'* sail was used to do the job of several smaller sails. Requiring less attention, it could only be used downwind, usually at night, so was very rarely seen by sailors.

FLYING DUTCHMAN

For more than 300 years this has been the most famous maritime ghost story, which inspired Coleridge to write *'The Rime of the Ancient Mariner'*. The story is that the ship tries to round Cape of Good Hope and never succeeds, then also attempts Cape Horn and fails. The accursed ship sails backwards and forwards on its endless voyage, manned by an ancient crew crying for help as they work the rigging. The superstition is that any mariner who sees this ghost ship will die within the day. The real Flyning Dutchman appears to have set sail in 1660.

FOG

The greatest hindrance to pirates who drifted up the American coast from the West Indies when they reached Newfoundland, even great storms will not clear it, as Bellamy and Williams discovered. The Mariner's Dictionary tells us *'the warm water of the Gulf Stream penetrating high latitudes is productive of fog, especially in the vicinity of the Grand Banks where the cold waters of the Labrador Current makes the contrast in the temperatures of the adjacent waters most striking.'* This was the setting for the book and film *'The Perfect Storm'*.

FOGEY

A fogey was an invalid soldier or sailor, and an **old fogey** has come to mean an old-fashioned person. The derivation may come from the Scots dialect word fuggy, meaning covered with moss, i.e. not moving much.

FOOTLOOSE

The bottom of the sail is its foot, and when it is not tied to a boom, it is loose-footed, dancing freely in the wind with no restrictions, with a mind of its own, from which we get the saying *'footloose and fancy-free'*.

FORE-AND-AFT-RIGGED

The inside (*luff*) edge of a sail is attached to a mast, and the lower edge to a boom. The boom can then be moved from one side of the ship to another to direct the ship or react to winds.

FORECASTLE

Formerly a raised deck at the front of the ship, from where arrows were directed at the enemy – it served the function of a castle tower. Over the years its height was lowered and lowered to make boats more manoeuvrable, and to enable the captain on the poop deck to see what was happening. So the forecastle (pronounced *'folksle'*) just came to mean the front decking. In medieval ships there were also *'aftercastles'* for the knights and soldiers on board fighting ships, making them very unwieldy and unseaworthy.

FORGING AHEAD

When one ship steadily goes ahead and away from another.

FORLORN

17th century term for the vanguard of a military expedition such as Morgan's march on Panama. The French equivalent of a *'forlorn'* was *'les enfants perdus'* - the lost children. Perhaps today's word forlorn equated to the chances of survival of those who were in the most dangerous position in any hostilities.

FOULED ANCHOR

First used by the Admiralty in England in the 1500's, it has been used by the Royal Navy ever since, and adopted by the US Navy and fleets across the world as an insignia and symbol. How this problem scenario, of an anchor one cannot raise, became a sign of pride, is unknown.

FOUL UP

If an anchor is entangled with its cable, it is *'fouled up'*. A *'foul berth'* is caused by another vessel anchoring too closely, where there could be a collision. A *'foul bottom'* means that it is difficult to secure anchors. **'Fall foul of'** is a nautical term for becoming impeded. From foul we get today's acronym SNAFU (Situation Normal, All Fouled Up). More recent slang includes FUMTU (Fouled Up More than Usual) and FUBAR (Fouled Up Beyond All Recognition). Te author would like to add his own version as regards top management and politicians in the developed world – FUPOM (Fouled Up By Our Masters).

FOUNDER
'*Foundering is, she will neither veer nor steer, the sea will so over-rake her, except (unless) you free out the water, she will lie like a log, and so consequently sink.*' (Smith – 1691). The origin is the Latin *fundus* or bottom – the boat takes so much water in her hull that she sinks to the bottom of the ocean.

FREEBOOTER
From the Dutch '*Friebuiter*' or pirate.

FREE THE SHIP
Bale or pump water out.

FRENCH GOODS, or GOUT
Syphilis. To be '*Frenchified*' was to suffer from venereal disease. '*Frenchman*' was applied to any foreigner, and was also a synonym for syphilis. The prevalence of venereal diseases was often the main reason for wanting a doctor on board, and sometimes ships were taken just for the contents of their medical chests to treat the illness.

FRENCH KING, TO HAVE SEEN THE
To have been blind-drunk.

FRESHEN THE HAWSE (HAWSER)
The hawse is the opening in the bow, through which the anchor chains or ropes pass (Old Norse *hals*, meaning throat). *Freshen* is a nautical term meaning to renew. *Freshening the hawse* means that more anchor chain or rope is let out, to prevent the same piece constantly being exposed to friction. Somehow the term came to be associated with taking an alcoholic drink, possibly because that part of the anchor line was taking a rest. *Freshen the hawser* has the same meaning – the hawser is a heavy multi-purpose rope used on sailing ships, from the Old English word *hauucor* or hoist.

FRIGATE
This three-masted '*man-o'war*' weighed 360 tons and was 110 feet long, carrying 195 men and 26 guns. With up to 26 guns, this fast warship was not big enough to be a '*ship of the line*' for the '*line of battle*' of the Navy, but often used for independent action such as against pirates. '*A well-dressed frigate*' could also mean a woman. It is unknown where the phrase '*battleship*' for a domineering woman originated.

FROM THE SEAS
If a pirate ship was hailed and asked her home port, this could be the answer given. By their articles, pirates forsook their homelands, and thereupon belonged only '*to the seas*'.

FUDGE
'Fudging the books' comes from a Captain Fudge, known as *'Lying Fudge'*. He was the captain of the 'Black Eagle' which was to transport 55 Quakers in August 1655 from the Newgate to the Colonies, for offences against the Conventicle Act. Delayed at Gravesend, by October, 19 prisoners and some crew had died of the plague. He was arrested for debt and his remaining crew mutinied. In February 1666 the ship left for the West Indies, but was seized by a Dutch privateer and the Quakers freed. Israel d'Israeli, the father of the Prime Minister Benjamin D'Israeli, wrote in 1791: *There was, sir, in our time one Captain Fudge, who upon his return from a voyage, how ill-fraught soever his books, always brought home a good cargo of lies, so much that no aboard ship the sailors, when they hear a great lie, cry out "You fudge it!"*

FUTTOCK
A curved piece of timber composing the frame of the ship, referred to by location, e.g. first futtock, second futtock and so on.

FURL (FARTHEL)
To *farthel* or *furl* a sail is to wrap it up closely, and bind it together with strings called *caskets*, fast to the yard.

GALE
A wind of 34-40 knots, force 8 on the Beaufort Scale. A strong gale is 41-47 knots, force 9. A storm is classified as over 49-55knots, force 10, and a violent storm is 55-63 knots, force 11. Hurricanes are over 63 knots. The violent storms and hurricanes in the Caribbean wreaked havoc with the little privateers and pirate ships. One of Morgan's flagships was only 120 tons, so would disappear from view in a stormy sea.

GALIZABRA
A fast Spanish frigate, heavily armed, used in the 17th and 18th centuries. These could bring treasure back to Seville from the Spanish Main by themselves, rather than wait for the escorted convoy of treasure galleons known as the *'flota'*.

GALIOT
A long, sleek ship with a flush deck, carrying from 2 to 10 small cannon. Used by the Barbary Corsairs, powered by oars, she carried from 50 to 130 men.

GALLEON
Either used for trade or war, these huge ships had three or four masts, square rigged on the foremast and mainmast, and *latine*-rigged on the after-mast(s). A galleon on the transatlantic route might vary between 400 and 1000 tons, with 400 being an average ship. Sailing qualities varied, with speeds of 4-8 knots, and they could carry 20-76 guns of varying calibre. If used as a man-of-war, there were 36 guns mounted on each side of her, with two remaining guns mounted aft, making 74 cannon, plus numerous swing guns mounted along the rail used to repel boarders. They were usually terribly overcrowded, often carrying an infantry company of at least 100 troops under an army captain. There was a *'split command'*, whereas on Dutch and

English ships the naval captain also commanded the soldiers. Because of its high sides and even higher poop deck, the galleon was easily rocked by the sea, and it pitched and rolled more than other ships. With a top speed of only 8 knots, it was difficult to manoeuvre well for several reasons. Massive square sails prevented sailing into the wind, the hull being broad at the bottom and narrow at the top still failed to lower its high centre of gravity, and it had a small keel.

A typical Galleon

GALLEY

Formerly a ship that could be rowed, the term came to mean, in late seventeenth century England, an armed merchantman with one or more flush decks. The slave ship *Princess*, upon which Bartholomew Roberts served, was a galley of this type. For this use, they were rigged like frigates, and Captain Kidd's '*Adventure*' was such a galley.

GALLEYPEPPER

The soot and ashes that fell into pirates' meals from the cook's open fire in his galley, or kitchen.

THE GALLOWS DANCE

The jiggling of feet of a man being hanged

GALOOT

This dismissive word, originally used by seamen, seems to have come from the Dutch '*gelubt*', meaning eunuch.

GAMMY

Lame, as in having a '*gammy leg*'. Some ships were '*gammy*' if they were difficult to steer, especially if cargo had shifted. From the Welsh mutation of '*cam*' meaning crooked, awry or wrong, as in Dafydd Gam (David who is lame, or has a squint). In E. Annie Proulx's '*The Shipping News*' we learn that '*The common eider is called a "gammy bird" in Newfoundland for its habit of gathering in flocks for sociable quacking sessions. The name is related to the days of sail, when two ships falling in with each other at sea would back their yards and shout the news. The ship to windward would back her main yards and the one to leeward her foreyards. For close manoeuvring. This was known as gamming*'. This author believes that '*gammy*' is the only word of the ancient Welsh language used commonly in English, along with '*mom*' or '*mum*' from the

Welsh *'mam'* meaning mother, and *'dad'* from the mutation of the Welsh *'tad'*, or father.

GANGWAY!
This is the portable ramp used for moving goods or people to and from a pier or dockside, from the Old English *'gangweg'* or passageway. Any crewman struggling through with a heavy load would shout this term to ensure that others moved out of the way.

GARBLED
Garbling was the banned practice of mixing rubbish with cargo, and came to mean anything that was wrongly mixed up.

GENOA, GENNY
The biggest jib-sail on a ship.

GEORGES
English gold coins

GET INTO A FLAP
Sails do not flap, they *'flog'*, but flags flap. Warships signalled to each other with flags, and when there is a flurry of flagging, as a fleet prepares for battle or manoeuvres, there's *'a bit of a flap on'*.

GET SPLICED
To *'get hitched'* or married, when two ropes are joined together.

GIBBET
A wooden structure for exhibiting hanged pirates over a length of time.

GILT - KNOCK THE GILT OFF THE GINGERBREAD
This means to spoil the best part of a thing or story. In German fairs, gingerbread was always on sale, splashed with gilt to make its appearance more attractive. From this custom, the gilding and painted carvings at the bows, stern and entrance ports of sailing ships of war (see *'brightwork'*) came to be known as *'gingerbread work'*. To *'knock the gilt off the gingerbread'* was therefore to incur the wrath of a captain by damaging the appearance of the vessel.

GIVE A DOG A BAD NAME AND HANG HIM
Some sources believe that the origin was from 'seadog'. To get rid of pirates after 1700, it was enough to claim that a man had been a pirate to summarily hang him.

GIVE A WIDE BERTH
Avoid a dangerous-looking ship, or give lots of room to manoeuvring vessels. It has come to mean to *'steer clear of'* any person in a foul mood. Ships also had to be anchored far enough away from another ship (given a wide berth) so that they were not damaged when the other ship swung at anchor with the wind or tide.

GIVE QUARTER

Pirates 'gave quarter' to a ship if it surrendered immediately, so that none of the crew would be hurt. The term dates back to when captured knights and nobles would be returned for a ransom of around a quarter of their yearly income.

GIVE THE SLIP

A vessel which slipped its anchor cables, i.e. did not pull up the anchor, but cut the line, could make a '*soft farewell*' at night, and 'give one the slip.'

GLORY HOLE

A small enclosed space where unwanted items were stowed.

GOD MADE THE VICTUALS BUT THE DEVIL MADE THE COOK

Popular saying when salt beef was virtually the only edible food on ship.

GOING LIKE THE CLAPPERS

To '*clap on*' more sail meant that the ship sailed faster, and it seems that this is the origin of the term.

GOING TO POT, GONE TO POT

The large kettles or cauldrons used for cooking were never cleaned out. Whatever was available was added to the existing contents, even leftovers were added. Table scraps were not wasted, but thrown into the ever-cooking stew-pot. The term referred to things that no-one wanted any more, thus we now say that a High Street is going to pot, with the advent of out-of-town shopping malls. It may be that also gold and silver were melted down in the pot for easier division between pirate crews.

GOLD

Its stable value and ready conversion into anything the pirate needed made this the most lucrative of all targets. John Ayres wrote in 1684: '*Gold was the bait that tempted a pack of merry boys of us, near three hundred in number, under command by our own election of Captain John Coxon*', when they raided Panama and the Pacific coast.

THE GOLD BUG

The 'first' story of buried pirate treasure, it was responsible for Edgar Allan Poe's literary career, being the first story that he sold. However, the real origin of buried treasure stories was '*The Journal of Penrose, Seaman*' by William Williams, published posthumously in 1815.

GOLLYWOBBLER

We have a phrase today, '*I have the collywobbles*' meaning to be afraid. There may be a connection with this term, the large square staysail, which was hoisted between the masts of a schooner in a reaching wind, to increase speed.

GO OFF HALF-COCKED
If a pistol is only half-cocked it will not fire, and thus the intended effects will not be as one desires.

GO ON THE ACCOUNT
Undertake a buccaneer or pirate voyage. The term stems from the fact that if their actions were illegal, the person would have to account for his actions as within the law. From the 15th century onwards, craftsmen and professionals worked '*on account*', and so did pirates and buccaneers when they signed the ship's articles for a voyage, with '*no prey, no pay*'.

GO LARGE
This is a current English term for being an extrovert while trying to get as drunk as possible. However, in 1691 Captain Smith wrote: '*Now it is fair weather out with all your sails, go large or Lask, that is, when we have a fresh gale, or fair wind, and all Sails drawing. But for more haste unparrel the Mizen-Yard and lanch it, and the Sail over her lee-quarter, and fir Gives at the other end to keep the Yard ready, and with a Boom, Boom it out; this we call a Goose wing.*'

GOLD ROAD
The track across the Isthmus of Panama used to transport Spanish gold by trains of pack mules.

THE GOLDEN AGE OF PIRACY
From about 1690 until the death of Black Bart Roberts in 1722. After this date the Royal Navy grew in parallel with the British Empire and patrolled the seas. Naval sloops were built specifically to be 'pirate-hunters'.

GONE BY THE BOARD
Anything which was lost over the side was called this, as it was generally irretrievable.

GRAPE SHOT
A bunch of small cast-iron balls, wrapped in canvas, and fired by boarding parties (or to repel tem). The 'grape' dispersed like buckshot, making the likelihood of hitting someone more likely.

GRAPNEL, or GRAPPLE
A light anchor with very sharp flukes, which could be thrown at the ship to be boarded. The barbed flukes hooked into the ship, were difficult to extract, and pirates would climb the attached ropes.

GRAVEYARD OF THE ATLANTIC
Off the coast of Cape Hatteras, North Carolina, the northbound Gulf Stream meets very cold currents from the Arctic to form the treacherous and shifting '*Diamond Shoals*'. Hundreds of ships have been wrecked here.

GRAVING

The word from which we get today's 'graving dock' was described by Smith (1691) thus: *'Graving is only under water, a white mixture of tallow, soap and brimstone; or train-oil, resin and brimstone boiled together, is the best to preserve her (a ship's) caulking, and make her glib or slippery to pass the water; and when it (the hull) is decayed by weeds, or barnacles which is a kind of filth like a long red worm, will eat through all the planks if she be not sheathed, which is as casing the hull with tar, and hair, close covered over with thin boards nailed to the hull, which though the worm pierce, he cannot endure the tar...'*

GREAT GUNS

These were the heaviest cannon that ships carried, and also came to mean the most famous naval officers of the day. The term was later used for heavy weather, as when a wind *'blew great guns'*, probably referring to the crashing and booming of the waves around and against the ship. Recently is has become unfashionable, but we still use it if a football team is *going great guns*, meaning that they are performing really well, and by inference pounding the opposition.

GREEK FIRE

Fire bombs aimed at sails and rigging from cannon, to disable a ship's movement.

GRENADE, GRENADO, GRANADO

A square bottle of glass, wood or clay filled with pistol shot, glass, bits of iron and gunpowder, it was a favourite assault weapon of pirates and buccaneers. Used between 1650 and 1750, Johnston/Defoe wrongly attributes their invention to Blackbeard - *'a new fashioned Sort of Grenadoes, viz. Case bottles filled with Powder, and small Shot, Slugs, and Pieces of Lead or Iron, with a quick Match in the Mouth of it.'* *'Granado Shells'*, or *'granadoes'* were in common use from about 1700, the name derived from the Spanish *'granada'* meaning pomegranate. They were also sometimes also called *'powder flasks,'* hollow balls made of iron or wood and filled with gunpowder. With a touch hole and a fuse, it was thrown at the men on the opposite deck before boarding. No less than 15 grenades have been found on the wreck of the *Whydah* (q.v.)

GRIN AND BEAR IT

Lord George Byron heard this nautical expression, meaning to put up with hardship, when travelling on a ship. For seamen, there was no point in being miserable in putting up with harsh conditions, it was better to be good-natured on board a small ship, or the voyage would seem longer for everyone. Byron used it for his inspiration for a verse in *'Childe Harold'*:

> *'Existence may be borne, and the deep root*
> *Of life and sufferance make its firm abode*
> *In bare and desolated bosoms; mute*
> *The camel labours with the heaviest load,*
> *And the wolf dies in silence not bestow'd*
> *In vain should such example be; if they,*
> *Things of ignoble or savage mood,*

Endure and shrink not, we of nobler clay
May temper it to bear, it is but for a day.'

GRIPE
A ship will 'gripe' if it is badly designed or its sails are ill-balanced, repeatedly nosing into the wind so her sails flog and her speed falls. This malady passed from a nautical term to mean continuously complaining.

GROG
Alcohol, usually Jamaica rum. We still say we are *'feeling* **groggy***'* today if we are not very well – this refers to the frequency of pirate hangovers in the seventeenth and eighteenth centuries when pirates used to carouse between and during voyages *'on the account.'* In the Royal Navy, rum replaced brandy as the daily ration because of its cheap availability from newly conquered Jamaica. However, in 1740 Admiral Vernon ensured that the rum was diluted with water, because of drunkenness in the fleet. The daily pint of rum was replaced by adding two pints of water (a quart), and dispensed upon two occasions during the day instead of at one time. As the rum in those days could easily be 60% proof and above, it is no wonder that some crews were incapable of action if they drank a pint quickly. Drunken sailors were punished until the early twentieth century by having *'six water grog'*, their allowance diluted with six parts water instead of three parts. Grog (in decreasing proportions) was served in the Royal Navy until 1970. Sadly, the last *'grog ration'* - one part rum to three parts water -issued twice a day to sailors in half-pint measures, was drunk on July 30th, 1970.

GROG BLOSSOM
Either an inflammation on the face, or the 'purple' nose associated with heavy drinkers – often a form of Acne Rosacea rather than by over-imbibing. W.C Fields suffered from this, as did John Pierpoint Morgan, the great American financier of Welsh descent. The author suffers from this annoying complaint, which is often triggered by alcohol and spicy food. Sometimes, life is just not fair.

GROG SHOP
Tavern or pub.

GROMMETS
Ship's boys or apprentices used for menial tasks, from the Spanish *'grumete'* meaning novice seaman.

GUANO
Not a pirate term, but the reason why sailing ships were not immediately wiped out by the invention of steam ships. Islands in the Humboldt Current off the west coast of South America were covered in several yards depth of concentrated bird droppings, which made superb fertiliser. Seabirds gathered there for centuries, to make use of the abundant fish stocks. The value of the guano was not enough for an expensive steam ship to collect it, so in the late 19th century it became the staple cargo of hundreds of sailing ships.

GUARDACOSTA - COSTA GARDA

Private revenue cutters used by the Spanish to enforce their Caribbean trading monopoly. They were commissioned by local governors, fitted out in Spanish or colonial ports and earned their money by the prizes that they took. An account by Defoe in his General History tells us: '*A Guarda del Costa, of Porto Rico, commanded by one Matthew Luke, an Italian, took four English vessels, and murdered all the crews. He was taken by the Lanceston Man of War, in May 1722, and brought to Jamaica, where they were all but seven deservedly hanged. It is likely the man-of-war might not have*

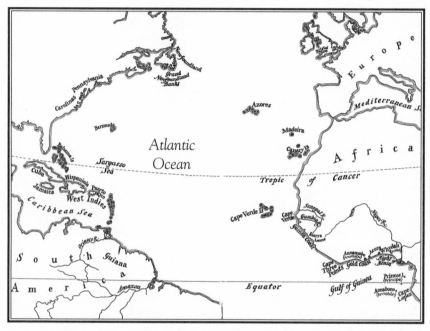

The Pirate Seas

meddled with her, but she blindly laid the Lanceston on board*, thinking that she had been a Merchant Ship, who thereupon catched a Tartar. Afterwards, in rummaging, there was found a Cartridge of Powder which was made up of an English journal, belonging, I believe, to the Crean snow; and upon this examination, at last, it was discovered that they had taken this vessel and murdered the crew; and one of the Spaniards, when he came to die, confessed that he had killed twenty Englishmen with his own hands.' (* to lay aboard is to draw alongside a ship to board it)

These 17th century 'Spanish' coastguard boats tried to stop all foreign trade to the West Indies. They regularly tortured English, Dutch and French merchant seamen and handed them over to the Inquisition. They were privateers, including Irish and English captains, commissioned by Spanish crown officials, and were restricted in peacetime, but from the 1670's had almost free rein to protect the Spanish West Indies and mainland from pirate, smuggling and logwood raids. They complemented the activities of the Armada de Barlovento, the Spanish royal squadron which patrolled the Caribbean. Guardacostas were given authority to patrol a particular stretch of coastline, and based in a specific port. Their crews were therefore fresh and ready for action, and had to be successful, for they were mercenaries who lived off the prizes they took. Acting Governor Molesworth of Jamaica, complained in 1684 that *'these galleys and piraguas are mostly manned by Greeks, but they are of all nations, rogues culled out for the villainies they commit. They never hail a ship; and so they can but master her, she is a certain prize. They lurk in the bushes by the shore, so that they can see every passing vessel without being seen. When our sloops are at anchor they set them by their compasses in the daytime, and steal on them at night with so little noise that they are aboard before they are discovered.'* The previous year, Governor Lynch had written to London that the Spanish had armed some small craft and *'ordered them to take all ships that have on board any "frutos de esas Indias" (fruits of these Indies), whereby they make all fish that come to net. They have committed barbarous cruelties and injustices, and better cannot be expected, for they are Corsicans, Slavonians, Greeks, mulattoes, a mongrel parcel of thieves and rogues that rob and murder all that come into their power without the least respect to humanity or common justice.'*

GUINEAMAN
A slave ship operating off the Guinea Coast of West Africa.

GUINEAS
English coins made from gold from Guinea.

GULF STREAM
The huge, warm *'North Equatorial Current'* which moves at a rate of about 4 knots from the Caribbean to the Gulf of Mexico, through the Florida Straits, up across the Grand Banks of Newfoundland and across the Atlantic at 80 miles per day, to warm the seas of the west coast of Britain and Europe. The author has bathed in the sea off the coast of Africa and South Wales in August, and the sea temperature has been far warmer in Wales.

GUN, SURE AS A
To be positive, or *'true'* as a gun. Not until the late 17th century did *'sure'* detach itself from *'as a gun'* and become a word in its own right in any context.

GUNNER
'Lord' Henry Dennis was the main gunner for Howel Davies, and then Black Bart Roberts, and the gunner led the group manning the cannon. His greatest skill was in aiming from a rolling ship at another rolling ship, and he would train and oversee each group of 4 to 6 men who were responsible for loading, aiming, firing, resetting and swabbing for the next load and fire. He would also check that guns were not dangerously over-heating (when they could burst their barrels) or recoiling excessively (a grave danger on the gun deck). He would coordinate timing, especially for broadsides. By 1700, cannon were available which could fairly accurately hit a target from 700 to 1000 yards away.

GUNNER'S DAUGHTER

The gun to which boys serving in the Royal Navy were tied or *'married'* when being whipped. On some ships it was superstition that if the boys were not whipped on a Monday, there would be no good winds for the following week. To *'hug'* or *'kiss the gunner's daughter'* thus meant a whipping. When *'married to the gunner's daughter'* for a flogging, the miscreant was tied to the four deck rings which held each cannon in place. As the sailor was tied to the gun barrel, the saying **'you've got me over a barrel'** comes from this time. Sailors were whacked with a rope's end on the gun deck, where the ceilings were only a maximum of four feet six inches. For more serious offences, requiring enough room to 'swing a cat' of nine tails, the punishment was carried out on the main deck.

GUN WALLS, GUN WALES, GUNNELS

In the 15th century, these were called *'gonne walles'*, the upper edge of a ship's side, that prevented guns and other deck items from falling over the side. They had openings, to let sea water wash from the deck, and to let guns fire. The saying *'awash to the gunnels'* means that the sea is coming over the deck. Derived from the same source is *'packed'* or *'full to the gun wales'* that is that the lower decks are crammed full of cargo and men, and so is the top deck, so that the ship can take no more plunder. A *'wale'* was any of the strakes on the side of a vessel, from the Old English *'walen'*, or ridge.

GUN SALUTE

A ship entering port may well do this, to let the people know that it was friendly. It took some time to recharge cannon, so it was an act of good faith, becoming defenceless for a time.

HAG-BOAT

Also referred to as a hog-boat. In the chapter on Black Bart Roberts, we find that his Royal Rover is classified as a hog-boat: The Weekly Journal reported in 1720 on the action *'The Lisbon Fleet from the Bay of All Saints, Brazil, has arrived. But one vessel of 36 guns was taken by a pyrate ship (formerly an English hog-boat) and two others plundered.'*

HAIL

A ship was hailed to ask where she was bound (see Ahoy!). Saluting another ship with trumpets and the like was called *hailing*.

HALE

Most old books use this term for *'haul'*, meaning to pull, so *overhaled* should mean overhauled. However, to *over hale* means that a rope is pulled too tightly, so it is haled the other way to make is more slack.

HALF-MUSKET SHOT

The preferred *'killing range'* for maximum effect of a broadside of cannon. At 100 years, this was point-blank range, and the Royal Navy generally aimed at the hull to sink the ship. Other navies used different types of cannon to fire at longer range at the masts and yards of British ships to prevent them from closing in.

HALF SEAS OVER
A term meaning half-way across the sea, or nearly finished, and used when halfway across the Atlantic, or halfway across the Irish Sea between Britain and Ireland. The term came to mean *'pretty well gone'* or drunk. Britan imported a strong beer from Holland in the 17th century, which was known as *'op zee ober'*, or overseas beer. Because of its potency, it was a favoured drink of seamen, and its effects upon one's physical and mental capacities meant a swift descent into unsteadiness of gait and reason. *"Lads, warning by me take!"*

HALF-SLEWED
When the yards which carry the sails are not properly braced to deflect the wind, they are said to be half-slewed, faltering and swaying ineffectively - hence the synonym for affected by alcohol. (See also Slewed.)

HALYARDS
The ropes by which sails are hoisted, e.g. the jib halyards, top sail halyards, etc.

HAMMOCK
Columbus noted that the Carib Indians slung a *'hamorca'* between trees, and he then introduced it into European ships. Their swinging action counteracted the sell of the waves and made for a more comfortable sleep than in a bunk or on deck. Hammocks on Royal naval vessels were first authorised in 1597.

HAND OVER FIST
Seamen used to climb the rigging or ropes, and haul in or let out sails *'hand over hand.'* A fast and skilful sailor was highly valued. Because one hand always had to be clenched to a rope, the term changed to *'hand over fist.'* Someone who accumulated yardage very quickly was said to be climbing *'hand over fist'*. Someone who rapidly ascends the rigging is a successful and skilled seaman, and the term was applied to the pursuit of financial success in the USA, and when one gains money *'hand over first.'*

HANGING, DRAWING AND QUARTERING
This barbarous practice was brought by the Normans to England, and practised upon various Welsh princes and their followers up until the fifteenth century. It is said that it was personally devised by King Edward for the ritual slaughter of Prince Dafydd, the brother of the murdered Llywelyn, at Shrewsbury in 1282. It stayed as the official sentence for treason, forgery, the murder of a master by a servant and (sometimes) piracy until 1814 in Britain. King Charles II watched the regicides who signed his father's death warrant suffer this sentence in 1660. The condemned man was dragged on a sledge and hanged, but not until he was dead. The condemned man would be cut down within a few minutes, then fastened to a stone block, when the executioner cut off his penis and testicles, cut open his stomach and pulled out his intestines, which had to be burnt before the prisoner's eyes. English law insisted

that the prisoner be disembowelled while still alive. The body was then cut into quarters, which were displayed in various public places. These executions drew huge crowds. Women who forged or committed treason were not to be '*mangled publicly*' but burnt alive. It was treason for a woman to murder her husband but not for a man to kill his wife. A woman was slowly burnt for '*coining*' (forging coins) in 1789 in front of huge crowds in London.

HANGMAN'S KNOT
From the inestimable 'The Ashley Book of Knots', 1944, which lists and illustrates 3854 different kinds of knots: *There are several knots recommended for this purpose, and there are several variations of the one given here that may be found in the chapter on NOOSES. But this knot of eight turns appears to be the standard one, and it may be counted upon to draw up smoothly and snugly when it fulfils its office. The noose is always adjusted with the knot slightly below and immediately in back of the left ear. This is to provide the sideways jerk, which is one of the refinements of a successful hanging.*
Hangings at sea were infrequent. Such an occasion furnished a bit of extra-routine labour, in which the boatswain took especial pride, and in which no bungling was tolerated. A boatswain's reputation would be forever ruined if there were any hitch on such an occasion... certain well-established conventions had to be observed... A fall was led through a single block at the fore yardarm and thence to a second single block under the fore cap. Between the two blocks was a yardarm knot, the upper bight of which was not half-hitched, as is customary, but was merely stopped with light twine. This stopping would carry away the instant the knot was hauled against the block, so spilling the sheepshank. The weight at the noose end at once dropped to take up the slack given by the spilled sheepshank, and it was brought up with a jerk by a toggle which fetched against the yardarm block. The toggle was marlingspike hitched and seized to the rope at a point which allowed for an exact six-foot drop outside the rail. In preparation for this the fall was laid at a length along the deck 'ready to be hurried aft' when twenty stout fellows seized the rope.'

HAPPY AS A SANDBOY
The Ostrich Inn, on the site of the original harbour of Bristol, is next to the Redcliffe Caves, which used to be a major source of sand. Landlords used to send little boys (sandboys) into the caves to collect sand to spread on the floor of the tavern to soak up the beer spillages. They were paid in beer.

HARD AND FAST
When a ship touched the sea bed (see '*touch and go*') and was held tight, and unable to proceed, being '**stuck fast**.' This fixed situation has come to be used in modern terminology for a rule or opinion, which cannot be changed.

HARDTACK
Biscuits baked without salt in a hot oven, also called sea biscuits, which were taken on long voyages as they resisted spoilage.(see Ships Biscuits)

HARD UP

Sailing ships could be pressed by the wind, and forced to turn away and alter course, putting the helm '*hard up to windward*'. Today the term means being pressed for cash, having to '*weather*' a financial storm. The other derivation is the phrase '*hard up in a clinch with no knife to cut the seizing.*'

HARD UP IN A CLINCH AND NO KNIFE TO CUT THE SEIZING

A nautical saying, denoting that a seaman was in a difficult situation, with no way to cut himself free. It has virtually the same meaning as today's '*between a rock and a hard place.*'

HAWSER

A heavy rope used for towing or docking. (See Freshen the Hawse)

HAZARD

The most common card game in Black Bart's time, to while away the hours. However, dice games were the most popular pursuit and the quarrels caused by gambling on his ship forced Black Bart to get his pirates to abandon them except on land.

HAZING

One of the reasons why seamen were reluctant to fight off pirates, and many willingly joined them, was this practice of making life at sea as bitter and miserable as possible for them. *Hazing* was the practice of giving seamen unpleasant, disagreeable jobs, often during their leisure time, by bullying ship's officers. It comes from the Old French *haser*, to punish by blows, or scare. Punishments included picking oakum (q.v.) or being forced to stand for hours on end, although the exhausted sailors had done nothing wrong. A pirate in '*Treasure Island*' shouts: '*I'll be hanged if I'll be hazed by you, John Silver!*'

HARD AS BRAZIL

A term dating from the mid-17th century, meaning extremely tough, stemming from the shipping of Brazilian hardwoods.

HARD TACK

A term for ship's biscuits made of flour and water, which could last for months if stored correctly. (see Ship's Biscuits)

HAVEN'T A CLEW (CLUE)

The sails are attached at their corners by brass rings (cringles) sewn into the clews. If the clew should become undone, and the vessel '*has no clew*', it will not sail anywhere until it is '**clewed up**' again. Clew lines are lines running from the corner of the sail, known as the clew, to the yardarm and down to the deck. To clew is to haul a square sail up to a yard, before furling, by means of clew lines.

HAWSE

The hawses are the great openings under the head of the ship, through which the cables run when she lies at anchor.

HEAD

Roman galleys had elaborate heads on the bow, which were fitted with bronze *beaks*, and used for ramming. As sailing ships developed, the *'beakhead'* became a term applied to a structure projecting from the stem and the bowsprit. This was usually a work platform, decked with grating and open to the sea below. Waves washing through the grating made a constant flushing action and thus an ideal lavatory. *'The head'* remains a popular term for a ship's sanitary utilities.

HEAD SEA

'When the Storm is past, though the wind may alter three or four points of the Compass, or more, yet the Sea for a good time will go the same way; then if your course be right against it, you shall meet it right a head, so we call it a Head Sea. Somimes when there is but little wind, there will come a contrary sea, and presently the wind after it, whereby we may judge that from whence it came was much wind, for commonly before any great Storm the sea will come that way. Now if the Ship may run on shore or mud she may escape, or Billage on a rock, or Anchors flook, repair her leak, she split or sink, she is a wrack. But feeling the Storm deceaseth, let us try if she will endure the Hullock of a sail, which sometimes is a piece of the Mizen-Sail or some other little Sail, part opened to keep her head to the Sea, but if yet she would weather coile, we will loose a Hullock of her Fore-sail, and put the helm a weather, and it will bring her head where her stern is; courage, my hearts.' – Captain Smith, 1691. See Sea.

HEAVE TO, or LIE TO

Sails were set to counteract each other, so the ship stayed almost motionless.

HELL'S BELLS AND BUCKETS OF BLOOD

'Hell's Bells' is a shortened version of the sailor's expletive *'Hell's Bells and Buckets of Blood.'* There is also an old saying that *'he swears like a sailor'* which seems to be the precursor of *'he swears like a trooper.'*

HELM

From 'The Gentleman's Dictionary', 1705, we read: *'HELM, or Tiller, of a Ship; is that Piece of timber which is fastened into the Rudder, and so comes forward into the Steerage, or Place where he at the Helm Steers the Ship, by holding the Whipstaff in his Hand. Some Ships have a Wheel, like those in Cranes, placed between the Quarter-Deck and Coach; which has several Advantages, to what the Common Methods have.'* When Black Bart raided one port in 1719, the captain had taken the new innovation of the ship's wheel off the best merchant at harbour, and Roberts tried to bargain it back to the boat, but was foiled. Wheels started to become common in the 1730's, replacing the tiller, and requiring considerably less effort. The modern term **'at the helm'** means in control of an organisation or team.

HEMPEN HALTER
The hangman's noose.

HEMPEN FEVER
The pirate joke was that one would rather die by this, i.e. by hanging, than suffering in the merchant or Royal Navy.

HERMAPHRODITE BRIG, HALF BRIG
A two-masted ship with the foremast of a brig and the mainmast of a schooner.

HIDE A LOUSE FOR THE SAKE OF ITS SKIN
To be thrifty or try to save something, a habit despised by most pirates, who lived their short lives by the day.

HIGH AND DRY
A ship that has been run aground so far as to be seen dry on the strand, left *high and dry*, or '**stranded**.' It was also applied to a ship that had been beached for careening, or one that was in dry dock, on blocks for repairs.

HISPANIOLA
Columbus called the island today shared by Haiti and the Dominican Republic 'Isla Espanola' (Island of Little Spain) in 1492, and Hispaniola is the Anglicised version of it. Under Oliver Cromwell's grandiose *'Western Design'*, he discussed a possible alliance with Spain, while sending out a force to seize Hispaniola from them. The 1654-55 expedition was a shambles, and rather than return home to his wrath, the leaders decided to take Jamaica instead, at the heart of the Spanish Caribbean

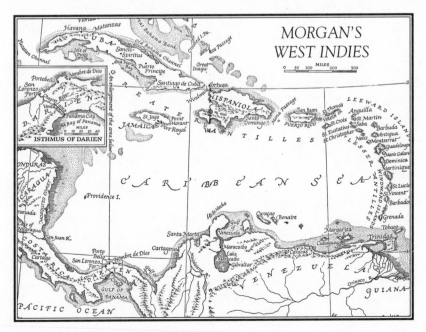

possessions. In 1665, the island was taken despite the inadequacies of the campaign, simply because there were very few Spanish settlers or defences. Many of Captain Morgan's buccaneer's were Cromwell's soldiers who stayed on in Jamaica, and fought wearing their old army 'redcoats'. The name Saint Dominic was afterwards applied to the island by the French, who were anxious to rid the island of Spanish connections as they vied with Spain for its possession.

TO HITCH
' to catch-hold of Anything with a Roape, to hold it fast' - Sir Henry Mainwaring, 'The Seaman's Dictionary' 1644. To 'get hitched' was, like 'to get spliced' to become married.

HIT THE DECK
At close quarters, if a swivel gun or murderer was to be fired, pirates would dive to the deck to avoid being severely maimed.

HOGSHEAD
Large cask (barrel) used generally for shipping wine and spirits, as well as tobacco, sugar and molasses. As a measure for beer or cider it is 54 gallons. A statute of King Richard III in 1483 fixed a hogshead of wine at 63 wine-gallons, or 52 and a half Imperial gallons. It seems to have been derived from the Dutch *oxehoved* or the Old Swedish *oxhooft*, meaning ox's head, so war corrupted to hogshead over time.

HOISTED BY ONE'S PETARD
The *petard* was the small cask of gun powder used to prime cannon fuses, and in battle one was stored by each gun. A careless seaman could set one off lighting a fuse, thereby being blown (hoisted) into the air. There is another explanation in that a petard was an ancient iron bell-shaped weapon filled with gun powder. It was hoisted, usually on a tripod, onto gates or barricades to blow them up. If it exploded prematurely, the engineer would be blown up.

HOLD
The part between the keelson and the lower deck where all goods, stores and victuals are carried. The modern word *rummage* comes from to *'rummidge in the hold'*, to remove and clear the goods in the hold.

HOLDING ITS OWN
The situation when neither ship can advance on each other. Also used to describe a ship trying to approach a port but not making any headway.

HOLY MACKEREL
Mackerel is caught in huge quantities, but *'goes off'* very quickly, especially in its summer *'runs'*. Thus it was the only fish that merchants were allowed to sell in the 17th century on the Holy Day, Sunday.

HOLY PIRATES
To distinguish them from the Muslim Barbaray Corsairs in the Mediterranean, the Knights Hospitallers, the Knights of St Stephen, the Knights of Rhodes and the

Knights of Malta were known by this term. The Knights Hospitallers were successively based in Jerusalem from 1070, then Syria, then Cyprus, and eventually were ousted from Rhodes in 1308, moving on to Malta. All these Christian orders were virtually permanently at war with Islam for hundreds of years.

HOLYSTONE
The soft sandstone used in the navy to scrub the decks of ships. It was either called holystone as it was full of holes, or because sailors had to kneel, as in prayer, to use it.

The third verse of the shanty '*The Flash Frigate*' is:
The next thing we do is to holystone the decks,
Mizzen-topmen from the fore-hatch their buckets must fetch,
And its fore and main topmen so loudly they bawl,
Come, fetch up your holystones, squilgees and all.

HONESTY AMONGST THIEVES
The sea thieves, pirates, had such severe punishments for stealing from the '*commonwealth*' booty, or each other, that there was very little theft amongst them, the origin of this saying.

HOOKER
This may have come from the prostitutes who used to frequent that great entrepot of European trading, the Hook of Holland. By the 19th century, some ships were known as '*old hookers*' by their crews, presumably because they were female and traded for money. In the 16th century, *hookers* were thieves who used a hook to gaff the possessions of their victims in the streets, and ran away with the loot. Perhaps some of these hookers were female.

HORNSWAGGLE
To cheat.

HORSE BEANS
'*Horse beans*' were fed to slaves on the '*Middle Passage*' from Africa to the Americas. Very large beans, they were used as animal fodder in Europe, and to make them semi-edible for humans, they were pulped then covered with '*slabber sauce*', made from palm oil, flour, water and red pepper.

HORSE LATITUDES
The areas of variable winds on either side of the *Doldrums* (q.v.), at around 30 degrees in each hemisphere, in both the Atlantic and Pacific Oceans. They are also known as '*the Calms of Cancer*' and '*the Calms of Capricorn.*' (See Flog a Dead Horse)

HORSE MARINE
An insult by a seaman to a marine, and an even greater insult when applied to a mariner, implying that he was a land-lubber.

HOT CHASE, HOT PURSUIT

The principle that a fight on the open seas could be carried on into neutral territory if the enemy tried to escape. In 1759, Admiral Boscowen chased three French vessels into Portuguese territory and destroyed them.

HOTCHPOTCH, HOTCHPOT, HODGEPODGE

This expression has been corrupted to *hodgepodge* over the years. In Anglo-French, it was used to describe a dish made in a single pot in which many ingredients were mixed. It was usually a mutton broth or stew, with vegetables, similar to the Welsh national dish, '*cawl*'. The origin appears to have been from the Old French '*hocher*' (to shake) and *pot*. Thus ingredients were mixed or shaken up in a large cooking pot. During the 13th century, it came to refer to the process of gathering property and sharing equally cargo that had been damaged and strewn about after the collision of two ships. (Both ships were to blame, so the salvage was shared jointly between the owners). The remaining goods were, by the process of *hotchpot*, divided equally between the owners of the two vessels, based on the premise that both ships contributed to the loss. The term is now synonymous with confusion and disorder, a jumble.

HOT PRESS

When it was absolutely vital for the Royal Navy to impress men in time of war, press gangs were given permission to take any men, notwithstanding that they might carry '*protections*' against impressment (-certificates granted to ships masters, mates lighthouse keepers, Customs Officers, harpooners, etc., etc.) In times of '*hot press*', men hid for their lives.

HOTSHOT

The term dates back to at lest the early 17th century, with '*hot-shots*' being men who went to war, perceiving themselves to be excellent at their profession. The nautical term applied to heated cannonballs. On cold days, cannonballs might be heated and each kept in an iron bucket to warm the crew on watch or at rest.

HOUSE OF LORDS

The name given to themselves by the senior members of Howell Davies's pirates, who then served under Bart Roberts. They addressed each other as 'my Lord' and treated the other crew members as the '*Commons*'.

HOY

A small, heavy coasting-vessel for goods and passengers, keeping near to the coast, from the Dutch '*heude*' and '*heu*'. The English hoy, or work-sloop, dated from around the end of the 17th to the start of the 18th century, being square-rigged with a gaff sail. They were used for smuggling and piracy, taking 6-10 cannons on the top deck, with swivel guns fore and aft, and a crew of 30 men. They were hit and run ships, used in night attacks near the coast, not for long voyages.

HULK

From the Old French *'hulque'*, these were large transport vessels, which when no longer seaworthy were sometimes used for storage or as prisons in harbours. Thus it is an old, obsolete or abandoned great ship, which often towered over the smaller boats in a dock. *Hulking* has come to mean something large and unwieldy, and everyone today knows of *'The Incredible Hulk'*, a rather unjolly green giant.

HUMBLE PIE

The origin of this term is that *'umble'* was the intestines of deer. The master ate pie made with venison - muscle meat - while the servants ate *'umble pie'*.

HURRICANE

A clockwise revolving storm up to Force 12, 65 mph, common in the Caribbean and up the North American coast.

HUZZAH

The fore-runner of hurrah, and then hooray, a shout of encouragement.

IDLER

Because they worked in the day, ships' artists such as the carpenter, sailmakers and cooks were excused night watches. They were thus *'idle'* and off-duty at night, and called *'idlers'*. William Falconer, in his 1789 'Universal Dictionary of the Marine' said an idler was a member of the crew who worked all through the ay, and thus was not required to keep the night watch unless there was an emergency – carpenters, cooks, sailmakers and the surgeon were therefore exempt.

ILE-A-VACHE

Also called Ile-de-Vache (Cow Island), this favourite pirate location off the south-west of Haiti was mispronounced by the British as *Isle of Ash*.

I'LL NAIL YOU FOR THAT

This threat dates from the days when justice consisted of hanging or flogging. For other crimes one could be *'nailed'*. The miscreant was taken to the hangman's gibbet and 'nailed' through the earlobes until night. Women were also nailed through the tongue for slander.

IMPRESSMENT

The official act of taking men for the service of their country, for the army or navy, usually against their will. It is not generally known that many of Oliver Cromwell's *'New Model Army'* were impressed men. (Many of these *'redcoats'* ended up as buccaneers in the West Indies, serving in their faded red jackets under Captain Morgan). Service is the navy was hated, so there was always a shortage of seamen, and thus *'press gangs'*, to press unwilling men into the service are part of British history. In 1536 Mary Tudor's government disallowed Thames watermen from exemption to from being *'pressed'*. Thus all London's taverns were a fruitful source of recruitment. Elizabeth I gave *'protection'* (exemption) to mariners from being pressed for army service in 1563, and allowed any itinerant vagrant to be pressed in

1597. Queen Anne gave protection to apprentices under 18 years old in 1703. George II exempted men over 55, Thames watermen employed by fire insurance companies, and masters and mates of merchant ships in 1740. A proportion of seamen in colliers (coal ships) were given protection in 1774. (See Hot Press, Press Gangs). The 1812 War between England and America was partially the result of the British practice of impressing American sailors off American ships, claiming that they were British subjects. (The author would like to note that Wales, a far older nation than England, has never declared war on America, nor any other country in its 2000 years of Christian history, and that it is England's only remaining colony).

INCH OF CANDLE
The fixing of a time limit by marking a line on a lit candle, it was commonly used at auctions of prize vessels at Port Royal. The Welshman Maurice Williams, one Morgan's captains, bought the Spanish ship 'Abispa' (Wasp) for £120 in May 1659, 'by inch of candle'. He had made the highest offer, then waited for the candle to burn the required inch. There being no other bids in the time, the ship was his.

INDENTURED SERVANTS
These were a source of manpower for the pirate captains – Esquemeling makes reference to their treatment by slave owners: 'The planters that inhabit the Caribbee Islands are rather worse and more cruel unto their servants than the preceding. In the Isle of Saint Christopher dwells one, whose name is Bettesa, very well known among the Dutch merchants, who has killed above a hundred of his servants with blows and stripes. The English do the same with their servants. And the mildest cruelty they exercise towards them is that, when they have served six years of their time (the years they are bound for among the English being seven to complete), they use them with such cruel hardship as forces them to beg of their masters to sell them unto others, although it be to begin another servitude of seven years, or at least three or four. I have known many who after this manner served fifteen or twenty years before they could obtain their freedom. Another thing very rigorous among that nation is a law in those islands, whereby if any man owes to another above five and twenty shillings, English money, in case he cannot pay, he is liable to be sold for the space of six to eight months.'

Black slaves were treated even worse than English servants, and many became pirates. The great chronicler of the buccaneers, Esquemeling, also turned to buccaneering from being an indentured servant, after he was bought and sold. The Welsh Royalist prisoners from the Civil War Battle of Saint Ffagans were sent to the West Indies as indentured servants, never to return. Cromwell also sent 7,000 Scottish prisoners, and any Irishmen he could lay his hands on. Landless paupers from France, Britain and Holland were attracted, by the promise of free land after seven years, with free passage and board, to go to the West Indies. The ruthless cruelty of employers ensured that many of them, escaped into a better life of buccaneering and piracy.

On that note, Esquemeling recorded how a planter treated a bondsman who ran away and was recaptured: 'No sooner had he got him, but he commanded him to be tied to a tree; here he gave him so many lashes on his naked back, as made his body run with an entire stream of blood; then, to make the smart of his wounds the greater, he anointed *him with lemon juice, mixed with salt and pepper. In this miserable posture he left him tied to the tree for 24 hours, which being past, he began his punishment again, lashing him, as before, so cruelly, that the miserable wretch gave up the ghost.'*

Known as 'engagees' in the French colonies, Bretons and Normans were decoyed into the West Indies by promises of a better life, not realising that they were needed to cultivate sugar-cane and tobacco as there were not enough Negro slaves there. *Engagees* in the French Antilles usually gained their freedom in 18 months or three years, compared to the standard English term of seven years. Being resold, some Englishmen could serve up to 12 years of slavery.

INDIGO
The genus Indigofera was harvested and refined in the West Indies and Spanish America, to make a purple-blue powder of huge value as a commercial dye in Europe. In November 1664, the Welsh Captain Maurice Williams took a Spanish prize full of logwood, chests of indigo and silver into Port Royal.

IN DEEP WATER (see Bitter End)

IN DUE COURSE
A nautical term from the days of sail, meaning that something will happen when it should happen.

IN HIS BOOTS
Dead-drunk, also 'topsy-boosy' meant drunk. Today, 'wellied' means drunk, derived from 'welly', the slang for a wellington-boot. To **'fill one's boots'** is still common slang today for getting extremely drunk.

IN IRONS
The awkward position of a square-rigged sailing ship when it is headed into the wind and unable to bear away on any tack. Fore-and-aft-rigged vessels can also fall into the same trap.

INTERLOPER
An illegal trading vessel.

IN THE OFFING
In pirate terminology, 'we sighted a prize in the offing' meant that a ship had been spotted a good distance from, and barely visible from shore. 'In the offing' means now that something might happen.

IN THE SAME BOAT
This comes from the days when on a sailing ship, everyone had to suffer the same problems – see 'Grin and Bear It.'

IRISH APRICOT
A potato, also known as an Irish apple, or Irish lemon.

IRISH ARMS
Thick legs.

IRISH BEAUTY
A woman with two black eyes.

IRISH CONFETTI
A hail of stones and other harmful missiles.

IRISH EVIDENCE
False evidence or a perjurer.

IRISH HORSE
The 'Irish Joke' has a long history. Most Irish jokes start off as jokes told by the Irish about men from Kerry, the most south-west, rural and unsophisticated part of the island. 'Irish horse' was the seaman's term for extremely tough salt beef (-later, corned beef earned the epithet). It was thought that the poor Irish worked their horses longer and harder than the English, which made them tough to eat. A part of an 18th century sailor's song runs:
'Salt horse, salt horse, what brought you here ?
You've carried turf for many a year.
From Dublin quay to Ballyack
You've carried turf upon your back.'

IRISH HURRICANE
Also called 'Paddy's hurricane', dead calm at sea.

IRISH PENNANTS
Loose ends of rope hanging from the rigging or side of ships, noting lazy work by the crew. Also the reef sail ends left flapping when the sails were furled on a square rigged ship. These reef ends, and gasket ends (the strip of canvas or rope holding the furled sail) were also known as 'dead men'.

IRONS
Bilboes were carried on all the Armada ships, and were soon taken up by British ships as a form of punishment. To 'iron' a man, or 'clap him in irons' was to put him in bilboes (see bilboes).

IRON-SICK
From Sir Henry Maiwaring's 'The Seaman's Dictionary', printed in 1644: *'A ship or boat is said to be iron-sick when the bolts, spikes, or nails are so eaten away with the rust of the salt water that they stand hollow in the planks, and so the ship doth receive in water by them; and this is the reason why they put lead over all the bolt heads under water.'*

ISRAEL HANDS
According to Defoe, Hands was shot through the knee by Blackbeard when they

were drinking in North Carolina. When asked why he shot him, Blackbeard *'only answered, by damning them, that if he did not now and then kill one of them, they would forget who he was.'* Hands was made Blackbeard's second-in-command, captain of the *Adventure*, and both settled in North Carolina after the siege of Charleston. Hands was away when Blackbeard was killed in 1718, and taken to Virginia for trial. He was convicted but pardoned for testifying against corrupt North Carolina officials, and Defoe said that he died a lame beggar in London. However, a pirate called Israel Hynde sailed with Black Bart Roberts. He joined Roberts' crew from the Mercy galley in 1721, and was hung in chains at Cape Coast Castle in 1722. Being hung in chains meant that he was an 'important' pirate, gibbeted as an example to others, and the author believes that this could be the real end of Israel Hands

ITCHLAND
Wales in the late 17th century, until Scotland took over the nomenclature in the early 18th century, and an *'Itchlander'* came to mean a Scot until the mid-19th century.

JACK DUSTY
Not a pirate term, but the name given in the Royal Navy to the sailor assigned responsibility for the flour stores, which was needed to make bread. The equivalent US tem is *'Jack-of-the-Dust.'*

JACOB'S LADDER
A portable rope ladder with wooden rungs, of use in a variety of situations when slung over the ship's side. In Genesis 28:12 Jacob saw angels ascending to, and descending from heaven on a ladder.

JAMAICA
The expedition sent by Cromwell to take possessions in the West Indies was an absolute disaster. In its attack on Hispaniola, its commander, General Venables, was so frightened that he hid behind a tree *'soe possessed with terror that he could hardly spake'*. Captain Butler, sent to recruit Frenchmen on their island of St Kitts, was so drunk that he fell off his horse and spewed over the feet of the delegation of French officers sent to meet him. Jamaica was taken more by accident than design, and Venables spent some time in the Tower of London on his return to England. After the taking of Jamaica by the English in 1655, French, Dutch and English buccaneers flocked to its capital, Port Royal. The French had forced them out of their Tortuga stronghold, and the English authorities saw them as a source of considerable trading wealth, and a first line of defence against the Spanish in the West Indies. By 1662, there was so much looted silver and gold in Port Royal that the government thought about establishing a mint there.

JAMAICA DISCIPLE, or the LAW OF THE PRIVATEERS
Customs passed down from the *'boucaniers'* of the 1630's onwards in the Caribbean. There were democratic controls on any type of authority in the *'pirate code'*, or *'code of the coast'*. Under the code, any *'prize'* was divided up evenly, with two shares to

the captain and one each to all men. Other rules covered the presence of women on board, hours of drinking, the settlement of disputes, and the apportionment of prize money to those maimed and injured. By Henry Morgan's day, his last expedition gave the captains eight shares each, and Admiral Morgan took 1%. This was agreed before the venture.

JAMESTOWN
The first English settlement in America, dating from 1607, on the banks of the james River in Virginia.

JERKY
What Americans call today '*beef jerky*' were strips of meat called '*viande boucanee*' and what English buccaneers called 'jerked meat' after the American-Spanish '*charqui*'. Hard and dry as a board after being slowly smoked in the '*boucanes*', they were sold by the Tortuga boucaniers in bundles of a hundred for six pieces of eight. They were essential for crew in the tropics.

JIB
A triangular sail set on the boom which runs out from the bowsprit.

JIBES, GYBES
Swinging a boom (*gybing*) when changing course can lead to someone being hurt, or damage to sail or rigging. Gybes came to mean unwelcome actions, and are the origin of today's jibes.

JIGGER
This was a light tackle consisting of a single and double block, that increased pulling power by a factor of four. It is included in this glossary because of the following delightfully explicit instruction from R. Dana's 1844 '*The Seaman's Manual*' - '*Lift the skin up, and put into the bunt the slack of the clews (not too taut), the leech and foot-rope, and body of the sail; being careful not to let it get forward under or hang down abaft. Then haul your bunt well up on the yard, smoothing the skin and bringing it down well abaft, and make fast the bunt gasket round the mast, and the jigger, if there be one, to the tie.*'

JIMMY BUNGS
Nickname for a ship's cooper.

JOLLY BOAT
A light, general purpose boat carried at the stern of the ship, more able to manoeuvre near land. Probably the word originated from the Danish '*jol*' or yawl.

JOLLY ROGER
An adaptation of the '*black flag*', commonly a black flag with a skull and crossbones, flown towards the end of the Golden Age of piracy. Other versions showed a whole skeleton with a sword on one hand and an hourglass in the other. Most probably

named after Black Bart Roberts, from his habit of dressing up in red silks before battle. He was known as *'le jolie rouge'*, the *'pretty man in red'*. In 1700 was the first recorded use of the black flag, used by the Breton pirate, Emanuel Wynne fighting HMS Poole off Santiago. It has a skull and crossbones and an hourglass. If an intended victim refused to surrender on the sight of the black flag being raised, a red flag was hoisted, signifying that no quarter would be given. The death's head, and skull and crossbones, were worn as a cap badge in some European regiments in the 17th century.

CADWALLADER JONES
This Welsh Governor of the Bahamas gave protection to the *'Arch-Pirate'*, *'Long Ben'* Every. Jones was said to have *'highly caressed those Pirates that came to Providence'* and *'gave Commissions to pirates without and contrary to the advice of the Council'*. Jones was said to have kept the inhabitants of New Providence in *'abominable slavery'*. He disagreed with the lawful advice of his Council so violently that on one occasion he even ordered his son to train the guns of a ship on the Council Chamber. At some point the Council had managed to imprison him, but in February 1692 he was taken from prison and restored to power as Governor by *'some desperate Rogues, Pirates and others... a seditious rabble.'*

JUAN FERNANDEZ ISLANDS
This small group of islands was a pirate haven about 400 miles west of Valparaiso in Chile. An American, Bernard Keiser, is convinced that *'the lost treasure of the Incas'*, worth over $10 billion, were hidden in a cave there, about 6 metres deep, by English corsairs in the 18th century. The largest island, Mas-a-Tierra, was renamed Alexander Selkirk Island in 1966 (see Robinson Crusoe).

JUNK (1)
From the Javanese *'djong'*, the Portuguese used the word *'junco'* to describe these flat-bottomed boats of the Far East. With no keel, a flat bow and a high stern, its width is about a third of its length, the the rudder can be lowered or raised. It had two or three masts with square sails made from bamboo, rattan or grass. An easy to steer, seaworthy vessel, used and captured by Far Easter pirates.

JUNK (2)
Salt beef, or *'salt horse'* (q.v.) was extremely stringy, coming from poor and tough cuts of meat. Junk was a type of bulrush from which rope was made. Thus salt horse also was known as *junk*, something of poor quality, from which we get the modern meaning. Another derivation is that it came in *'chunks'* which were quite difficult to soften in one's mouth.

JURY RIG
The *jury mast* is a 17th century term, when a temporary mast is made from any available spar after the mast has broken. The origin may come from *'injury mast'* or from the Old French *'ajurie'* meaning help or relief. *Jury rigged* came to mean assembled in a makeshift manner.

KEEL
The first step in constructing a ship such as a galleon was to lay the keel (from the Spanish *quilla*) - the ship's backbone.

KEEL-HAUL, KEEL-RAKE
Possibly a Dutch invention, this soon caught on amongst other navies in the fifteenth and sixteenth centuries, as a means of discipline. A rope was attached to a high yardarm on the starboard, passed under the ship, and up to a port yardarm. A seaman, sometimes with lead weights on his legs, was dropped from the yard-arm, dragged under the keel of the boat and hauled up on the other side to the other yardarm. Apart from the 'near-drowning' effect, the victim was banged against the keel, and lacerated by encrusted barnacles and keel splinters. Sometimes this was done several times until the man died from drowning, a broken neck or shock. The punishment was repeated until the victim had suffered enough, or he had died. Often, when under water, a *'great gun'* was fired, causing more pain in his ears. This *'is done as well as to astonish him so much the more with the thunder of the shot, as to give warning unto all others of the fleet to look out and be wary by his harms'* – 'A Dialogical Discourse', Nathaniel Boteler, 1634. To keel-rake was to drag the victim under the length of the ship, a terrible punishment.
It was the standard Royal Navy punishment of the times, until flogging with a *'cat 'o nine tails'* took over around 1700. Punishment for drawing a weapon in a quarrel was usually the loss of the right hand.
A Dutch expedition to find the North-East Passage in 1595 keel-hauled two men when they were discovered staling furs off the natives. Being keel-hauled three times in a row in the frozen waters, the first man had his head ripped off when he was pulled under the ship. The second survived, only to be cast ashore to freeze to death. Some of the crew complained, so five were hung as an example. Piracy was an attractive alternative to being a merchant seaman.

KEEP A WEATHER EYE OPEN
This is an old sailing term - trouble will always come from the side of the ship where weather is developing. If a sailor is stationed at the weather bow, he will become tired of the constant pitching of the bow and the spray and wind in his face - he will feel **'under the weather'**. The weather is the wind, and to **'make heavy weather'** is to make unnecessary work.

KEEP MUM
From the dice game *Mumchance*, which had to be played in complete silence.

KENNING
16th century term for the sea distance from which high land could be seen from a ship. It varied between 14 and 22 miles, according to weather conditions.

KETCH
A two-masted boat, the after-mast being shorter.

(A FINE) KETTLE OF FISH (see Black Arse)

Fish were boiled in huge pots or kettles. When the results sometimes went wrong and tasted foul, the contents were referred to sarcastically, as a *'fine kettle of fish'*, which no man would eat. The term has come to mean a messy situation, which is difficult to solve.

KEYS, see CAY

CAPTAIN KIDD

William Kidd's reputation is surprising, compared to that of Black Bart Roberts. Kidd only took one significant prize and only made one major voyage. He was hung at Wapping Old Stairs in 1701, leaving a legend of hidden treasure, buried anywhere between Boston and India.

KILL-CALF

A murderous ruffian, a butcher. Also 'kill-cow'.

KILL-COBBLER

Gin.

KILL-DEVIL

The most popular drink in the pirate haven of Port Royal. Governor Modyford described this strong rum punch: *'the Spaniards wondered much about the sickness of our people, until they knew the strength of their drinks, but then wondered more that they were not all dead.'* The Dutch equivalent, *'kilduijvel'*, seems to be the forerunner of kill-devil. Also a type of gun.

KILL GRIEF

Strong drink, usually rum.

KING NEPTUNE

The ruler of the oceans.

KING OF SPAIN'S DAUGHTER

Pirate term for looted wine. A tun of wine was 252 gallons, so a 72-tun ship could carry 72 x 252 gallons of wine. 126 gallons was called a *pipe* of wine. Wine was stored in lead *'pipes'* in the West Indies, giving the seasoned alcoholic illnesses such as the *'dry gripes'* (q.v.)

KISS THE WOODEN LADY

To be forced to stand facing the mast with ones arms encircling it and wrists lashed together. It was a minor punishment, but shipmates were encouraged to kick the offender in the buttocks when passing. Happy days.

KITES

The highest and lightest sails, set above royals, including *skysails* (see skyscrapers), *moonsails* and *stargazers*. Also referred to royal and topgallant studding sails.

KNOCK DOWN
Ships had to carry a cooper, as all food and drink at sea was carried in wooden casks. Space was at such a premium in the cramped quarters and store-rooms, that the casks were usually knocked down (disassembled using a mallet) and the staves stacked and stored neatly, when the contents were disposed of. The casks would then be made up again when new provisions were taken on.

KNOCKED INTO A COCKED HAT
In the early days of sailing, the ship's position was charted by marking three plotting lines on a map. The ship should thus be at the junction of all three, but due to inaccuracies of measurement, it was often place din a small triangle. The triangle was known as a cocked hat after the common three-cornered hat of those times.

KNOCK OFF
Galleys used to be rowed to the rhythm of a hammer hitting a wooden block. When the hammer or mallet ceased hitting, the galley slaves could rest. Even today we 'knock off' working.

KNOT
Nautical term of speed, one knot is 6080 feet, about 1.2 miles per hour. Knots were recorded on a stick and entered in a 'log'.

KNOTS
In his 'Sea Grammar' of 1627, Captain John Smith stated that there were only three knots (of thousands) which were needed by the sailor, the last of which was the 'shepshanke'. The sheepshank 'is a knot they caste upon a Runner, or a Tackle, when it is too long to take in the Goods, and by this knot they can shorten a Rope without cutting it, as much as they list (wish), and presently undo it again, and never the worse.' There are literally thousands of knots described in 'Ashley's Book of Knots'. A love knot was sent by a sailor tied loosely. If it came back tightened up, the feeling was reciprocated. A 'slippery hitch' was used 'in small boats, especially open boats that are easily capsized, the necessity frequently being for instant casting off, and the slippery hitch is found indispensable.'

KNOW THE ROPES
If pirates did not know all the functions of the hundred of ropes, and were not experts at the dozens of knots, their ship could neither catch another ship nor escape from superior forces. Someone who 'knows the ropes' now means a person who is expert from both knowledge and experience. There are only three ropes aboard a sailing vessel - the bolt rope, the boat rope and the manrope. (Manropes are made of four-strand rope, canvas-covered. Boltropes are three-stranded and 'soft-laid', used for splicing.) However, the rigging could comprise upwards of ten miles of cordage in the largest vessels, with hundreds of different names and functions. The ropes were usually the same thickness and colour, and could only be told apart from the precise position in which they were secured.

LACED MUTTON

A wanton woman.

LADDER, CLIMB THE

To be hanged, as in *'Walter Kennedy climbed the ladder to bed.'*

LAID UP

A ship that is moored or being repaired, as it is disabled, is said to be *laid up*, not fit to sail, until it is fully back in commission.

LAND LUBBER

'Lubber's holes' were holes in the platforms surrounding the mast. They enabled poor sailors to clamber through them to go up and down the mast, rather than quickly climb up the *'rat lines'* (or *'futtock shrouds'* and *'topmast shrouds'*) of the rigging around the platforms. A *lubber* was someone who was very clumsy, so a *land lubber* was known to sailors as someone awkward from the land who knew nothing about sailing and rigging. Some sources say that the term originated in 'land lover'.

LAND TO! (1)

This saying, not the more familiar 'Land Ho!' seems to have been used at sea: *'One to the Top to look out for Land, the man cries out Land to; which is just so far as a Kenning, or a man may discover, descry or see the Land.'* – Smith (1691). Perhaps *Land Ho* was a diminution of *Land Ahoy.*

LAND TO (2)

A ship is said to lie *'land to'* when she is at so great a distance that the land can only just be seen.

LANDMARK

This is a point on the landscape that a ship takes reference from – so a **landmark decision** meant that the captain was sure what he was going to do, from the lie of the land that he could see.

LANGRACE, LANGREL (see SHOT)

For privateers, this was possibly their favourite type of cannon shot in the 18th and 19th centuries. Also known as *case shot* or *canister shot*, the case was filled with bits of iron, ostensibly to cut through the rigging of a ship and make it inoperable. Buccaneers and pirates, however, preferred to use it as an anti-personnel device. The wide scatter of the shot ripped holes out of defending seamen, while preserving the nautical integrity of the *'prize'* ship. If pieces of iron or grape shot were not available to fill the case, anything was used in an emergency, even stones and gold coins. There is a record of a ship's surgeon cutting up a corpse to extract the gold coins that penetrated the man.

LANYARD

Many pirates wore crossed sashes, to hold pistols, daggers, knives and so on, to prevent these being lost overboard. A lanyard was a short line of rope used for making anything fast. Items were fastened by lanyards to their belts and boots. From the Ashley Book of Knots: *'A sailor has little opportunity at sea to replace an article lost overboard, so knotted lanyards are attached to everything moveable that is carried aloft: marlingspikes and fids, paint cans and slush buckets, pencils, eyeglasses, hats, snuffboxes, jackknives, tobacco and money pouches, amulets, bonus's whistles, watches , binoculars, pipes and keys are all made fast around the neck, shoulder, or wrist, or else are attached in a buttonhole, belt or suspender.'*

LAP-CLAP
A copulation. To *'get a lap-clap'* was to become pregnant.

LARBOARD
The port or left side of any ship when facing the bow, from the Old English *'laddebord'* (loading side); or from the Norse *'hlada bord'* which had the same meaning.

LARGE
The ship sails *'large'* when the sails are eased off with the wind from abaft the beam. The bowlines are not used, so the sails receive the full effects of the wind. Also known as *'sailing free'*.

LASH UP
Secure something with ropes called *'lashings'*, as a temporary repair.

LASK
To sail *'large'* (q.v. *'go large'*) with the wind about 4 points abaft beam.

LATITUDE
A ship's position North or South of the Equator.

'THE LAW OF THE SEA'
Privateers or pirates would not harm a crew which surrendered without fighting.

LAY OF THE LAND
We also call this the *lie of the land*, and it means that seamen study the horizon when making landfall, to look for familiar signs and possible harbours.

LAY THE LAND
To lose sight of land.

LEADING LIGHTS
It became customary to enter a port using a system of leading lights to show the way.

LEAGUE
About three miles. English nautical leagues in the 17th century were measured at 20 to a degree of latitude, or around 6000 yards. Each league was divided into three

nautical miles. The Spanish used an identical measurement at sea, the '*legua marina*' being 5.57 kilometres. (6,650 Castilian *varas*, to be precise).

LEAD LINE
A piece of lead was attached to a long line, which was marked in fathoms, to sound the depth of the water. The piece of lead was often hollowed out, and a piece of animal fat placed in the hollow. In this way the lead-swinger could tell whether the sea bottom was muddy, or sandy or whatever. If there was no indication, it meant that the bottom was rocky, and extra care had to be taken.

LEE
The side of a ship or promontory away from the wind; the side sheltered from the wind. *Leeward*, with the wind, towards the point to which the wind blows, is opposite to windward. A *lee shore* is a dangerous coastline to which the wind blows directly, forcing the ship towards it. It is important to *allow a little leeway*, i.e. margin for error when operating off a lee shore. '*Have a care of the leelatch*' means to take heed that the ship does not bear too much to leeward. '*A ship lies by the lee*' means that all the sails are lying flat against the masts and shrouds.

LEEWAY
The distance a ship is forced to leeward, i.e. the lateral drift of a vessel. If one is '*given leeway*' one has time to catch up, or greater freedom of action.

LET FLY
The order to immediately release the sheets which hold the sails, so that the sails shake uncontrollably. This halted a ship's movement, and was used as a salute from a junior officer to the flagship. It has come to mean to lose one's temper.

LET THE CAT OUT OF THE BAG
A sailor found drunk on board was ordered to fashion a cat o' nine tails or **'make a rod for his own back'**, which would then be kept in a leather bag. When sailors **'let the cat out of the bag'** they were in for misfortune, usually on *Blue Monday*. The Royal Navy's cat-o-nine-tails was kept in a red baize bag, and not removed until the offender was safely secured to the gratings and there was no possibility of reprieve, so '*the secret was out*'. Authority to use the cat was not removed from the Naval Discipline Act until an Order-in-Council of March 29th, 1949. The only form of British corporal punishment which still remains, is a maximum of 12 cuts with a cane for boy ratings. The French name for a cat-o-nine-tails was '*martinet*', from the 17th century disciplinarian colonel the Marquis de Martinet.

LET PASS
This was a simple licence issued usually by the Governor of Jamaica, identifying the bearer as an English vessel and requesting that it be allowed to reach its destination. Captain William James and Edward Mansveldt used them as a sort of licence to be a privateer. However, they were thrown overboard by the *guardacostas* so that ships could become prizes.

LETTERS OF MARQUE, MARK, MART (or LETTERS OF REPRISAL)

Documents, commissions or licences given to privateers by their governments, giving permission for privately owned ships to attack enemy merchant vessels. Sometimes a commission given to a commander could be used to 'cover' ships from other nationalities. For instance Henry Morgan used to take French pirate ships from Tortuga under his 'commission' when attacking the Spanish. Other times privateers attacked anyone, as when Mansvelt and Morgan attacked the Spanish although their letter of marque was to attack the Dutch. One captain in the Caribbean justified his plundering because of a letter of marque from the Danish West Indies, written in Danish – it actually only gave permission to hunt goats and pigs, but no-one could read Danish.

The minutes of the Council of Jamaica, February 22, 1666, explain why letters of marque were needed. There were no naval frigates posted to protect this British outpost surrounded by Spanish colonies, so Jamaica needed defence, as well as the easy supply of cheap goods that privateers brought in to trade. Currencies, gold and silver, wood, cocoa, hides, dyes, wheat and tallow were all traded at Port Royal, giving its merchants a living. Poorer planters sold the privateers provisions and needed the slaves that they brought in. The first mention is in 1293, and the Convention of Paris outlawed them in 1856. The very last letters of mark and reprisal were issued by the Welsh President Jefferson Davis of the Confederate States of America, in 1861, on the outbreak of the American Civil War. President Lincoln reacted by proclaiming that such acts would be considered piracy. W. M. Robinson's book 'The Confederate Privateers', Yale University Press, 1928 explored the fighting further.

LETTER OF REPRISAL

A fairly rare privateering commission allowing the holder to redress a wrong which could not be satisfactorily resolved in the courts. For instance, any English ship seized by the guardacostas could be claimed as a prize, even if it was on legitimate business, with the countries at peace, if a single piece-of-eight was found on board. For the guardacosta who lived on commission, it was fairly easy to 'find' such a coin. The aggrieved owners, who had lost their shop and cargo, were given permission to seek compensation by whatever means they thought necessary, i.e. by taking a Spanish ship in retaliation.

LIAR

Captain John Smith's 'A Sea Grammar' described the punishment for sailors who had told a lie: "The liar is to hold his place but for a week, and he that is first taken with a lie, every Monday is so proclaimed at the main mast by a general cry 'A Liar! A Liar! A Liar!' – he is under the swabber, and only to keep clean the beak-head and chains." (see Blue Monday)

LIFELINE

Ropes were left trailing from sailing ships, just in case someone fell overboard off the rigging or was washed over in heavy seas. However, to grab a lifeline was to be very lucky indeed.

LIGHT MONEY
Coins which had been '*clipped*' to be worth less than their face value. In 1683, it was reported in London that the colonists in Jamaica would refuse payment in '*light money*' for their crops.

LIGNUM VITAE
This very hard '*wood of life*' (species *Guaiacum*) was a valuable cargo to seize, like dyewoods. It was used aboard ship for deadeyes, block-sheaves and bulls-eyes.

LIMEYS
Since 1795, British warships have been required to carry lime juice to prevent scurvy, and American sailors still call British sailors limeys.

LINE OF BATTLE
Sailing ships could only effectively fire broadsides, so fleets formed lines for maximum firepower to fight against each other, thus we get the term '*ship of the line.*'

LIQUOR
'*Good liquor is to sailors preferable to warm clothing*' - Woodes Rogers, c.1718. Wearing damp clothing in the Atlantic day and night, subsisting on small portions of awful food, alcohol provided much-needed calories to keep the body temperature up. A daily liquor ration was a contractual obligation in both the merchant and Royal navies. Until the 19th century, water was a carrier of all types of illnesses, so everyone drank cider, beer or wine for preference, on land or at sea. From the 17th century, Caribbean rum became more popular than beer at sea, because beer went sour quickly.

LIVORNO (LEGHORN)
Pirate haven near Pisa in Italy, used by the Medicis to sponsor piracy, and which became a 'free port' open to any nation and religion in 1590. Muslim slaves were sold here by Cristian pirates (see Holy Pirates), and Livornese bankers arranged ransoms for Christian captives of the Barbary Corsairs.

LOADED TO THE GUNN'LS, LOADED TO THE GUARDS
A ship that was loaded to the *gunwhales* (*gunn'ls*), which is the the plank of a ship's side, would be heavily overloaded. Later, the '*guards*' were the Plimsoll markings for safe loading levels. The term came to mean a drunken seaman, with little control of his movements.

LOBLOLLY
Porridge or gruel, another word for *burgoo* (q.v.)

LOBLOLLY BOY
The surgeon's assistant, who served *loblolly* to patients.

LOBSCOUSE, 'SCOUSE

A stew of small bits of salt meat, broken ship's biscuits, potatoes, onions and spices. Because of the poverty of Liverpool, something similar was a common dish at home, and the modern slang for a Liverpudlian, 'scouser', comes from this dish. The origin of the word is the Welsh 'lobscaws', and many poor Welsh families settled there, looking for work.

LOBSTER

18th century seaman's slang for a soldier or marine, who wore red coats. Many former 'lobsters' turned to buccaneering and piracy.

LODEMAN

This predates the pirates, and used to mean a ship's pilot. The reason it is included is that *The Black Book of the Admiralty*, the list of maritime law, custom and usage, was codified from *The Laws of Oleron* in 1336. *The Laws of Oleron* were introduced into England by Richard the Lionheart in 1189, copied from his mother Eleanor's legislation in 1152 in Aquitaine. The tenor of these laws survived through the years in the Royal Navy. The following quote from *The Laws of Oleron* is priceless *'If a ship is lost by default of the lodeman, the maryners may bring the lodeman to the windlass or any other place and cut off his head.'*

Richard I's instructions to his 1189 and 1190 fleets, to go to the Crusades, have been preserved as the earliest naval laws, which persisted in this draconian form for over six hundred years. For murder on land, to be tied to the corpse and buried alive. For murder at sea, the offender was tied to the victim and thrown into the ocean. For threatening with a knife, to have the hand cut off. For striking any person without drawing blood, to be plunged three times into the sea. For cursing or reviling anyone, to pay an ounce of silver for each offence. For theft to have the head shorn, and boiling pitch and feathers poured over the offender.

LODESTAR

A guiding star, from the Middle English 'lode sterre' (*leading star*). In the Northern Hemisphere, it was usually the North Star (Polaris).

LOG-BOOK

The author believes that the name, for this record of a ship's progress, comes form the practice of daily throwing a log overboard, to estimate the speed of a ship.

LOGGERHEADS

These were large iron heads of long handles which were heated until they were red-hot. A sailor then wrapped cloths around the handle and took the loggerhead to insert into a bucket of pitch to make hot tar for caulking the ship. This way there was little risk of the pitch catching fire as it melted. Sailors sometimes used to spar with the cold loggerheads, during horseplay on the beach when careening. Thus the phrase 'at loggerheads' with each other came into being.

LOGWOOD or DYEWOOD
Of huge commercial value in Europe, this grew in great quantities in the Bay of Campeachy, the Bay of Honduras (modern Belize) and across the West Indies. This dark-red tree, Haematoxylum Campechanium L. produced a black or brown dye, which did not fade in cloth like existing dyes. Around 1700 it was worth £20 a ton in the West Indies, and up to 20 times as much in London, making it a valuable target for piracy and smuggling.

L'OLONNAIS (d.1668)
Perhaps the most horrible of all buccaneers, Jean David Nau came from Les Sables-d'Olonne in France, hence his nickname. He seems to have never taken prisoners, often cutting heads off and licking the blade. He was known as *'Fleau des Espagnoles'* *(Flail of the Spanish)*. On the Central American coast, he allegedly cut open the heart of a prisoner and gnawed at it before throwing it on the ground. Captured by native Indians shortly after this, they slowly cut him up into little pieces.

LONGBOAT
Towed behind a ship, this could hold up to 60 or 70 men, and was normally propelled by oars, but also a movable mast and sail might be used. These were needed in the days before quays to get stores and go ashore.

LONG CLOTHES
Clothes which were loose, and could be worn ashore. On board ship, baggy pants and coats could get caught in the rigging, so clothes were generally tight-fitting.

LONGITUDE
Because of the lack of knowledge of longitude until the invention of Harrison's Chronometer in the 18th century (see Sobel's book), merchant ships were forced to cluster upon well-known routes, where they were more at threat from pirate or buccaneer attack. (See *Dead Reckoning* and *Derroterro* in these Pirate Terms). Dava Sobel's exposition in his book *'Longitude'* is excellent. Suitable chronometers were not widely used until the late 18th century, so the navigational feats of pirates and circumnavigators like Roberts, Dampier and Woodes Rogers are truly remarkable. In the 18th century, the English measured west of Greenwich, the French measured west of Paris, and the Spanish west of Tenerife and sometimes Cadiz.

There is a lovely anecdote concerning the irascible Welsh captain of the Queen Mary, John Treasure Jones. On its final transatlantic voyage in 1967, he announced on the ship's public address system when near the Equator: *'Ladies and gentlemen, it is my duty to inform you that we are hopelessly lost.'* He waited a few moments, and continued, *'However, I am happy to report that we are making wonderful time.'*

LONG SHOT
Cannon had no sights, and could not be traversed right and left, and there was only small up-down adjustment, which could be negated by the movement of waves. Also each ball was slightly different and the gunpowder charges varied. Cannon

balls were most likely to hit and cause real damage with a maximum effective range of 200-500 feet. Thus very few *'long shots'* were effective, and the term came to be used by gamblers.

LONG SPLICE
Marriage.

'LOOK AROUND FOR LOOSE ENDS'
When a ship had to flee in an emergency without setting up its sails properly, and had escaped to a safe place, this was the instruction to sort out the pieces of rope, tie up things properly and to get the vessel ship-shape again. These loose ends would be *baggy-wrinkled* or woven into fenders to form collision mates. (See Cut and Run)

LOOK ONE WAY AND ROW ANOTHER
This has come to mean a 'hidden agenda' and comes from the fact that rowers face the opposite way that they wish to proceed.

LOOPHOLE
A small opening, often in the bulkheads, where small arms could be employed to fire at the enemy. It has come to mean a small legal ambiguity where clever lawyers can be paid by rich clients or firms to escape legal consequences. Alas, this loophole is not available to the majority of the population.

LOOSE CANNON
An unsecured cannon in a storm could do untold damage to men and the ship as it rolled about. The term now means an unorthodox person who can cause potential damage. In 1545, as the Mary Rose was watched by Henry VIII sailing out to fight the French, she was flooded through the lower gunports. As it started to list to starboard, 20 huge cannon broke free from their gun carriages, and began to roll across the gundecks, causing it to sink.

LOPSIDED (LAP-SIDED)
'The state of a ship, which is built in such a way as to have one side heavier than the other; and by consequence, to retain a constant heel or inclination toward the heavier side' – Falconer, 1789. A *'lop'* also refers to a choppy sea.

LOSE ONE'S WAY
Sailing vessels cannot sail directly into the wind, and those that do will eventually *lose their way*, failing to *make headway*. Headway is the forward motion of the ship regardless of wind, and leeway is the sideways motion of a ship away from the wind.

LOUIS D'OR
French coin.

LOUSE-TRAP
A fine comb. A *'louse-walk'* was a hair-parting. A *'prick-louse'* was a tailor, so *'louse-*

pricking' was mending clothes. *'Louse-land'* was Scotland. A saying of the times was *'if a louse misses a footing on his coat, it will break its neck'*, meaning that the coat in question was thread-bare. *'Lousy'* meant either contemptible or filthy.

LOWER THE BOOM
If you *'lower the boom'* on someone, you are halting their ambition, or reprimanding them severely. The saying comes from Elizabethan times. The boom is the long pole or spar that is used to extend the base of certain sails. However, it can be a spar pointing upward from a mast, enabling heavy objects to be lifted. If either dropped on one's head, it could cause severe damage. Derrick, Queen Elizabeth I's hangman, invented the second type of boom, used as a hoist, and we still use the word *derrick* today when referring to gantries, cranes and other lifting gear. The 'derrick' he invented was a single spar, a topping lift and purchase to hoist men to the gallows. Before that, only a rope was used.

LOWER (STRIKE) THE FLAG
To pull it down before or during a battle is the sign of surrender. However, flags could also be lowered as a mark of great respect, as a Port Royal when Sir Henry Morgan died.

LUBBER
An unskilled and clumsy man – see *'land lubber'*.

LUFF UP
To steer more into the wind, causing the sails to flap or *'luff.'*

LUGGER
A small and fast three-masted ship, favoured by pirates.

LUTERANOS
'Lutherans', a common name the Spanish used for Dutch and British buccaneers, whom they turned over to the Inquisition for extremely slow torture to death.

MADAGASCAR
This is the fourth largest island in the world, and was the most important pirate haunt outside the West Indies. French and English freebooters congregated here, in the Indian Ocean just 250 miles off the east coast of Africa. The natives were tolerant, there was abundant fresh water and food, citrus fruits prevented scurvy and there were hundreds of hidden harbours on Madagascar and its nearby islets. There were rich pickings on the nearby Indian Ocean and Red Sea. Each year, a fleet carrying Indian pilgrims with gold and silver to Mecca and Jeddah gathered at Mocha. Also Portuguese carracks carried precious goods from Goa to Europe. The French, British and Dutch East India Companies had ships loaded with silks, spices and jewels. The French attempt to colonise it ended with the abandonment of Fort Dauphin in 1674. As it had the first usable harbours after passing the Cape, many ships stopped there for fruit, water and provisions. It was a magnet for piracy. However, with the ending of the French wars in 1697, British men-of-war started patrolling Madagascar and St

Mary's Island, capturing David Williams in November 1703.

The island was a superb pirate base during the Golden Age of Piracy (q.v.), and far less dangerous than the Caribbean. Popular pirate havens in the area were St Mary's Island (Ile Sainte Marie), Mathelage, Johanna Island, Ranter Bay, St Augustine's bay, Fort Dauphin, Reunion Island and Mauritius. At St Mary's Island, Adam Baldridge lived like a king from 1685 through the 1690's, trading beef, food and supplies for pirate loot, being supplied from New York. He left in 1697, selling his kingdom to Edward Welch. The pirate captains Tew, Every, England, Plantain, Condent and Kidd all used the island as a base at some time in their careers.

MAINSTAY
This is the supporting timber framework of the main mast, and has come to mean the 'chief support' of any person or organisation.

TO MAKE BOTH ENDS MEET
Dating from at least the 17th century, the habit of splicing two pieces of rope to make a longer rope, and thus not necessitating the purchase of a longer rope. Thus this economical chore has passed into modern terminology.

MAKE HEADWAY
'Headway' is the forward progress of a ship at sea – from this we get the modern term.

MALTA
Just south of Sicily, Malta, Gozo and Comino were excellent and strategically placed pirate havens. They commanded the passage between the East and West Mediterranean, and were used by corsairs and Christian pirates for centuries, until the French occupation of 1798.

MAMORA
On the Atlantic coast of Morocco, a renowned pirate base until captured in 1614 by the Spanish.

MANATEE
Esquemeling describes these: 'Thence we directed our course for a place called Boca del Dragon, there to make provisions of flesh, especially of a certain animal which the Spaniards call manentines, and the Dutch sea-cows, because the head, nose and teeth of this beast are very much like those of a cow ....Nigh unto the neck they have two wings, under which are seated two udders or breasts, much like unto the breasts of a woman'. These poor manatees, or dugongs, seems to have been an origin of the legends of mermaids.

MANILA GALLEONS
For over two-hundred years, huge heavily-armed Spanish treasure ships passed from Manila to Acapulco, Mexico and back.

MAKE FAST
'Instead of tying, Seamen always say, " Make Fast!" ' (Captain John Smith, 'A Sea Grammar', 1627)

MAKE HEADWAY
A ship makes headway against a tide or current, so effectively to get on.

MAKE HEAVY WEATHER
To sail closer to the wind, or weather, than is really necessary, thus slowing the boat up, and making more work than is necessary.

MAN-O'-WAR
A naval warship – see rate.

MAN-OF-WAR FOWL
The Frigate Bird, also called the sea-hawk by pirates.

MARINATED
Term for being transported as a convict, probably from pickling of fish in salt.

MARINER'S MIRROR
Lucius Wagenaer first published this collection of sea charts in Holland in 1583, and it was translated into English in 1588. For the next hundred years or so, it was widely used by seamen across the world.

MARLING SPIKE, MARLINE SPIKE
'Marling is a small line of untwisted hemp, very pliant and well tarred, to cease the ends of ropes from ravelling out, or the sides of the blocks at their arses, or if the sail rent out of the bolt-ropes, they will make it fast with marlin until they have leisure to mend it. The marling spike is but a small piece of iron to splice ropes together, or open the bolt-rope when you sew the sail.' – Smith, 1691. As merchant crews had no weapons, the marling spike was often the chosen weapon for a mutiny of would-be pirates.

MAROON
To abandon a sailor or prisoner on a desolate, deserted cay or uninhabited island. He was usually given a musket, a few shot, a little gunpowder and a bottle of water. It was a rare punishment, leaving the seaman the option of killing himself if he could not survive or no rescuers arrived. A 'maroon island' was an uninhabited island. From the Spanish 'cimarron', wild. Cimaroons, abbreviated to 'Maroons' were a West Indian community founded by escaped Negro slaves who cohabited with Amerindian women. Maroon is thus a corruption of cimaroon, 'dweller in the mountains' – a fugitive or lost person.

MASTER
The ship's master was also sometimes called its pilot. He was responsible for sailing the ship, a specialist in navigation and pilotage, who directed the ship's course. The

'sailing master' was in charge of navigation. Charts were inaccurate or non-existent, so it was a difficult job, and many were forced into pirate service.

MATCH
The slow-burning rope-end used to ignite cannons.

MATE
This was said to come from the term 'meat' as the original boucaniers used to share each other's meat, but may have come from 'matelotage' (q.v.) The ship's mate is responsible for overseeing the sailors, ensuring that the captain's orders are carried out, for stowing cargo and organizing the crew's work.

MATELOTAGE
From this French term we have today's 'mate', meaning close friend/bosom buddy. The 'cow-killers' or first 'boucaniers' had no wives or children, but usually lived with another male who inherited from him. This custom was called 'matelotage'. Any arguments between these 'mates' were settled by a duel, 'la coutume de la cote'.

I'LL SEE YOU MEASURED FOR CHAINS
A threat – measuring for the gibbet's cage.

MERCHANT SHIPS
In the 17th and 18th centuries, commercial ships were called merchant ships, but seamen usually reserved this term for the specific three-masted, square rigged vessel. They could carry passengers or cargo, and a typical ship would be about 280 tons and 80 feet in length, with 20 crew. They might carry 16 cannon, but it is doubtful if the 'short-handed' crew could handle more than 4 at a time. With excellent sail power, they could cross the Atlantic from Britain to America in about 4 weeks.

MERCHANT SEAMEN
Just like the Royal Navy, many of these had been forcibly 'impressed' into service, with disgusting food, disease, dysentery, minimal wages, cramped conditions and cruel masters. Dr. Samuel Johnson said 'no man will be a sailor who has contrivance enough to get himself into jail; for being in a ship is being in jail with the chance of being drowned ...... A man in jail has more room, better food, and commonly better company.' It is little wonder that they were unwilling to fight pirates, and that former merchant seamen formed the vast bulk of the pirate brethren. Punishment was so harsh for trivial offences, as in the Royal Navy, that the popular saying 'You might as well be hung for a sheep as for a lamb' comes from this time. The punishment was still the same for great offences as for small, and many willing merchant seamen became pirates.

In times of peace, seamen's wages remained unchanged between 1700 and 1750. A merchant captain took about £5-£6 per month, and his first mate and surgeon around £3-£4. Cooks, carpenters and boatswains received around £2, and ordinary crew members around £1-50p. They were often not allowed to leave the ship in port, especially at home, in case they might desert, and were often unpaid if a ship was in port or at anchor. Long stays in port, seeking a cargo, could sometimes lead to mutiny by the unpaid crews.

MESS
From the Anglo-Saxon *mese*, table, the space where the crew ate and slept. A mess means a quantity of food for a table, or the provision of food, from which the ship's mess possibly gets its name. A *mess of pottage* is a prepared dish of soft food, pottage being a thick soup of vegetables and often meat.

MESSING ABOUT
This term seems to have originated in the *'mess-deck'*, the crowded quarter which was the only part of a ship where the crew could mingle off-duty.

MESTIZOS
The offspring of a European settler and a native Indian, called by the Spanish *'mestisas'*.

MIDDLE PASSAGE
From the 16th to 18th centuries, slave ships from England sailed to Africa's west coast with rum, firearms and brass goods. These were bartered for slaves, who were then shipped (the middle passage) to the Spanish West Indies then the southern states of the USA. Slaves were then exchanged for rum and sugar in the Caribbean, and tobacco and cotton in America. Each of the three passages was fantastically profitable, bringing great wealth to Liverpool and Bristol.

For the Middle Passage, the naked male slaves were pulled out of their dungeons and chained together herded onto ships. They were prodded down a ladder to the upper hold, then pushed onto a long shelf and chained by the ankle and wrist to the board. Many slaves passed out in the stench and the suffocating heat. Up to 400 slaves could be pushed into the belly of the ship, each with a pace 5-6 feet long, 16 inches wide and 3-4 feet high. A little air came in through the overhead gratings, and the only place for bodily wastes was to seep between the planks they were chained to, dripping onto those on the lower shelves. They might wait in port or up to 10 months in these conditions before sailing. Women and children were taken aboard separately to the men, and were at the mercy of the whims of the captain and crew. Apart from measles, gonorrhoea, syphilis and smallpox contracted from the Europeans, the prisoners suffered from malaria, yellow fever and amoebic dysentery. The worst disease was *'the bloody flux'*, with fever and a bloody running discharge of the bowels. It stunk so much that barrels of vinegar could not remove the stench. *'Blackbirders'* could be smelt up to a mile away. The only time that the prisoners could move was when they were taken to the deck to eat. If they refused to eat, they were whipped. If they continued to refuse, iron bars were lodged into their jaws and food jammed down their throats. One captain cut off the arms and legs on *'the most wilful'* protesters to *'terrify the rest'* into obeying his orders.

Casualties were appalling, and up to 55% of the slaves could die on the Middle Passage. Captain Thomas Phillips lost 318 of his 700 cargo in the *Hannibal* in 1693. The Royal Africa Company's records show an average loss of 23% of the slaves.

MIND YOUR P's and Q's

Sailors received credit at quayside taverns until they were paid. In these blissful pre-metrification days, beer was sold in pints and quarts. The innkeeper kept a record of p's and q's for each debtor, and ensured that they were entered on his account. Some tavern owners would put extra ticks in the pints and quarts columns if they thought the seaman was drunk. Thus it was important to be mindful of how many drinks you actually owed for.

MISS THE BOAT

Sometimes sailors became so drunk that they missed their ship sailing. William Williams recounts his own being left marooned, in an inebriated condition, in his 'The Journal of Penrose, Seaman.' (First published 1815)

MIZZEN (MIZEN) MAST

The rear mast on a ship. The 3rd, aftermost mast of a square-rigged sailing ship. To 'mizzen' is to fit the mizzen sail; 'change the mizzen' means to bring the yard to the other side of the mast; and 'spell the mizzen' is to let go the sheet and peek it up.

MODERN PIRACY

There are around 300 known cases of piracy and armed robbery of ships every year, with many being unreported. These are unreported as a ship's owners wish to avoid long delays in ports due to police investigations. A ship's operating costs may be $15,000 a day, so it may not be cost-effective to seek justice. Again, some cargoes could be dubious in the first place, as maritime law-enforcement is fragmented across the world. Pirate hot-spots today are the South China Sea, the Indian Ocean and the Malacca Straits. Countries associated with piracy (all pirates need a land base) are Indonesia, the Philippines, India, Malaysia, Brazil, Ecuador, Bangladesh and Somalia/Djibouti. Surprise attacks by fast boats upon ships navigating slowly through narrow channels are favoured, and pirates now possess grenade launchers. However, the key to most successful attacks is stealth, between the hours of 10pm and 6am when most of the crew are asleep. Attacking from the stern, they use grappling hooks to board tankers, cargo ships, bulk carriers and container ships, as well as yachts and other vessels.

Countries like Brazil cannot attack piracy as it has no coastguards, and its police have no boats. In the Far East, much piracy is controlled by crime syndicates, which pay bribes to quash investigations. In the Far East, entire cargoes can disappear, along with the ships which can later appear as 'phantom ships' with fake documents after the crew has been killed or set adrift. Brazilian pirates prefer to take high-tech equipment for the black market, while West African pirates literally strip a ship of everything.

MOIDORES

Portuguese gold coins.

MONEY FOR OLD ROPE

Older, unneeded old rope would be sold on shore to local traders, and the money shared out amongst the crew.

MONKEY (1)

A small wooden cask to hold rum, or a small cannon (also known as a *dog*). A monkey-jacket was the short red jacket worn by midshipmen. Jackets were cut short for sailors to enable them to climb in the rigging. A monkey poop was a shoot poop deck. Monkey was the generic term for anything small, such as the smallest casks, pumps or sailing-blocks. Incidentally, the phrase **'to freeze the balls off a brass monkey'** has a naval origin. This monkey was a small brass tray which held a pile of iron cannon balls next to the guns. In extreme cold, the different coefficients of expansion of brass and iron meant that sometimes the neatly piled cannon would roll out of the tray.

MONKEY (2)

A small cannon, also known as a '*dog*'. Anything small on board a sailing ship was known as '*monkey-sized*'. The smallest pumps, casks and blocks were also called '*monkeys*'. (See Powder Monkey)

MONKEY JACKET

A short red jacket worn by midshipmen in the Royal Navy. Other sailors wore these coats, which were cut short to enable seamen to climb the rigging more easily.

MONKEY PUMP

A quill or straw, used for drinking from a coconut, bottle or cask. (See Sucking the Monkey)

MONMOUTH CAP

A popular pirate hat, a sort of big woollen beret with a bobble on top, made in Monmouth, Gwent, and worn on the back of the head.

MONTBARS THE EXTERMINATOR

This buccaneer surpassed Rock the Brazilian, who entertained his company by roasting Spanish captives alive on spits. Montbars' favourite torture was to slit a man's stomach open, take out his intestines and nail them to a post. Then he pressed burning wood into the victim's buttocks to force him to dance to the furthest extent of his intestines. The Spanish Inquisition practised similar tortures and possibly worse upon their European prisoners, so the Spanish were '*fair game*' for such horrors.

ADMIRAL SIR HENRY MORGAN – *THE GREATEST BUCCANEER OF THEM ALL*

An accomplished general of troops as well as the most successful buccaneer of all time, the Welshman Morgan almost single-handedly kept Jamaica a British possession until his death in 1688. As 'Admiral of the Brethren of the Coast' he led the first successful attack upon 'impregnable' Panama, and also took Portobelo and Puerto Principe in his long career. (See the author's forthcoming book, published in 2004).

MOROCCO
European corsairs used its Atlantic (and sometimes its Mediterranean) ports, as its ruling dynasty was hostile to the Ottoman Empire. Sale and Mamora were the main pirate havens, until Sultan Malay Ismail took over as the main prey upon merchant shipping at the beginning of the 18th century.

MORRO
Large castle or fortification protecting a port, such as San Felipe at Porto Bello.

MORTAR
Very short cannon with a wide mouth, filled with a number of fused bombs, which exploded after hitting the target.

MOSES' LAW
A punishment on some pirate ships, which could only be carried out by the quartermaster, where an offender received 39 lashes on his bare back. (See Articles of John Phillips)

Captain Henry Morgan before Panama

MOSQUITO (MISKITO) COAST
Eastern (Caribbean) coast of Nicaragua, from the San Juan River in Nicaragua to the Aguan River in Honduras. Because of its dense mangrove swamps, hundreds of inlets and lack of arable land, it was never settled by the Spanish, and became a sanctuary for runaway slaves and a pirate hideout. The English alter controlled it. It was the place where the privateer William Williams was marooned c. 1730, and on which he based his factional novel 'The Journal of Penrose, Seaman.'

MOTHER CAREY'S CHICKENS
The storm petrel can run lightly over the sea's surface. The name comes from 'Petrello' (little Peter in Italian – St Peter could walk on water). When seamen saw them near a ship, they expected a storm to be in the offing. Storm petrels are called 'les oiseaux de Notre Dame' in French, the birds of Our Lady. In Latin, these 'Aves Sanctae Mariae' belonged to 'Mater Cara', which the British corrupted to Mother Carey. Where 'chickens' comes from is beyond the author's skills as a researcher or etymologist.

"Morgan's buccaneers attack Puerto Principe in 1668".

MUD HOOK
Slang for anchor.

MULATTO
The offspring of a European and an African slave.

MUM
17th century strong ale made from wheat and oats, and flavoured with herbs. From the German *'mumme'* in Brunswick, where it originated, the Dutch equivalent is *'mom'*.

MURDERER (MURTHERER), MURDERING PIECE
A swivel gun with a long barrel and a wide mouth for firing nails, spikes, stones and glass. They were known as *'pedreros'* (q.v.) by the Spanish, Anglicised as *'patareros'* or *'perriers'*. The iron pin in the stock was fitted into a socket, and there were sockets at several places on a ship, so the gun could be quickly taken to wherever it was needed most. They were used in nearly all merchant ships to repel boarders, up to the early 19th century. In warships they were supplanted by marines, who acted as marksmen, in the early 18th century. In 1644, Mainwaring wrote: *'Murderers are small iron or brass pieces with chambers. In merchant-men they are most used at the bulkheads of the forecastle, half-deck or steerage (steer-reach), and they have a pintle which is put into a stock (socket), and so they stand and are traversed; out of which they use murdering shot to scour the decks when men enter; but iron murderers are dangerous for them which discharge them, for they will scale extremely and endanger their eyes much with them. I have known divers (many) hurt with shooting them off.'*

MUSICIANS
Their prime function was to play extremely loudly, if pirates were forced to attack. They preferred to take ships peacefully, but in an attack the black or red flag was raised and as much noise was made as possible, a cacophony to frighten the victim's crew. The Royal Navy had a ship's trumpeter. Black Bart allowed his musicians to rest on a Sunday, but at all other times, night or day, they were supposed to answer a bored crew's calls for entertainment.

MUSKET
The general term for a single shot rifle of the times, and the model for the more accurate rifle to follow, the musket was only slightly more accurate than a *blunderbuss*. The musket ball was smaller and designed to shoot straighter, but was less likely the cause the kind of damage that a *blunderbuss* could inflict. It was used

to 'pick off' the helmsman and officers before boarding, and for hunting. Early muskets were 5-6 feet long, using a double iron bullet, and had to be supported and fired with the aid of fork rest. For short-range work, barrels were sawn off, (like today's sawn-off shotguns), and an effective load of one musket ball and three heavy buckshot pellets was inserted. The handle, or stock, was also sawn off, to make it easier to handle and attach to a sash across the pirate's chest. The term comes from the Spanish *'mosquete'* or sparrow-hawk.

MUSKETOON

The musketoon was less accurate than a musket, but had the effect of a small cannon at close range. It was much shorter than the musket, and did not have the flared barrel of a blunderbuss, and was used by boarding parties.

MUTINY

Some merchant ships got rid of their captains because of various reasons. If they did not shoot the captain, they usually set him and his followers adrift in a pinnace or small boat with water and biscuits. They usually then turned to piracy. More unusually, Royal Navy ships did the same, as with Fletcher Christian and Captain Bligh. Even pirate ships often mutinied if they were not successful, and elected another captain. The definition of a mutiny was refusing to obey the legal order of a superior. Mutineers were hanged at the yard-arm. If a whole ship's company mutinied, only the ringleaders were executed. Samuel Johnson commented that going to sea was *like going to prison, with worse food, worse company and the probability of drowning*. Seamen in both the merchant and Royal Navy were treated abominably. The following is a partial list of naval mutinies:

1747 HMS *Namur*, Portsmouth. 3 hung, 12 men received 50-100 lashes.

1748 HMS *Chesterfield*, West Africa. 2 shot, 5 hung.

1779 HMS *Defiance*, North America. 1 hung, others *'severely flogged'*.

1779 HMS *Jackal*, France. Several men hung.

1780 HMS *Prothee*, home station. 1 hung, 3 men 400-600 lashes.

1781 HMS *Sylph*, Leeward Islands. 6 hung.

1781 HMS *Namur*, Plymouth. 5 men 200-600 lashes.

1782 HMS *Narcissus*, North America. 6 hung, 2 flogged.

1783 HMS *Camilla*, Jamaica. 5 men 800 lashes.

1783 HMS *Adamant*, home station. 2 men 600 lashes.

1793 HMS *Winchelsea*, home station. 2 men 200 lashes.

1795 HMS *Defiance*, home station. 5 men hung, 6 men 300-600 lashes.

1797 HMS *Beaulieu*, home station. 4 men hung.

1797 HMS *Pompee*, home station. 5 men hung.

1797 HMS *St. George*, Mediterranean. 4 men hung.

1797 HMS *Powerful*, home station. 1 man 300 lashes, 1 man 200 lashes.

1797 HMS *Hermione*, Jamaica. Over the next few years, over 12 men hung.

1798 HMS *Amelia*, home station. 2 men hung.

1798 HMS *Renominee*, Jamaica. 4 men hung.

1798 HMS *Marlborough*, Berehaven. 1 man hung.

1798 HMS *Princess Royal*, Mediterranean. 4 men hung.

1798 HMS *Adamant*, home station. 2 men hung.

1798 HMS *Defiance*, home station. 11 men hung, 13 flogged and/or transported.

1798 HMS *Queen Charlotte*, home station. 2 men 300 lashes.

1798 HMS Glory, home station. 8 men hung, 3 men flogged.

1798 HMS *Captain*, home station. 10 men 100-400 lashes.

1798 HMS *Diomede*, home station. 1 hung, 1 man 500 lashes.

1798 HMS *Haughty*, home station. 2 men hung.

1800 HMS *Albanaise*. 2 men hung.

In the 19th century, men were still receiving up to 500 lashes. In 1809, on the HMS *Nereide*, there occurred flogging with a special kind of cat-o-nine-tails, and also *'the most unmerciful starting with sticks of a severer kind than is ever used in the Royal Navy'* on ten men. Dozens of men were hung.

NAUTICAL MILE
A minute of latitude, or 6076 feet, compared to a land mile of 5280 feet.

NAVAL MAN OF WAR
The largest could weigh up to 3500 tons and have 140 guns. There were different types of *'Ship of the Line'*, based upon their size and firepower. The heaviest man of war was the 200-foot class with over 100 heavy guns, and with 850 seamen on its three decks. The Frigate was smaller and faster, at 110 feet and 300 tons, with 200 men. There were between 18 and 40 mid-size guns, on one or two decks. The Corvette was smaller, two-masted with up to 20 guns on one deck.

NAVAL SLOOP
Bigger and more heavily-armed than a standard sloop, a superior ship to the normal pirate sloop. It was developed as a pirate-hunting ship, with a crew of 70 men. 113 tons, 65 feet in length, the ship had been *'sharpened'* to allow for faster attacking. It was also fitted with 7 pairs of oars to put through the gunports, to chase in windless conditions. Its crew could fire the 12 nine-pound cannons every 90 seconds.

NAVAL SNOW
Comparable to a brigantine, with a crew of 90 and 8 mounted six-pounder cannon. Just 60 foot long, it was distinguished by its fore and aft trysails. It managed well in a light quartering wind, and the common patrol ship when the Royal navy eventually decided to exterminate piracy.

NAVIGATION
Smith in 1691 recommended that the Captain carried the following: *'Compasses, so many a Pair and Sorts as you will, an Astrolabe Quadrant, a Cross-Staf, back Staff, an Atrolabe, a Nocturnal.'*

NEAP TIDES
Tides when the moon is in the second and last quarter, not so high, low or swift as Spring tides. *'A ship is beneaped'* when the water does not flow high enough to bring it off the ground, or out of a dock, or over a bar.

NEGRO

The author is aware of the pejorative nature of this description, but is merely using the terms of the day. In the author's '100 Great Welsh Women', Nell Gwynne and Lucy Walters are described as the 'mistresses' of Charles II rather than the modern term of 'partner'. It is sometimes difficult to modify history in line with modern-day correctness. Up to a third of some pirate crews were black, and had the same right as white pirates to booty, and the same voting rights. Some were elected pirate captains. Some were captured slaves and some were fugitive slaves. The deck of a pirate ship was the most empowering place in the New World for a black to be in the 18th century. Bart Roberts had at least 40 black men serving as 'free' pirates with him, and around half of the crews of Paulsgrave Williams and Black Sam Bellamy were black. There are records of blacks being elected captains and quartermasters of pirate vessels.

NEGRO'S HOLIDAY

Sunday. Just as slaves worked seven days a week, so sailors still had to run the ship at sea on a Sunday.

NEW ORLEANS

Barataria Bay near New Orleans was a favourite pirate haunt, the most famous being Jean Lafite, a former New Orleans blacksmith. He commanded, with his brother Pierre, up to 10 ships in the Gulf of Mexico, attacking American, British and Spanish shipping. He died in 1820 or 1821 after burning Glaveston.

NEW PROVIDENCE ISLAND, 'THE NEST OF PYRATES'

This small 60-mile square Bahaman island was used by pirates since the 1680's, until by 1716 Governor Spotswood of Virginia called it the 'Nest of Pyrates'. It was formerly called Providence Island. In the centre of the Bahamas, it was abandoned by the English in 1704 after repeated French and Spanish attacks. However, its port of Charles Town (now called Nassau) was considered the ideal pirate harbour by Captain Henry Jennings after the end of the War of Spanish Succession in 1714. From 1716 - 1718 it was the most important pirate haven in the Caribbean, and pirates were said to 'dream of Heaven being in New Providence'. The settlement took over after the destruction of Jamaica's Port Royal in 1692, as the 'Sodom of the New World.' Nassau was a prominent pirate port, and was important for careening in safety.

Near all the trade routes, there was abundant water, meat, wood and fruit. The port of Nassau was too shallow for warships to attack, but held up to 500 smaller vessels, and was divided at its entrance by Hog Island. Thus to be effectively blockaded, two men-of-war were needed. Woodes Rogers arrived in 1718, and its pirate haven days were effectively ended. The exodus of pirates in 1718 included Howell Davis, Thomas Anstis, Olivier Levasseur (La Buze), Blackbeard, Paul Williams, Samuel Bellamy, Thomas Cocklyn, 'Jolly' Jack Rackham, Christopher Winter, Christopher Condent and others. In 1717, Stede Bonnet, Benjamin Horniglod, Charles Vane and John Martel had also used New Providence.

NEW YORK

One of its early governors, Colonel Benjamin Fletcher, earned his living by fencing stolen goods from pirates to corrupt officials. Pirate ships were even charged a fee to anchor in New York City's harbour, after which their goods were passed without problems through customs. They roamed free, spending their money in the port's taverns and brothels. Fletcher became a close friend of Captain Thomas Tew (see Rhode Island). The governor also asked another friend Captain William Kidd, to privateer against the French off the coast. Fletcher was removed from office by the English crown in 1698. New York was at the forefront of attempts to evade the hated Navigation Taxes, and its merchants traded openly with smugglers, and traded extensively with Adam Baldridge, the main pirate 'fence' in Madagascar. However, as the city grew, normal trade became more important, and by the 1730's the great days of New York and piracy were over.

NIPPERS

The anchor cable in large sailing ships was too large to bend around a capstan on the quayside. Smaller lines (*messengers*) were used to heave the cables, and these were 'nipped' to the cable by dextrous small boys, who became known as 'nippers'. Mainwaring in 1644 wrote that '*nippers are small ropes - the use thereof is to hold off the cable from the main capstan, when the cable is either so slippy or so great that they cannot strain it, or hold it off, with their hands only.*' These small agile boys were also used by pickpockets.

NODDY

The tern '*sterna stolida*', sometimes eaten by buccaneers when meat was in short supply.

NO GREAT SHAKES

As food barrels and other barrels were emptied, they were taken apart, to gain extra precious storage space. The empty casks were '*shaken*' apart, and the pieces of timber came to be called '*shakes*'. Little value was attached to shakes, so something or someone of little value came to be known as being of '*no great shakes*'. The other explanations of this term come from the 13th century word '*schakere*', a maker of boasts; and from shaking dice. Someone who throws a non-winning number is '*no great shakes*'.

NO MAN'S LAND

In 1789, Falconer noted that this expression '*derives from a situation of being neither on starboard nor larboard, nor in the waist or the forecastle, but being situated in the middle part of both places.*'

NO PEACE BEYOND THE LINE

This was the language of diplomacy between 1559 and 1684, saying that European treaties did not apply beyond a line 100 leagues west of the Azores and Cape Verde Islands. West of this line, seamen travelled at their own risk and could not be protected. In 1493, Pope Alexander VI had granted all lands west of this line to

Spain, with which judgement the major seafaring nations Dutch, Portuguese, French and English disagreed. From 1559 the French and Spanish were at peace in Europe, but at war in the Caribbean and west of the line. With the 1670 Treaty of Madrid, the Spanish recognised England's American colonies for the first time, and the Spanish were angered that Morgan's raid on panama occurred after signing this treaty.

NO PREY NO PAY, or NO PURCHASE NO PAY
Pirate motto, referring to the fact that without capturing other ships, there was no money to be made – see 'purchase'.

NORTH AFRICAN PIRATES
The Mediterranean ports of Tripoli (Libya), Tunis (Tunisia) and Algiers (Algeria) were the main havens of the Barbary Corsairs, who from about 1480 to 1630 virtually controlled shipping in the area. These cities were on the edge of the desert, so the sea was regarded as their main resource. The Ottoman rulers became so reliant upon the corsairs that eventually the ruler came to be elected from the pirates. The corsairs had protected status in the Ottoman Empire, so had secure bases from which to attack Christian ships and ports. The Barbarossa brothers were each in turn Sultan of Algiers, and attacked the Spanish for around 50 years in the early 1500's. After the death of Suleiman the Magnificent in 1566, the Ottoman Empire slowly declined until by the early 1800's it was 'the sick man of Europe'.

NUESTRA SENORA DE ATOCHE
This Spanish treasure ship was wrecked in 1622, but rediscovered in 1985, with nearly $400 million in gold, silver and other artefacts, some of which is now on display at a museum in Key West, Florida.

NOW YOU'RE TALKING!
With the ship nicely balanced, with no weather or lee helm, and the sails set correctly, old salts would commend their ship as she splashed rhythmically and perfectly though the waves.

OAK ISLAND MONEY PIT
The most intriguing of all the sites associated with buried pirate treasure, and associated with Captain Henry Morgan and Captain Kidd, was first discovered in 1795. A few years later, digging through layers of logs and clay, a stone tabled was found, decoded to read: 'Forty Feet Below Two million Pounds Are Buried'. Over the years, booby traps and an artificial beach have been discovered, along with an extremely complicated drainage system. Four men died in 1965 excavating the site. There is no space to describe this remarkable site, but several books have been written, and the easiest accessible information is on the 'Swasbuckler's Cove' website, 'The Money Pit of Oak Island'.

OAKUM
Strands of old hemp rope or manila fibres were soaked in tar, and stuffed in between

the planks of a hull to stop leaks. Unpicking old rope into strands was a slow, tedious job which hurt the fingers and thumbs, and this '*picking oakum*' was a regular punishment for minor misdemeanours. In the Royal navy, each man in a ship's cells had to unpick a pound of oakum every day. The word comes from the Anglo-Saxon '*acumba*', the coarse part of flax.

OCTANT
A navigational instrument, not particularly accurate, but vital before the introduction of sextants in the late 18th century. Chronometers were of no real use until the 19th century. The wonderful best-selling book '*Longitude*' by Dava Sobel describes some of the problems of sailing the oceans without accurate instruments, and the invention of Harrison's series of chronometers..

OFF AND ON
A ship was 'off and on' while waiting for daylight to enter port. She *stands on* to shore for a while, then heads out to the *offing* for safety, then comes to stands on to shore and so on.

OFFING
From the shore, or out into the sea. '*The ship stands for the offing*' means that the ship sails from the shore to the sea. If a ship keeps in the middle of a channel, and does not near the shore, she is said to '*keep an offing*'. '*Offward*' is contrary to the shore, so if its stern lies to the offward, its head faces the shore. **'In the offing'** has come to mean that something is likely to happen, as a ship *in the offing* will either come to land, anchor, send a boat ashore or sail away.

ON AN EVEN KEEL
When a ship is well-trimmed and steady at sea, well balanced. A ship in this condition is unlikely to **'keel over.'**

ON THE ACCOUNT
Being involved in piracy or buccaneering.

ON THE FIDDLE
This may have a nautical origin. Dining tables on HMS Victory and other ships were edged with a fixed or hinged rim, called a '*fiddle*', to stop platters and jugs from sliding off. Some sailors had their square platters filled so full, at the expense of the rest of the less favoured crew, that their plates had to be balanced '*on the fiddle*'.

ON THE ROCKS
A ship in desperate trouble gives us the modern phrase.

ON THE SPOT (see Black Spot)

OK
There are many origins of this term, but one of the more likely seems to be from the French '*au quai*' meaning in dock and safe. Another French derivation is from the

Haitian port of 'Aux Cayes', fmous for its superb rum. The Scots 'Och (Auch) Aye' may also be the original term.

OUT OF TRIM
A ship that is unbalanced for sailing because its cargo, loot or ballast is not allocated correctly.

OVER A BARREL (See Gunner's Daughter)

OVERBEARING
Sailing downwind directly at another ship, thus *'taking the wind from his sails'*, a favourite manoeuvre of pirates. The prize slowed and could be taken more easily.

OVER HAUL
The crew went aloft to *'overhaul'* buntlines to stop sails chaffing, when rigged over long periods on a downwind course. The term has gradually come to mean maintaining something in perfect condition.

OVERREACH
When a ship holds its tack course for too long, it overreaches the desired turning point, and the distance and time to travel to the next tack point is increased.

OVERWHELMED
This refers to a ship which has capsized or turned upside down in the water.

PADDY'S PURCHASE
Seaman's abuse for any length of rope which is left over and not needed for a job.

PAINTER
Rope at stem of boat for towing it, or mooring.

PANAMA
One of the three ports used by the Spanish treasure fleets, on the Pacific coast. Every year, silver was taken from Panama on mule trains across the Panama Isthmus to Nombre de Dios, and then Portobelo on the Caribbean coast. If the Chagres River was full, small boats were used instead of mules. Panama City was sacked by Henry Morgan in 1671, just three years after he had taken Porobelo. .

PAPAGAYO
A north-east gale off the Central American coast, which springs up without warning.

PARCEL A SEAM
After the seam is caulked, this is to lay over it a narrow strip of canvas, and pour hot pitch and tar over it for waterproofing.

PARROT

Most of us remember Captain Flint, the rascally Long John Silver's parrot in Treasure Island, with its incessant *'Pieces of Eight ! Pieces of Eight !'* Parrots were very popular on sailing ships, and William Dampier in his second voyage tells us that those near Vera Cruz in the Bay of Campeche were the biggest in the West Indies *'Their colour was yellow and red, very coarsely mixed; and they would prate very prettily and there was scarce a man but what sent aboard one or two of them. So that with provision, chests, hen-coops and parrot-cages, our ships were full of lumber, with which we intended to sail.'*

They were easier to keep on ship than monkeys, and were sold everywhere. A 1717 advertisement in London's *'Post-Man'* reads: *'Parrotkeets with red heads from Guinea, and two fine talking Parrotkeets from Buenos Aires, and several young talking Parrots'*, which were being sold at the *'Leopard and Tiger'* tavern at Tower Dock. Another 1717 issue offered *'Parrotkeets which talk English, Dutch, French and Spanish, Whistle at command, small parrotkeets with red heads, very tame and pretty'*, at the Porter's Lodge, Charing Cross.

THE PARROT MUST HAVE A NUT

From the Shakespearian saying, *'the parrot must have an almond'*, referring to the need to bribe certain officials and governors to turn a blind eye to pirates trading on their territories. Kurt Cobhain's *'Polly wants a cracker '*, part of a splendid Nirvana song, seems to have evolved from this saying. However, the best use of slang in a modern record still remains the opening line of *'Reward'* by the Welshman Julian Cope's old group *'The Teardrop Explodes'*. It is *'Bless my cotton socks, I'm in the news.'*

PARTNERS

The stout wooden framework, necessary to hold a mast, pump, capstan or bitt to the deck. Without partners, none of these would hold tight.

PASSED WITH FLYING COLOURS

The present term comes from the fact that ships which wished to be identified would fly their pennants when passing others.

PAY A SEAM

To put hot pitch and tar on a seam between two of the ship's planks, without using a strip of canvas, which is *'parcelling'* a seam.

PAY OUT

To feed a line over the side of the ship, hand over hand.

PEDRERO

This Spanish swivel gun, copied by the English, shot iron balls. The *pedreros pequenos* used 4 pound shot, the *esmeriles pedreros* used 3 pound shot and the *esmeriles pequenos* used 2 pound shot. In the 18th century, a *pedrero* was a gun that shot stone balls or a great number of tiny balls to sweep the deck of enemies, and the *esmeril* was considered the equivalent of a *falconete*.

PEG LEG

Nickname for pirates who had lost a leg in battle or accident, and the leg replaced by a wooden stump. Francois le Clerc and Cornelius Jol were pirate 'peg-legs'. The Dutch equivalent was *'houtebeen'* and the Spanish *'pie de palo'*. Like losing a hand, losing a leg would mean that most pirates would die of gangrene, so relatively few survivors would were a peg-leg. Captain Ahab in *'Moby Dick'* had an ivory leg. Nowhere in *'Treasure Island'* does Long John Silver have an artificial leg. He wore crutches, and the peg-leg is the addition of film-makers. In this 1883 book, Long John was based on William Henley, a friend of R.L. Stevenson, who had a foot amputated in boyhood.

PESO

This silver coin weighed about an ounce, 27.46 grammes. The 8-real peso was the well-known *'piece of eight'* but there was also a 10-real peso. Later the pesos were made of gold.

PETER PEPPER (Pierre Poivre)

Of *'picked a peck of pickled peppers'* fame, was an East India Company administrator in Mauritius in the 1770's who introduced plant varieties from South America, including pepper, and gave incentives to grow them. Not much to do with pirates, but a fascinating gobbet, or snippet, of information with which to annoy one's friends and colleagues.

PETIT GOAVE

Pirate port in the south-west of St Domingue (today's Haiti), which replaced Tortuga as a buccaneering base in the 1670's.

PETTICOAT BREECHES

These baggy trousers, widening out and ending at mid-calf, were ideal for barefoot pirates scrambling up the rigging.

PICAROON, PICKAROON

17th century term for a pirate, from the Spanish *'picaro'*, meaning rogue or rascal.

PICKLE

The salt brine in casks, in which beef and pork was immersed to preserve it in the tropics.

PIECES OF EIGHT

Silver Spanish coins, or dollars, marked with an 8, and worth four pesetas or eight *'reales'*. In the 17th and 18th centuries, so many were in circulation that they were accepted almost anywhere in the world. The American dollar sign $ was derived from 8 stamped on the side of the *'piece of eight'*, the silver peso (or *piaster*). Two pieces, or bits, made a quarter, and this is the origin of the American *'two-bit'* or quarter dollar coin. They were minted at Mexico City and Lima in Peru, and were common currency in all of England's colonies, being valued at 4 shillings and sixpence. Often they were cut into 8 pieces for ease of transaction, so that *'two bits'* made a quarter. The origin of the modern American term, *'not worth two bits'* is from the days when the English colonies around Massachusetts used this Spanish money. Pieces of eight were produced for about 300 years, in Mexico, Peru and Colombia, and they became the standard unit of trade between Europe and China. They were legal tended in the USA until 1857. Gold was used for escudos, which were the same value as pieces of eight, and gold doubloons were worth 8 escudos.

Before the Spanish started exploiting Potosi in Peru (in today's Bolivia), silver was almost as valuable as gold in the Old World. Such were the quantities taken from the New World, that silver dropped to about a fifteenth of the value of gold. (The Spanish took 4 billion pesos of silver and gold from the New World between 1492 and 1830. When one sees some of the remarkable religious architecture in Spain, remember the misery that was the source of the resources, much like the buildings of Bristol and Bath originating from the slave trade. Cardiff was also built upon *'black gold'*, the product of the inhuman conditions and child labour in the coal mines).

PIGTAILS

Even more popular in the 17th and 18th century than today amongst art teachers, advertising executives and balding rock stars, pigtails were *'tarred'* at sea, which may be the origin of *'Jack Tar'*, the popular name for a seaman. However, it is more likely that seamen were called *'tars'* because their hands were always covered with tar off the ropes and ship's timbers. In *'The Shipping News'* we read: *'Sailors once wore their hair in queues worked two ways, laid up into rattails, or plaited in four-strand square sinnets. The final touch called for a pickled eelskin chosen from the brine cask. The sailor carefully rolled the eelskin back (as a condom is rolled), then worked it up over his queue and seized it. For dress occasions he finished it off with a red ribbon tied in a bow.'* It is unknown at present whether the eelskin had a complementary usage as a condom.

PILE UP

Now applied to road accidents, the origin is nautical, when a vessel piled up on top of rocks.

PILLORY

For minor offences ashore, many pirates had suffered from the pillory before they escaped to sea. A frame held a standing man, with his head and two arms protruding through three holes. The prisoner's ears were then nailed to the wooden frame, so he could not avert his head from missiles hurled at him by the crowd. Men and women died from this punishment, and blinding was common. The last occurrence was in 1814.

PINK (Dutch *pincke*, Italian *pinco*)

There were two types of pink. The small Mediterranean cargo ship with a flat bottom and a narrow stern was the Italian *pinco*. In the Atlantic, it was any vessel with a very narrow stern, derived from the Dutch *pincke*. In the 17th and 18th centuries, large square-rigged pinks were used as merchantmen and warships

PINNACE
In the 18th century, a small, fast boat that could be rowed or sailed. Also used to describe the ship's longboat that ferried men to the shore. In the 16th and 17th centuries, pinnaces were much larger, from 20-60 tons.

PIPE DOWN
Sailors said this to someone who was talking too much. Its derivation is that the last noise at night was the boatswain's pipe, the signal for silence on the mess-decks and lights out.

PIRACY ACT 1721
Pirates were tried in civil courts until 1340, when Edward III destroyed the French fleet at Sluys, and claimed thereafter to be *'Sovereign of the Seas'*. From now on Admiralty Courts were empowered to try piracy cases. Henry VIII passed the first Piracy Act in 1536, creating a Vice-Admiral of the Coast to hold trials and sentence pirates. In 1611 another act authorised Courts of the Admiralty to try cases in the colonies and plantations of North America and the West Indies. The 1721 Act stated that anyone who traded with a pirate, if found guilty, would be treated as a pirate and charged accordingly. Until then, it was fairly easy to dispose of stolen goods. Also, anyone who provided a pirate with ammunition, stores or provisions, or who fitted out a ship for piracy, or corresponded with a pirate, was deemed to be a pirate, felon and robber.

PIRAGUA, PIROGUE, PIRAGAYA
Native dugout, a sea-going canoe used by natives in Central and South America. The term comes from the Carib language. Also sometimes in the West Indies it referred to a plank-built boat with one sail and a flat bottom. Many pirates started their careers with a pirogue, which could not be chased around the shallow waters of the cays, and could land on any beach.

PIRATE COUNCIL
Each crew-man was a member, unlike the officers' councils of war in the Royal Navy. The council decided where to go, what to do, what punishments to make, who should be captain, whether the captain should be deposed and so on.

PIRATE FLAGS
The *Old Roger* or *Jolly Roger* (q.v.) is the most famous pirate flag, the 'skull and crossbones', but most pirates amended this to their own personal banner. Black Bart Robert's main flag had him sharing a glass of wine with the skeleton of the devil, which was holding a burning spear. His personal pennant was a picture of him with a raised sword, standing on two skulls, marked ABH and AMH. These signified a Barbadan's head and a Martinican's head, as the governors of these colonies both sent vessels to capture Roberts. However, he hung the Governor of Martinique from his yardarm. They were meant to strike fear into the enemy's heart, and when a merchant ship saw Roberts' flags being raised, they did not generally wish to fight *'the great pyrate.'* This black flag was raised in battle, and if the prize did not strike

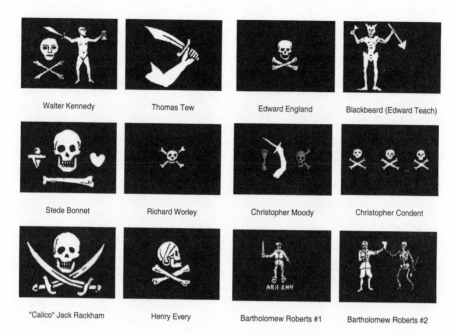

Walter Kennedy

Thomas Tew

Edward England

Blackbeard (Edward Teach)

Stede Bonnet

Richard Worley

Christopher Moody

Christopher Condent

"Calico" Jack Rackham

Henry Every

Bartholomew Roberts #1

Bartholomew Roberts #2

its colours, the **red flag** would be flown, signifying '*no quarter*'. The first known use of the skull and crossbones was by the Breton pirate Emmanuel Wynne in 1700, where the skull and bones surmounted an hour-glass.

PIRATE FOOD
Neither flour nor dried beans could be kept for long in the dame hulls of ships, so only heavily salted meat and fish would last for any length of time. Water also went off quickly in the wooden casks, so alcohol was preferred. Any stews were strongly spiced to disguise the saltiness of the food and picked vegetables. (See Turtles)

PIRATE HOOKS
This hand replacement would have been strapped to the stump of the arm with leather, but there are no records of pirates surviving amputation and having them. The popularity in fancy dress costume probably comes from J.M. Barrie's Captain Hook in '*Peter Pan*'.

PIRATE ROUND
The route from North America to the Indian Ocean – where pirates could be encountered anywhere along the way.

PIRATES
These attacked any ships, including those from their own countries.

PIRATE COMPENSATION

In general, the following rules applied amongst pirate crews for injuries received in battle:

InjuryCompensation

To lose an eye 100 pieces of eight	To lose a finger100 pieces of eight
To lose the right arm 600 pieces of eight	To lose a right leg 500 pieces of eight
To lose the left arm500 pieces of eight	To lose a left leg 400 pieces of eight

PIRATE AND BUCCANEER PRIZES

The most successful captures and raids were as following:

Date, Captain, Ship	Prize or place looted	Value at Time
1579 Sir Francis Drake *Golden Hind*	*Cacafuego* treasure ship from Peru to Panama, taken off Ecuador	£450,000 contemporary estimate
1585 Sir Richard Grenville *Tiger*	*Santa Maria* and other treasure ships, off Bermuda	c. £50,000
1587 Thomas Cavendish *Desire*	*Santa Ana,* Manila Galleon off California	c. £125,000
1587 Sir Francis Drake *Golden Hind*	*San Felipe* East India carrack, off Azores	c. £114,000 upwards
1591 William Lane	*Trinity* and another ship from the Mexican treasure fleet, West Indies	c. £40,000
1592 Captain Crosse *Foresight* and 8 other English privateers	*Madre de Dios* Portuguese carrack en route from India to Lisbon, off the Azores	c. £500,00, of which £140,000 was taken by the Crown
1595 Sir James Lancaster with 7 English and 8 French privateers	From a Portuguese carrack and goods stored at Pernambuco in Brazil	c. £50,000 upwards
1601 William Parker	Looted Portobelo the Spanish treasure port on the Caribbean side of Panama, and treasure ships in the West Indies	c. £50,000
1607 John Ward *Gift*	*Reniera y Soderina*, Venetian ship off Cyprus	c. £100,000 upwards
1612-1613 Peter Easton and 4 ships	Dutch, English and African ships, Atlantic and Mediterranean	c. 100,000 golden crowns
1613 Sir Henry Mainwaring	Spanish ships in the Mediterranean	c. 500,000 Spanish crowns
1628 Hendrick Lucifer	Spanish treasure ship off Cuba	1.2 million guilders
1628 Piet Heyn with 31 ships	Spanish treasure fleet from Mexico, off Cuba	c. 14 million Dutch guilders
1636 William Ayres and David Jones*, *Roebuck*	Indian and Arabian ships in the Red Sea and off the Comores	c. £40,000
1658 Sir Christopher Myngs *Marston Moor*	Venezuelan ports	c. £375,000
1662 Sir Christopher Myngs and Sir Henry **Morgan***, with 11 ships	The port of St Jago in Cuba (Santiago del Cuba)	c. £30,000
1663 Sir Christopher Myngs *Marston Moor* with Sir Henry **Morgan*** and 12 ships	Town of San Francisco de Campeache, Mexico	c. £37,500
1665 Colonel Edward Morgan* (Henry Morgan's uncle)	The port of Oranjestad, St Eustacia	c. £25,000
1663-65 Sir Henry **Morgan*** with Captains Morris* and Jackman	Villa de Mosa (Honduras) and Granada (Nicaragua)	c. £100,000 upwards

1667 Francois L'Olonnais (Jean David Nau) with 8 ships	Various ships, and sacked Maracaibo and Gibraltar, Venezuela	c. £65,000
1668 Sir Henry **Morgan*** and 10 small ships	Sacked Puerto Principe (now Camaguey), Cuba	c. 50,000 pieces of eight and treasure
1668 Sir Henry **Morgan*** *Oxford* with John Morris* and 6 small ships (cromsters)	Sacked treasure port of Portobelo, Panama	c. 500,000 pieces of eight plus 300 slaves, gold and silver
1669 Sir Henry **Morgan*** and 8 small ships	Sacked Maracaibo and Gibraltar, Venezuela, took the galleons La Marquesa, destroyed the San Luis and Magdalena	c. 250,000 pieces of eight, including the value of the slaves and bullion
1671 Sir Henry **Morgan*** with John Morris* and Bledri Morgan* and 1400 men	Old Providence (1670), Chagres Fort and sacked Panama City	c. £30,000 claimed in ransoms at the time, and 750,000 pieces of eight, the richest raid in history
1680 John Coxon	Portobelo, Panama	c. £18,000
1683 De Graff, van Horn and de Gammont and 5 other ships	Sacked the port of San Juan de Ulua and its town of Veracruz in Mexico	c. £200,000
1686 Edward Davis *Delight*	The port of Sana, Peru	c. £25,000
1687 Edward Davis (*Delight*), Captain le Picard, George Hout	The port of Guayaquil, Ecuador	c. £50,000
1695 Henry (Long Ben) Every *Fancy* with 5 other ships	*Fateh Mohamed* and *Gang-I-Sawai (Gunsway),* Indian treasure ships, Red Sea	c. £400,000
1698 William Kidd *Adventure Galley*	*Quedah Merchant*, an Indian ship off Cochin, India	c. £45,000
1698 Dirk Chivers (*Soldado*) and Robert Culliford (*Mocha*)	*Great Mohamed* Indian ship in the Red Sea	c. £130,000
1701 John Halsey *Charles*	2 British ships at Mocha in the Red Sea	c. £50,000
1701 John Bowen* *Speaker*	Indian vessel in the Re Sea	c. £100,000
1703 John Bowen* (*Speedy Return*) and Thomas Howard (*Prosperous*)	2 Indian ships in the Red Sea	c. £70,000 upwards
1707 John Halsey and David Williams* *Charles*	2 Indian ships off Mocha in the Red Sea	c. £50,000
1717 Black Sam Bellamy and Paulsgrave Williams*	*Whydah* slaver, off Long Island, Bahamas	£25,000 from the sale of slaves, £30,000 from the sale of cargo
1719 Howel Davis* *Buck*	*Loyal Merchant* off Cape Verde Islands, and other merchantmen	c. £40,000
1719 Howel Davis* *Rover*	Dutch ship off Principe Island, West Indies	c. £20,000
1719 Black Bart Roberts* *Royal Rover*	*Sagrada* Familia and two other Portuguese treasure ships, Bay of All Saints, Brazil	40,000 moidores and a fortune in diamonds and gold (c. £5 million today)
1720 Edward England *Fancy*, and *Victory*	*Cassandra*, an East Indiaman at Johanna Island in the Comoros	c. £75,000
1720 Edmund Condent *Flying Dragon*	Arab ship off Bombay	c. £150,000
1721 John Taylor (*Cassandra*), Olivier la Bouche (*Victory*)	*Nostra Senhora de Cabo*, a Portuguese ship at Reunion Island	c. £500,000 in diamonds and gold; £375,000 in other cargo

* denotes a Welsh pirate. Black Bart Robert's prizes in a period of not much more than 3 years amounted to about £100,000,000 in today's money.

PIRATE HAVENS (1)

Medieval pirates favoured Wales and the West Country, with many harbours protected by hills and difficult to reach by road. They were usually welcomed by local inhabitants and officials, being a welcome source of cheap trade. The majority of British buccaneers and pirates came from the great port of London, and from Wales and the West Country. In the 16th century, the buccaneers favoured Tortuga in the Caribbean, being hilly and difficult to attack and also near shipping lanes. However, as the French and English presence grew, they moved on to New Providence in the Bahamas and Madagascar in the Indian Ocean, neither under control of any government. One of the major problems was in selling contraband, as there were few traders in these havens, who took a vast profit. As a result, pirates often tried to cut a deal with corrupt governors of settlements and colonies, where there were better prices available from a multitude of traders. Jamaica's Port Royal was a haven in the mid to late 17th century, because of its distance from London.

PIRATE HAVENS (2)

We must mention the modern meaning of 'pirate havens' as the US Government has issued a *'priority watch list of pirate havens'* – countries where the pirating of copyrights, patents and the like are common. They are: Argentina, Brazil, Colombia, Dominican Republic, Egypt, Hungary, India, Indonesia, Israel, Lebanon, Philippines, Russia, Taiwan and Uruguay. The EU is also surprisingly included, which is the major trading bloc of 15 European nations including Germany, France and England. It is surprising that Thailand is omitted from the US list as it is in the UK's list of top ten pirate havens, especially with regard to illicit CD manufacture, along with China and Taiwan.

PIRATE JOKES

How much does it cost for a pirate to get an ear pierced? A buck an ear.

A pirate finds an oil lamp amongst his booty, and cleans it up by rubbing it with his sleeve. A genie appears and grants him any three wishes he wants. *'Aaargh, me hearty'* says the pirate, *'I'll be having a huge tankard of grog.'* *'That's not much to ask for,'* mutters the genie. *'Aaargh, belay that order,'* replied the pirate, *'make it so that it can never run dry.'* *'Your wish is my command, it is so'* says the genie, and full tankard of grog appears. The pirate downs it in one, and it refills magically. *'What about your other two wishes?'* asks the genie. The happy pirate answers, *'Aaargh, I'll have another two just like this'*.

What does a pirate call his wife? Peggy.

A pirate walks into a tavern with a ships wheel jammed down the front of his trousers. 'Doesn't that give you pain?' asks the serving wench. 'Aaaargh' replies the pirate, 'it's driving me nuts.'

Two pirates are reminiscing in an inn about their injuries at sea. The one complains that he was the unluckiest pirate alive. The other asks him the reason. The lame pirate replies, *'We were trying to board this Portuguese man-o-war for three days, the ships locked together, and on the first day, I got my leg shot off, but the surgeon gave me a skinful of rum and fixed me up with this peg leg.'* The second pirate asked, but what about your hook? '*Aaaargh, on the second day, I was hurled back into the fray and a Portuguese cutlass sliced my hand off, but the surgeon topped me up with rum again and clamped this hook on, and sent me back into battle.*' '*Aaaargh, you were really unlucky*', said the second pirate, '*but what about the eye-patch?*' '*Well, on the third day we saw them off and I looked up to the skies to thank God, and a seagull defecated straight into my eye.*' The second sailor looked quizzically at him, and said '*But that wouldn't blind you?*' '*Aaaargh*, the lame pirate replied, '*I forgot, it was my first day with the new hook.*'

What has 8 arms and 8 legs? 8 pirates.

'*A boat is called a "she" because there is always a great deal of bustle around her; there is usually a gang of men about; she has a waist and stays; it takes a lot of paint to keep her looking good. It is not the initial expense that breaks you, it's the upkeep. She can be decked out; it takes an experienced man to handle her correctly, and without a man at the helm she is uncontrollable. She often shows her bottom, and when coming into harbour heads for the buoys*'. What do pirates call their vacations? Aaaargh and Aaaargh.

A pirate captain had the habit of amusing his crew by doing 'magic'. However, the ship's parrot always gave the game away, shouting '*it's up his sleeve*', or '*it's behind his back*' or whatever. In a great storm the ship sank, and the only survivors in the longboat were the captain and the parrot, which he hated vehemently. However, after a few days, dying of thirst, he asked the dumb parrot to say something, and the parrot refused. After a few days of pleading from the dying captain, who was desperate to hear any voice, just one last time, the parrot relented. Looking around him, at the empty ocean, he at last squawked. '*All right … I give up … What have you done with the ship.*'

In his last moments, the captain found in the bottom of the boat a lamp, and rubbed it. A genie appeared, but said he could only grant one wish. The captain, dying of thirst, asked that the sea be turned to rum. This was effected and the genie disappeared. The parrot gazed at the captain bleakly, and said, '*Now you've done it, we're going to drown*'. '*Why's that?*' asked the captain. "*Because we'll have to wee in the boat*' answered the parrot.

The pirate captain and his parrot were rescued, both sick of the sight of each other, and the parrot took to swearing terribly whenever he saw the captain, cursing him for all his troubles. The constant cursing annoyed the captain so much that one day he grabbed the parrot by the throat, screamed '*Belay that swearing*' at him, and threw him at the cabin wall. The parrot was quiet for a few hours, and then started, worse than before. The captain, really infuriated, grabbed the parrot and locked him in his pirate chest. However, he can still hear the bird swearing, and pecking the wood, so he lets him out. The parrot remains mute for a few hours again, and then starts cursing, even worse than the last time. At last, the captain hurls the bird into the ship's freezer. For a few minutes, the parrot swears and then shuts up. The captain thinks that the bird has suffered enough and lets him out. The parrot, humbled, sits perfectly on the captain's shoulder, and apologises profusely. '*I am dreadfully, awfully sorry about my obscene vocabulary. My language will never be like that again. I am going to be a reformed parrot. You are a truly wonderful villain, a prince among pirates – by the way, what did the chicken do?'*

How much does a pirate pay for his hook and peg? An arm and a leg.

PIRATE SHIPS

These had to be fast, and easy and quick to careen, so small boats of 30-50 tons were favoured in the Caribbean. If a large boat was taken, it was usually used to store plunder, before being destroyed, sold or set adrift. A shallow draught was essential to operate around the cays of the West Indies, and allow escape from larger vessels. All deckhouses were cut down to streamline the ship and leave the deck easy to shift cannon and resources from one side to the other in a fight. The gunwales were raised to give the crew extra protection.

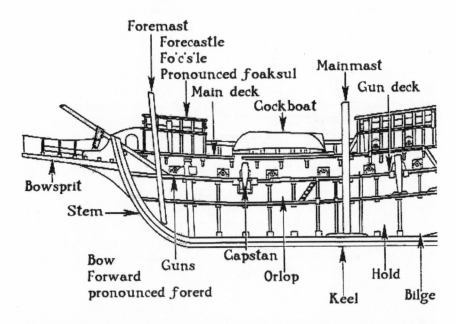

An alphabetical list of some of the pirate ships with their captains is as follows: *Adventure, Queen Anne's Revenge* (Edward Teach, Blackbeard); *Adventure Galley* and *Adventure Prize* (William Kidd); *Bachelor's Delight* (William Dampier); *Barbara*, John Phillips; *Black Joke* (Benito de Soto); *Blessing* (Captain Brown); *Bravo* (Captain Power); *Cassandra* (John Taylor); *Charles* (John Halsey); *Childhood* (Captain Carracioli); *Delight* (Francis Spriggs); *Delivery, Happy Delivery, Ranger* (George Lowther); *Desire* (Thomas Cavendish); *Dolphin*, Thomas Booth; *Fancy* (Henry Every); *Flying Dragon* (Edward Condent); *Flying Horse* (Captain Rhoade); *Flying King* (Captain Sample); *Fortune, Royal Fortune, Good Fortune, Royal Fortune (1), Royal Fortune (2), Great Ranger, Little Ranger, Rover, Sea King* (Black Bart Roberts); *Gift* (John Ward); *Golden Chalice*, John Callice; *Happy Delivery* (George Lowther); *Liberty* (Thomas Tew); *Mary Anne, Whydah* (Black Sam Bellamy); *Mayflower* (Captain Cox); *Mocha* (Robert Culliford); *Most Holy Trinity* (Bartholomew Sharp); *New York*

Revenge (Captain Cole); *Night Rambler* (Captain Cooper); *Oxford*, Henry Morgan; *Ranger* (George Lowther, Charles Vane); *Revenge* (Cowley, Phillips, Gow, Bonnet, Blackbeard and others used this name); *Rising Sun* (William Moody); *Royal James* (Edward England); *Scowerer* (John Evans); *Sea King* (Captain le Vasseur, Bart Roberts); *Snap Dragon* (Captain Goldsmith); *Speaker, Speedy Return* (John Bowen); *Sudden Death* (Captain Derdrake); *Victory* (Olivier la Bouche).

PISS IN A QUILL
16th-19th century slang for making and agreeing a plan. Obviously pirates had the same opinions of planning committees and paperwork as this author does.

PISS MONEY AGAINST A WALL
To waste money on alcohol, a favourite pirate pastime when in a safe harbour.

HE PISSES MORE THAN HE DRINKS
A pirate who boasts.

PISS-POT
A 'saw-bones', *or ship's doctor.*

PISTOL
The pistol was a pirate's best friend, not a rifle. Blackbeard used to carry six in his sash, loaded and ready for action. Howell Davis carried four, and Black Bart two. It had a flintlock (presentation) mechanism, with a single shot loaded via the barrel. The *powderbox* or *powder horn* kept powder dry, and ready for action - damp powder was useless. A pirate probably did not carry his powder horn with him during combat, but used a smaller container preparatory to action. After loading his pistols and perhaps musket, he would move into action. In prolonged battles, men were probably designated to loading small arms, ready for the pirates to discharge them.

PISTOL PROOF
The description applied to Black Bart by his crew – a pirate who knows what he's doing and cannot therefore be hurt.

PISTOLE
Any foreign gold coin, especially French of Spanish, worth about a quarter of a doubloon.

PITCHER-BAWD
A worn-out prostitute, only good enough to take pitchers of beer to a tavern's customers. Pitchers were leather jugs, treated with tar pitch to help them hold their shape. Glass was too expensive and fragile.

PLAIN SAILING
The origin was '*plane sailing*', the method of recording the course and speed of a ship on a plane projection of the spherical earth.

PLATE
Silver, usually in bars, but sometimes in coins.

PLATE FLEET
One royal convoy, the *flota* (q.v.) left Seville every year, stopping at the Canary and Leeward Islands for water and provisions, across the Caribbean to Veracruz in Mexico. Later in the year, the *'galeones'* left Cadiz for Cartagena, then on to Portobelo in Panama to meet the merchants who brought treasure across the Isthmus from Peru. They carried expensive European manufactured goods, and each fleet usually was of over a dozen large galleons and smaller ships, accompanied by two men-of-war, the Capitana (q.v.) and Almirante. They returned to Spain with silver, gold, logwood, indigo, hides and cacao.

PLUMB THE DEPTHS
To fully investigate, by *'plumbing'* or sounding the depths in shallow waters. Perhaps the current meaning shows us that this was a really boring job, the lowest of the low, unskilled and repettitive.

POINT-BLANK
The direction of a gun when levelled horizontally. The shot flies to its target without a curve, so iss used from close range. The phrase may have come from the French *'point blanc'*, the white centre of a bullseye target for archery, meaning that one would definitely hit the target.

POLEAXE
Short-handled axe or hatchet with a spike or hammer opposite the blade, used for slaughtering cattle. The boucaniers, or cattle-killers, began using the variety with the pike, to drive a series of them into the side or rear of a ship. They could then swarm up this *'ladder'* of axes and take their prize.

POOP DECK
The raised rear deck, above the quarter deck, where the ship was steered, and from where the captain usually directed battles.

POOP, POOPED
To be *'pooped'* is to be swamped by a high following sea, as waves break over the stern. This is extremely dangerous for a vessel, for obvious reasons, and could cause her to founder or be ripped to pieces. We now use the term to mean overwhelmed by exhaustion. This term derives from the Latin *'puppis'*, which refers to the stern or aftermost part of a vessel. *Poop* was the name given to the short, aftermost deck raised above the quarterdeck of a sailing ship, but is now commonly used to describe any aftermost deck.

POOP DECK
The deck at the stern of the ship, usually above the captain's quarters, and usually the highest deck.

POOR JOHN
Salted and dried fish, usually hake and cod. Seamen far preferred meat to fish.

PORT
When standing at the back (*aft*) of a vessel looking forward (*for'ud*), the left side of the vessel is the port (*larboard*) side. To port weapons is to carry them in your left hand. Port may be an abbreviation of *'porta il timone'* - carry the helm. Port Holes comes from the French *'porte'* and Latin *'porta'* or door, which opened to allow cannon to be stationed within the ship, not just on deck, whereby a ship could become top-heavy.

PORTOBELO
Because Francis Drake had sacked Cartagena and Santo Domingo, and Nombre de Dios had a worse natural harbour, the Spanish developed Portobelo as the their main Caribbean treasure port from 1595. In the 18th century, at terrible cost, a road linked it to Panama City on the other side of the Isthmus. Henry Morgan sacked it in 1668.

PORT ROYAL, 'THE SODOM OF THE NEW WORLD'
Known as Cagway to Christopher Myngs, in Henry Morgan's early days on the island, the original Carib-Spanish name for Port Royal was *'cayagua'* (literally, island of water). When Cromwell's force under Penn and Venables took Jamaica in 1655, they thought the name *'cayagua'* was that of the entire cay, not just the tip of Palisadoes Point. The new port of Cagway was renamed Port Royal in 1660, on the restoration of Charles II, but was still called Cagway by Morgan and his cronies for some time after. Because of fear of a Spanish invasion, buccaneers were requested to come from Tortuga to bolster its defences, but after the 1660 peace with Spain, many buccaneers were granted letters of marque to attack shipping. By the early 1670's, Port Royal even rivalled Boston for wealth, with a city of 7000 people

'*Pirate heaven*' with a huge harbour that could take up to five hundred ships, and at the heart of all the West Indies shipping routes, this was an easy market for pirate plunder. It was a series of sandbars and cays, which formed a peninsula off modern Kingston. The waters were 30 feet deep, just a few yards offshore, allowing for easy anchorage. Buccaneering was unofficially sanctioned by the governors of Jamaica, and the lawyer Francis Hanson of Port Royal wrote in 1683 *'The town of Port Royal, being as it were the Store House or Treasury of the West Indies, is always like a continual Mart or fair where all sorts of choice merchandises are daily imported, not only to furnish the island, but vast quantities are thence again transported to supply the Spaniards, Indians and other Nations, who in exchange return us bars and cakes of gold, wedges and pigs of silver, Pistoles, Pieces of Eight and several other coins of both metals, with store of wrought Plate, jewels, rich pearl necklaces, and of Pearl unsorted or undrilled several bushels.....almost every House hath a rich cupboard of Plate, which they carelessly expose, scarce shutting their doors in the night.... In Port Royal there is more plenty of running Cash (proportionately to the number of its inhabitants) than is in London.'*
Port Royal was also known for its '*grog shops*', gaming houses and brothels, earning it the nickname of '*the Sodom of the New World*'. In July 1661 alone the Council

The West Indies

issued licences for forty new grog shops, taverns and punch houses. Amongst them were the Black Dog, Blue Anchor, Cat and Fiddle, Cheshire Cheese, Cat and Fiddle, Feathers, Jamaica Arms, Three Crowns, Windmill, Three Tunns, Three Mariners, Sugar Loaf, Sign of the George, Sign of Bacchus, Sin of the Mermaid, The Ship, The Salutation, King's Arms, Jamaica Arms and Green Dragon. Around this time Governor Modyford was making a fortune in bribes from Henry Morgan and other buccaneers. In 1680, there were over 100 licensed taverns for a population of 3000. Around this time John Starr operated its largest whorehouse, in the official 1680 census maintaining an establishment with 21 *'white women'* and 2 *'black women'*. Port Royal was the largest English or French settlement in the New World outside Boston. By 1690, one in four of its buildings were *'brothels, gaming houses, taverns and grog shops'*. A seventeenth century clergyman returned to England on the same ship as he sailed out on, writing *'This town is the Sodom of the new World and since the majority of its population consists of pirates, cut-throats, whores and some of the vilest persons in the whole of the world, I felt my permanence there was of no use.'* It was heaven for traders, who cheaply bought pirate loot, sold it in London at huge profits, and also profiteered by selling expensive supplies to pirates.

Charles Leslie, in his 1740 *'History of Jamaica'* recorded of pirates, that in Port Royal, *'wine and women drained their wealth to such a degree that in a little time some of them were reduced to beggary. They have been know to spend 2000 - 3000 pieces of eight in one night; and one gave a strumpet 500 to see her naked. They used to buy a pipe of wine, place it in the street, and oblige everyone that passed to drink.'* A pipe is a cask of 105 gallons, or 840 pints of wine. Barre's Tavern was one of the more high-class establishments in the town, frequented by Henry Morgan, and perhaps operated by the family of Charles de la Barre, secretary to Governor Lynch. It offered light refreshments *including 'syllabub (q.v.), cream tarts and other quelque choses.'*

Port Royal lay on a small cay and the tip of the long sandspit called the Palisadoes, which forms Kingston Harbour. On June 7th, 1692, a combined earthquake and tidal wave destroyed this buccaneer capital, probably killing two-thirds of its 3000 population, sweeping Captain Morgan's grave into the sea. The tremors had rocked the sandy peninsula on which Port Royal was built, and caused building to slide and slip into the sea. Apart from the 2000 that died on that day, another 2000 died later from wounds, disease and fever. In the tidal wave that followed the earthquake, *'nothing else was seen but the dead and dying, and heard but shrieks and cries.'* So few people were left alive that the bodies just floated in and out with the tide, and rolled along the beaches. A joiner, John Pike, wrote to his brother and told him that his house was lost beneath the waves: *'I lost my wife, my son, an apprentice, a white-maid and 6 slaves and all that I ever had in the world. My land where I was ready to raise 5 houses, and had room to raise 10 more, is all sunk, a good sloop may sail over it as well as over the Point.'*

The capital of St Jago de la Vega, corrupted to Santiago, now resumed its authority over Jamaica's affairs. Port Royal was rebuilt after the earthquake, only to suffer a great fire in 1703. In 1712 Governor Hamilton reported that a hurricane had destroyed 38 ships at Port Royal and 9 at Kingston. Storms, hurricanes and two more earthquakes in 1722 and 1744 meant that the town was reduced to a British naval station with a dockyard, which closed in 1905. Chaloner Ogle (see the chapter on Black Bart Roberts) was anchored on HMS Swallow, off Port Royal on August 28th, 1722, and reported *there was as much wind in my opinion as could possibly blow out of the heavens ... all the merchantmen in the harbour foundered or drove ashore excepting one sloop.'* It is the only sunken town in the New World, and efforts are being made to have it declared a World Heritage Site, *'an underwater Pompeii'*. Underwater excavation has enabled us to 'rewalk' the narrow street of Port Royal today, and perhaps even Henry Morgan's grave may be found. Texas A&M University's Nautical Archaeology Programme has reconstructed the life of the town's main pewterer, Simon Benning, from the silver cutlery and pewter plates found on the site.

POWDER
Gunpowder - the saying **'to keep one's powder dry'** stems from the need to ensure that gunpowder was not opened and exposed to the damp in the air until the time it was needed, otherwise it might not ignite.

POWDER-BOX, POWDER HORN
This was crucial for dry gunpowder, and was made of wood, leather or from an ivory horn. In time of battle, the less able such as the cook would use powder-boxes to reload weapons for the fighting men. All fighting guns were single shot in these times, and a pirate would drop his musket and use his cutlass until it was reloaded. He could not keep a powder-box on his person, as any spark or shot at it would send him to *kingdom come*. There was also a leather belt, a 'baldrick', which held separate measures of powder, which some pirates used, especially the sharpshooters who were

stationed in the ship's rigging prior to boarding. A **powder-flask** was another name for a grenade (q.v.), flask being another term for bottle, which would break on impact.

POWDER MONKEY
Gunner's assistant. The term given by the Royal Navy, for the young men who made up most of the gun crews in the 17th century. Poorly treated, ill-paid, and with no chance of promotion to a less dangerous job, they were always keen to desert if possible and join a pirate crew. Often mere children (see Monkey), they carried small buckets of powder from the ship's magazine to the guns, thus minimising the chance of major explosions.

PRESS
To forcibly recruit men for the Royal Navy by the *'press gang'*, often from taverns in British docklands. They were *'impressed'*, or *'pressed into service.'* The press gang, if forcing men into the navy, was led by an officer. Most pirates were former Royal Navy or merchant seamen, attracted by a far better life than the one they had been pressed into joining.. Estimates are that 50% of men taken by *'press gangs'* (which preferred to take seamen rather than 'land-lubbers') died at sea between 1600 and 1800. When Captain Lowther led a mutiny on the *'Gambia Castle'*, a Royal Africa Company ship, records show that 72% of the 110 crew who refused to join him were dead within a year. Another telling statistic is that in the Seven Years War, 1522 men were killed in action, but over 150,000 were lost through disease or desertion.

PRESSING
In 1657 a sentence for refusing to plead was *'You shall go to the place from whence you came, and there being stripped naked and laid flat upon your back on the floor, with a napkin about your middle to hide your privy members, and a cloth on your face, then the Press is to be laid upon you, with as much weight as, or rather more than, you can bear. You are to have three morsels of barley-bread in twenty-four hours; a draught of water from the next puddle near the gaol, but not running water. The second day two morsels and the same water, with an increase of weight, and so to the third day until you expire.'* The last pressing took place in 1726, and it was replaced with screwing the thumbs with whipcord in front of the open court until the victim pleaded guilty or not guilty. The most famous pressing was that of Saint Margaret Clitherow in 1586 in York. She was sentenced to the *'peine forte at dure'* for refusing to plead, saying *'having made no offence, I need no trial'*. She died within fifteen minutes. The pirate Captain Gow (aka John Smith) was sentenced to pressing.

PRIMING-IRON
The iron rod forced down the touch-hole of a cannon. It pierced the bag or gunpowder ready for firing the cannon by applying the match. A *'rammer'* was a wooden cylinder that pushed the powder bag down the barrel of the cannon.

PRIVATEERS
Semi-official pirates, who supplemented a country's navy with *'private'* ships of war. Given *'letters of marque'*, they were allowed to attack the enemy in times of war, and

keep a large percentage of any plunder. They cost nothing, and their only reward was what they could take, or *'purchase'*, as in the term *'no purchase, no pay'*. With the end of the War of Spanish Succession' in 1713, there were literally thousands of privateers in the Caribbean and European ports, but the *'letters of marque'* had been withdrawn because of the peace. Thus many turned to piracy, culminating with almost complete pirate domination of the West Indies and American coasts between 1718 and 1722. Francis Drake and John Hawkins were noted privateers. It was also the name given to the privately-owned armed vessel with a letter of marque, which enabled it to take *'prizes'* in wartime. From 1589, 10% of the prize value went to the Crown, and 90% to the owner. Privateering was abolished by the Treaty of Paris in 1856.

PRIZE
A ship and its booty captured by a naval ship or privateer. Technically, they then belonged to the Crown, but after a review by the Admiralty Court, the ships and goods were sold at auction and the proceeds shared out. From the Latin *'pretium'* meaning reward or value. **Prize money** was the profits from the sale of the ship and its cargo, when captured by a warship or a privateer, so pirates assumed the same terminology. The vessel was brought to a 'friendly' port with a prize court, which awarded the prize money.

PROSTITUTES
Visitors complained that Port Royal's punch-houses were swarming with *'vile strumpets and common prostitutes'*. John Starr's brothel there contained 21 white and 2 black women. The most famous was the *'German Princess'*, Mary Carleton, who had been convicted of theft and bigamy and transported to Jamaica in 1671. She was returned to London in 1673 to be hanged at Tyburn. Born in Canterbury around 1634, she was a teenage criminal before appearing on the London stage, where a play, *'The German Princess'* was written especially for her. Her two years as a prostitute in Port Royal made some impact - she was described as being *'as common as a barber's chair: no sooner was one out, but another was in. Cunning, crafty, subtle, and hot in the pursuit of her intended designs.'*

PROVIDENCE ISLAND - ISLA DE PROVIDENCIA, SANTA CATALINA
A large island and pirate haven 250 miles off Portobelo, it lay between the Cuba to Venezuela trading route. Its pirates successfully beat off a Spanish attack in 1635, but it was taken in 1640. Henry Morgan used it for his attack on Panama in 1670-71.

PULL YOUR FINGER OUT
When cannon were loaded, a small amount of powder was poured into the ignition hole. To keep the powder secure before firing, a crew member pushed a finger into the hole. When the time came for ignition, he was told to pull his finger out.

PUNCH
To distilled alcohol or wine, various elements were added, such as tea, fruit juice,

sugar, spices and lime juice. Pirates drank from a ladle out of the bowl. Taverns were often referred to as punch-houses.

PUNCH HOUSE
Common term for a brothel, where alcohol was sold - a visitor to Port Royal wrote that its punch houses contained *'such a crew of vile strumpets and common prostitutes that 'tis almost impossible to civilise'* the town.

PURCHASE (1)
The plunder or bounty taken by pirates and buccaneers – the old meaning of *'purchase'* was *'the action of hunting, the chase, the catching and seizing of prey'*. Also any sort of mechanical power employed in raising or removing heavy bodies. The masts had to be *'purchased'* to careen a ship's bottom. To purchase the anchor is to loosen it out of the ground.

PURCHASE (2)
To draw in, e.g. *'the captain purchases apace'* means the captain draws in the cable quickly. Using mechanical power to move heavy items like the anchor.

PURSER RIGGED AND PARISH DAMNED
Someone who entered the navy to escape problems ashore, or one who entered because he was destitute.

PUT A NEW SLANT ON THINGS
Slant is the position of the wind relative to the ship, so this would be a change of position.

'PUTTING A MAN TO DRY'
This phrase was an English torture practised on slaves or indentured servants in the west Indies as a punishment for rebelling on the plantations, or trying to escape. In 1700 the French priest Pere Labat recorded in Barbados that *'the slaves who are captured are sent to prison and condemned to be passed through a cane mill, or be burnt alive, or be put into iron cages that prevent any movement and in which they are hung up to branches of trees and left to die of hunger and despair.'*

PUT AN OAR IN
In 1542, the phrase *'put an oar in someone's boat'* was first recorded, in a translation of Erasmus' work.

QUADRANT
The quadrant (or *cross staff*) was a simple instrument for navigation, basically a quarter circle with a 0 – 90 degree scale, two sights and a plumb line. It was in use from the middle of the 15th century to measure the altitude of heavenly bodies. It was succeeded by the Davis Quadrant, then by Hadley's Quadrant, and finally by Campbell's sextant.

John Davis the explorer (1550-1605), designed a new quadrant in 1594 which enabled sailors to find latitude. It was also known as a *'backstaff'* and was a method of finding the angle of the sun above the horizon, without having to sight directly on the sun. It vastly improved navigation and was used for 200 years. John Hadley (1682-1744) invented an improvement in 1731, which was also known as an *octant* (q.v.). This used two mirrors which allowed for measurements up to 90 degrees, although the device was only 45 degrees (one eighth of a circle). This evolved into the *sextant* around 1757, invented by Captain John Campbell RN. The sextant could measure angles of up to 120 degrees, and with observations of the stars, sun, moon and planets gave the navigator an accurate reading of latitude. Longitude was only enabled by the development of accurate time-keeping devices at sea. The first such device was invented by John Harrison in the 18th century, but they were not commonly available until the 19th century.

QUARTER
Mercy given to a surrendering or defeated crew. Pirates preferred not to fight, as did the merchant sailors who usually faced them.

QUARTERS
The officers' accommodation on the starboard or port quarters.

QUARTERMASTER
The representative of the **'Interest of the Crew'** to the captain, and democratically elected by pirates, he was literally in charge of the operations of the ship when not in action. The virtual equal of the captain, when a prize was captured, the quartermaster usually took it over. He kept order, judged disputes and disbursed food and cash. Because he was second-in-command, he usually received a larger share of plunder than other crew members. He often was given a prize vessel when it was taken and became captain himself. Usually, only the quartermaster could flog a seaman, and then only after a vote by the crew. Walter Kennedy explained in his trial that the role of the quartermaster prevented the captain having too much power. Pirates hated authority.

QUEEN ANNE'S REVENGE
This British ship, the Concord, was launched in 1710 during the War of Spanish Succession (Queen Anne's War), but in 1711 captured by the French and renamed Concorde. She was captured by the pirate Ben Hornigold while en route from West Africa to Martinique, laden with gold, silver, jewels and slaves. In 1717, Blackbeard, one of Hornigold's crew, took over the Concorde, renamed her Queen Anne's Revenge, and placed another 20 cannon on her. Six months later she was lost on the Outer Banks of North Carolina, and was found in 1996 off Beaufort Inlet. 18 cannon, wine bottles, pewter plates and other valuable items have been so far salvaged from Blackbeard's flagship.

QUEEN ANNE'S WAR
Better known as *The War of the Spanish Succession*, its end in 1713 allowed

thousands of experienced European sailors to be discharged, into unemployment. There was a massive surge in seamen turning to piracy at this time, because they had few other options. They added to the men who fled the West Country after Monmouth's Rebellion in 1685. Rebels captured were sent to the plantations in Barbados, and many of these escaped to a life of piracy also.

QUEUE
A 'tail' from the French, or pigtail, affected by most pirates, who stiffened it with a mixture of flour and water, and tied the end with a ribbon.

RACK AND RUIN
The origin of the term 'ship-wrecked' was 'ship-wracked', and a 'wracked' ship meant that the insurers suffered from 'rack and ruin'.

RAKING FIRE
Directing musket and cannon fire down a ship's length, from bow or from stern. The balls score the whole length of the decks.

RATCASTLE
Prison.

RATLINES
The small ropes fastened to the shrouds, by which men go aloft to trim the sails.

RAT'S TAIL
A pig-tail.

RATTLE THE BONES
Play dice.

RATE
The classification of naval warship according to how many guns it possessed. This is the origin of the term **'first rate'**, **'second rate'**, et al. In 1610, the HMS Resolution was described as a first rate of 80 guns, but with better technology, bigger ships with more guns came to be called first rates. In the 1700's, a first rate man-of-war carried over 100 guns, a second rate 84-100, a third rate 70-84, a fourth rate 50-70, a fifth rate 32-50, and sixth rate ships carried up to 32 guns. (In 1810, there was another change, with first rates having over 110 guns, second over 90, third over 80, fourth over 60 and fifth rates over 50 guns.) Only the first three rates were used in the 'line of battle' in a main battle fleet. There were few fourth rates, and were only used in the 'line of battle' in smaller fleets. Fifth and sixth rates were usually known as *frigates*. The sixth rates were known as *sloops*, if commanded by a commander rather than a captain. 'Feeling first-rate' has its origins here, as has 'that was a third-rate performance'.

RATS LEAVING A SINKING SHIP

As the bilges were full of rats, and were the first parts of the ship to be flooded, rats would appear from everywhere as the ship began to settle in the water.

REACH

The distance between two points at sea.

READY TO FIRE

Pirate captains ensured that their gunners were always ready for action - they never knew when a prize might appear from around a headland, or if they might be surprised by a naval frigate. Cannons were kept loaded, with wooden plugs, *'tompions'* on their muzzles to keep salt spray from spoiling the powder charge. Again to keep the powder dry, a sheepskin was laid over the touch-hole at the breech, with a lead apron holding it in place.

RED CROSS

An English ship. 'Red' also meant anything made of gold. A 'red one' or 'red rogue' was a gold coin. 'Red fustian' was port or claret.

RED FLAG

The red flag as a symbol of socialism was first used in the Merthyr Riots in Wales, when Dic Penderyn was wrongly executed. However, until around 1700 it was the emblem of a pirate ship, around when it was replaced by the black flag, and various derivations of the black flag to denote different captains. It then seems to have been run up only if the merchant crew refused to surrender at the sight of the black flag, and meant that there would be no mercy, no quarter given to her crew.

RED FUSTIAN

Port or claret.

REEF

To reduce the size of a sail.

REST ON ONE'S OARS

This means to suspend one's efforts, while to *'pull one's oar'* means to help one's colleagues. To *'have an oar in everyman's boat'* is meddling in other people's affairs.

RHODE ISLAND

Newport and Providence were well-known pirate and smuggling haunts in the second half of the 17th century, and until the first decades of the 18th century pirate captains such as Blackbeard, Henry (Long John) Every, Thomas Tew and Blackbeard frequented their harbours. In 1694, Newport's Thomas Tew returned with huge treasure from the Red Sea. He then received a Letter of Marque from the Governor of New York to sail to Madagascar. As merchant shipping increased, pirates were no longer welcome, and early in the 1720's, 26 pirates were hung outside Newport as a warning to others.

TO RIDE

When the anchor holds the ship fast, not being driven by the wind or tide, the ship is said to '*ride at anchor*'. '*To ride athwart*' is to ride with the ship's side to the tide. '*To ride hawse-fall*' is then in a rough sea water enters the cable hawses.

RIDE A PORPOISE

To steer a ship with a yard-arm struck down to the deck.

RIDE A STORM

A ship will lower or shorten her sails and rise out a storm, when it is impossible to heads into it or run before it.

RIG

The rig of a ship is her masts, spars, stays (or rigging) and sails, and they was they are arranged. The modern term of *rig* meaning clothing, and the term '*well rigged out*' meaning well accommodated with equipment and clothing, come from the days of sailing ships.

RIGGING

The two basic ways to rig sails are: Square Rigged, in which the sails are bent to the yards carried athwart the mast and trimmed with braces. Square-rigged sails are sturdy and catch a lot of wind; Fore and Aft Rigged, in which the sails are not attached to the yards but are bent to gaffs and set on the mast or on stays in the midship line of the ship, giving increased manoeuvrability.

RIME OF THE ANCIENT MARINER

Coleridge's 1798 poem recalls a ship's crew dying after falling under a curse for killing an albatross. The privateer and second-in-command Simon Hatley shot a black albatross on Captain Shelvocke's passage around Cape Horn in 1719, and the tale is based on this incident. Hatley shot the bird because he was depressed after days of being buffeted by contrary winds.

RINGLEADER (See Round Robin)

ROAD, ROADSTEAD

A place to anchor, with some shelter for all but heavy weather. It was normally near a port, for ships to meet or rest, and relatively easy to escape from.

ROANOKE ISLAND

This was the first English settlement in North America, off what is now North Carolina. It was used by the English and the early settlers as a base to attack Spanish shipping, but the settlers mysteriously disappeared in 1590.

ROBINSON CRUSOE, WILLIAM and ALEXANDER SELKIRK

Crusoe's prototype seems to have been Alexander Selkirk (1676-1721), who volunteered as a privateer for a voyage to the South Seas in 1703. Buccaneers under

Captain Watling were scared off the uninhabited Juan Fernandez Island in January 1681, and in their haste left a Mosquito (Miskito) Indian called William there. He had been in the woods, hunting for wild goats. On March 22nd, 1684, buccaneers under Captain Cook of the *Batchelor's Delight* and Captain Swan of the *Cygnet* came into sight of Juan Fernandez. Some of Cook's men had sailed under Watling, and wanted to send a boat ashore to look for William. Dampier related in his journals that he went ashore on this boat with another Mosquito Indian named Robin. '*Robin, his countryman, was the first who leaped ashore from the boats, and, running to his brother Mosquito-man, threw himself flat on his face at his feet, who, helping him up and embracing him, fell flat with his face on the ground at Robin's feet, and was by him taken up also. We stood with pleasure to behold the surprise, tenderness, and solemnity of this interview, which was exceedingly affectionate on both sides; and, when their ceremonies were over, we also, that stood gazing at them, drew near, each of us embracing him we had found here, who was overjoyed to see so many of his old friends come hither, as he thought, purposely to fetch him. He was named Will, as the other was Robin; which names were given them by the English, for they have no names among themselves, and they take it as a favour to be named by us, and will complain if we do not appoint them some name when they are with us.*'

William had seen the buccaneers anchor, and had killed three goats, which he dressed with vegetables, preparing a treat for them when they landed. The Spanish had known that William was on the island for three years and had tried to trap him and find where he was holed up. '*He had built himself a hut, half-a-mile from the seashore, which he lined with goats' skins, and slept on his couch or barbecu (wooden hurdle) of sticks, raised about two feet from the ground and spread with goats' skins.*' The goats were left there by the Spanish to multiply and supply fresh meat (much like the wild hogs and cattle in other islands), and there was fresh water flowing at two places on the island. He had been left on the island with just a musket, knife, a little powder and some shot. Dampier tells us that '*when his ammunition was expended, he contrived by notching his knife to saw the barrel of his gun into small pieces, wherewith he made harpoons, lances, hooks and a long knife, heating the pieces of iron first in the fire, and then hammering them out as he pleased with stones.*' Fishing lines were made from the skins of seals laboriously cut into thongs and knotted. He had no clothes left, and wore a goatskin around his waist.

The crews re-provisioned with goats, wild vegetables, fish, sea-lions and seals, before they weighed anchor on April 8th. It seems that William fits the lifestyle of Daniel Defoe's 'Robinson Crusoe' perfectly. Dampier's Journals were published in 1697 and 1699 and Defoe's book in 1719. However, most people believe that the Robinson Crusoe story was inspired by Alexander Selkirk, a Scot marooned by a Welsh buccaneer on the same island. Dampier features again in this version. In late summer 1704, he was captain of the privateer *St George*, with Thomas Stradling was captaining the consort ship *Cinque Ports*. In September, the *Cinque Ports* needed caulking and was put into Juan Fernandez for repairs, where the ship's master Selkirk and its captain Stradling had a terrible row. Dampier said that the repairs were not good enough and that the ship would leak badly. He shouted that if Stradling insisted on setting sail in her, he could '*go to the bottom alone*'. In high dudgeon, Stradling left Selkirk ashore with his sea chest. Selkirk thought that other men would join him, forcing Stradling to change his mind, but as the ship's boat pulled away from the beach, he shouted to Stradling that he had changed his mind. Stradling shouted back that he had not changed his, and Selkirk was marooned.

At first he expected the ship to return, read copiously from his Bible, prayed for rescue and almost starved, before he realised that this was a terrible error. He must have known that William had survived here for three years a decade ago, and he set to the job in hand. Two grass-covered huts were built and lined with goat-skins, one for living in and one for cooking. He replaced his worn-out clothes with goatskin garments, using a nail as a needle and unravelled stockings for his thread. He wore out his knife, but made fresh blades from iron barrel-hoops left on the island. When his ammunition ran out, he ran down goats on foot to kill them. Meanwhile, after leaving Selkirk, Stradling soon discovered that his ship was foundering, as Selkirk had predicted, so he was forced to run it aground in the Mapella Islands. The Spanish threw the survivors into dungeons in Lima for six terrible years.

On January 31st, 1709, Dampier was sailing under Woodes Rogers after rounding Cape Horn, trying to put into Mas a Tierra, one of the Juan Fernandez Islands. The privateer ships *Duke* and *Duchess* could not get closer than twelve mile away, because of winds, so it was decided to send a pinnace ashore. The crew were sick, and seven had succumbed to scurvy. Fresh water, vegetables and meat were urgently needed. The pinnace took hours to get within three miles of the island, and at nightfall a huge bonfire was seen on the coast. The pinnace returned to the *Duchess*, thinking that the French or Spanish were on the island. Next morning Captain Rogers could see no enemy ships at either bay on the island, and managed to get closer to the islands before the ship's yawl was sent out with seven armed men. It did not return, so Rogers risked sending the pinnace to the island, with chosen musketeers on board. It did not return for hours, and Rogers hoisted signal flags. When the pinnace eventually came back, it was loaded with fresh crayfish and a barefoot, bearded semi-intelligible man dressed in goat-skins. He was asked how long he had been there and answered four years and four months – he had kept the time by marking wood. He was asked his name and replied with difficulty, Alexander Selkirk, master of the *Cinque Ports*. Dampier then came forward to fill in the details. When Selkirk saw Dampier, he asked to be put ashore again, but was talked out of it.

Rogers used this period to help his crew recuperate. Apart from the seven who died, there were another dozen suffering from scurvy, of which two could not be saved. Ashore they found turnips and parsley planted by previous parties of buccaneers, and there was abundant wild cabbage, flocks of goats and all the crabs, lobsters and crayfish they could eat. Rogers' men pronounced that seal tasted as good as English lamb, and picked their teeth clean with sea-lion's whiskers, forgetting the horrors of the rounding of Cape Horn. After six weeks, on February 14th, Rogers continued upon his remarkable circumnavigation of the world. It is believed that Daniel Defoe was Captain Charles Johnson, who wrote the definitive history of pirates, 'The General History of the Robberies and Murders of the Most Notorious Pyrates' (1724). It was also believed that Defoe's 'Robinson Crusoe' was based on Alexander Selkirk, the Scot from Largo in Fife. Defoe had read William Dampier's 'Voyage Round the World', and also Woodes Rogers' account, with the same title. Both give the story of Selkirk. Defoe's latest biographer, Richard West, makes absolutely no mention of Johnson, and believes that Robinson Crusoe was not based upon Selkirk.

ROCK THE BRAZILIAN
From Groningen, Holland, he was called Roche Brasiliano from the long time he spent in Brazil, corrupted to *Rock the Brazilian* by the English buccaneers. He had a pathological hatred of the Spanish, as evidenced by his practice of roasting them alive on spits.

ROSEWATER SAILOR
An incompetent officer.

ROSTRUM
This was the Latin for the 'beak' of the war galleys, used for ramming other vessels. The rostra (plural of rostrum) of captured ships were taken to Rome to display in triumph. They were laid out in front of the speakers' platform at the Forum, and over the years the dais became known as the rostrum.

ROUGH TALK
Swearing. Insults and cursing were popular amongst pirates, especially after the Reformation, whereby their usage was very much curtailed in ordinary life. Coarse swearing set them apart on the life they had chosen, escaping from a life where God did not seem to be on their side.

ROUNDING UP
'Rounding in' was pulling on any rope which passes through one or more blocks in a direction nearly horizontal, e.g. 'round in the weather braces'. 'Rounding up' was a similar phrase, but applied to ropes and blocks which act in a perpendicular direction.

ROUND ROBIN (ROBBIN)
This French practice was adopted by English seamen with a complaint. All signed their names in a petition, on a piece of paper in a circle. There was more safety in numbers if they wanted something changed, so not one seaman could be pinpointed as the *'ringleader'* of dissent and punished. William Williams wrote about the practice in his 'The Journal of Penrose, Seaman', with reference to buried treasure. In France, names were signed on the ribbon (*rouban*) which went round (*rond*) the grievance document, hence *rond rouban* and thence *Round Robin*.

ROYAL AFRICA COMPANY
Charles II signed the Royal Charter for this company at Westminster on September 20th, 1672: 'We hereby for us, our heirs and successors, grant unto the same Royal African Company of England... that it shall and may be lawful to... set to sea such as many ships, pinnaces and barks as shall be thought fitting... for the buying,

selling, bartering and exchange of, for or with any gold, silver, Negroes, Slaves, goods, wares and manufactures.' *The venture was a considerable source of income for the Stuart monarchy.*

RUB SALT INTO THE WOUND
After a flaying with the *'cat 'o nine tails'*, vindictive officers would order salt to be rubbed into the offender's raw flesh to make the punishment even more painful. However, it served to help the healing process if the victim lived long enough. Also, Roman sailors were paid a quantity of salt as part of their *'salarium'* (salary, from the Roman *'sal'* for salt). The sailors thought that they were being doubly punished at losing part of their salary if they had to rub salt into their wounds after battle.

RUM, KILL-DEVIL, BARBADOS WATER, DEMON WATER, NELSON'S BLOOD, THE PIRATES' DRINK
This seems to have been dished out regularly every day upon pirate ships, following the Royal Navy tradition. Rum (sometimes known as *grog*) was plentiful in the Caribbean because it was easily made from sugar cane (*saccharum officinarum*). It was distilled from the 1640's onwards, so is considered to be the world's oldest distilled spirit. Sugar growers cured sugar in clay pots, and as it crystallised, a brown liquid called molasses drained out of the remaining sucrose. This was recycled by natural fermentation, and then distillation to give a clear liquid, which darkened in wooden casks. The French called it *'tafia'*, and the English *rum-bullion*, shortened to rum. (*Rum bullion* may have meant a *'great tumult'*). Later, *rumbullion* was transferred to another drink. It was also known as *'kill-devil'*. Perhaps the term originated because it was *'rum'* (odd) to get precious booty (bullion, or alcohol) out of waste products. Brandy was also easy to get hold of, and beer was carried on boats because it lasted a month or so before it turned vinegary. On the other hand, water was usually taken from a river near a port, or from a polluted river, and was only of any use in cooking. Barrels of water quickly became slimy, and was simply not potable. Pirates were often drunk because there was little alternative liquid. Fruit juices were added to prevent scurvy.

'*Rum*', in the sense of '*odd*', or '*different*' was used as a prefix in much 17th and 18th century slang. A '*rum beak*' was a justice of the peace, a '*rum bite*' a swindle, a '*rum blower*' was a pretty woman, a '*rum bluffer*' or '*rum dropper*' was an inn-keeper, a '*rum bob*' was an apprentice, '*rum booze*' was good wine (later an egg '*flip*' containing port, egg yolks, sugar and nutmeg), a '*rum bubber*' stole tankards from taverns, a '*rum buffer*' was a good-looking dog, a '*rum chunk*' was a gold or silver tankard, a '*rum clout*' or '*rum wiper*' was a silk handkerchief, a '*rum cod*' was a full purse of money, '*rum cole*' was newly minted money, a '*rum cove*' was a clever rogue, a '*rum cull*' was a rich fool, a '*rum doxy*' was a beautiful woman, or a pretty whore, and so on and so on. Other terms pirates would have used are '*rum slum*' for punch, and '*rum quids*' for a great share of booty or captured goods. Those interested in pursuing the meanings attached to '*rum*' should consult '*The Penguin Dictionary of Historical Slang*' by Eric Partridge, 1972. Of particular interest in this fascinating book is the term '*It's naughty but it's nice*', the phrase that an extremely popular author claims credit for when working in advertising, for a cream cake campaign. This was the title of a song of Minnie Schultz's, popular in the USA in the 1890's, which came to mean the *pleasures of copulation*. The book states that it has been a catch-phrase since the early 1900's.

Some interesting facts about rum are that 'Rum and Bible' ships carried alcohol and missionaries to the new World as part of the Triangular Trade; American colonists each consumed the equivalent of 4 gallons of rum a year; and the French recipe for Planter's Punch was based on an old slave song:

> *One of sour (lime)*
> *Two of sweet (sugar)*
> *Three of strong (rum)*
> *Four of weak (ice).*

Nelson's body was preserved in a cask of his favourite rum after the Battle of Trafalgar, from when we get the slang 'Nelson's Blood' for rum, but actually he was placed in a cask or brandy and spirits of wine. 'Captain Morgan' is the most famous brand of rum, and 'Captain Stratton's Fancy' is a wonderful poem by John Masefield, about the greatest of all privateers, Captain Henry Morgan and the traditional pirate drink of rum:

> *Oh some are fond of red wine and some are fond of white,*
> *And some are all for dancing by the pale moonlight:*
> *But rum's alone the tipple, and the heart's delight*
> *Of the old bold mate of Captain Morgan*
> *Oh some are fond of Spanish wine, and some are fond of French,*
> *And some'll swallow tay (tea) and stuff fit only for a wench;*
> *But I'm right for Jamaica till I roll beneath the bench*
> *Says the old bold mate of Henry Morgan.*
> *Oh some are for the lily and some are for the rose,*
> *But I am for the sugar cane that in Jamaica grows;*
> *For it's that that makes the bonny drink to warm my copper nose,*
> *Says the old bold mate of Henry Morgan.*
> *Oh some are fond of fiddles, and a song well sung,*
> *And some are all for music for to lilt upon the tongue;*
> *But mouths were made for tankards, and for sucking at the bung,*
> *Says the old bold mate of Henry Morgan.*
> *Oh some are fond of dancing, and some are fond of dice,*
> *And some are all for red lips, and pretty lasses' eyes;*
> *But a right Jamaica puncheon is a finer prize,*
> *Says the old bold mate of Henry Morgan.*
> *Oh some that's good and godly ones, they hold that it's a sin*
> *To troll the jolly bowl around, and let the dollars spin;*
> *But I'm for toleration and for drinking at an in,*
> *Says the old bold mate of Henry Morgan.*
> *Oh some are sad and wretched folk that go in silken suits,*
> *And there's a sort of wicked rogues that live in good reputes;*
> *So I'm for drinking honestly, and dying in my boots,*
> *Says the old bold mate of Henry Morgan.*

RUMBULLION

This is the demon offspring of Rumfustian, described by Burl when Black Bart Robert's crew distilled it at Damana Bay, Hispaniola, in February 1721: 'For that catastrophic brew two huge vats were rowed ashore and filled with molasses, skimmings of overripe fruit, a minimum of water and a liberal splashing of sulphuric acid. The liquid fermented for 8 days while a still was constructed. A complicated system of pipes arranged vertically in a trough of water led from a capacious copper vessel over a fire to a spiral tube under a cooling waterfall that continually dribbled over it. A pewter tankard was set under the spiral and drop by paralytic drop the rumbullion filled it. Only the most foolhardy drank more than one mug.'

RUMFUSTIAN

A popular hot pirate drink blended from raw eggs, sugar, sherry, beer and gin. (This reminds the author of a disgusting drink called 'diesel' that a Welsh friend Derek Rhys Williams insists that I always drink at his Breton farmhouse. It is half a pint of lager mixed with half a pint of banana liqueur. After several years of idly quaffing it for supper and breakfast, I queried why we have to drink the concoction. He replied 'I read a magazine article. It's what East German skinheads drink if they want to get pissed quickly'. This passes for Monmouthshire logic).

RUMMAGE

'Arrimage' is French for the ship's cargo. Damaged and unwanted goods were sold at an arrimage sale, hence the derivation of today's rummage sale. 'Rummaging' – searching through a jumble – comes from this nautical source.

RUMMER

A glass for drinking rum cocktails. Pirates usually used pewter mugs or coconut shells as rummers. The 'Rummer Tavern' in Cardiff referred to the days of piracy in the Bristol Channel.

RUN A RIG

To play a trick.

RUNNING A TIGHT SHIP

A term from the days of sail, when there were no 'loose ends' and everything was 'ship-shape'.

RUN UP A TAB

In dockside taverns, credit would be chalked up 'on the slate'. 'Tablet' was another word for the writing slate, so unsecured credit was '**chalked up** on the tab', and the term to have something '**on tick**' also comes from this custom. The loans had then to be paid off to talley-men or to the inn.

RUTTER see DERROTERRO

A SAIL!

The cry when a ship is spotted at sea. Likewise, a fleet of 20 ships is termed a fleet of twenty *sail*.

SAILING ON ANOTHER BOARD

Behaving differently.

SAILING UNDER FALSE COLOURS

Pirates did this to get close to intended prizes, as did the Royal Navy when hunting Black Bart Roberts. The national flag was known as 'the colours', so we have today the terms **true colours**, *show your colours, go down with colours flying, come off with flying colours*, *nail your colours to the mast*, etc.

SAINTE BARBE (French), SANTA BARBARA (Spanish)

Term used in the 17th century for a powder room or magazine. St Barbara was tortured and killed by her heathen father for being a Christian, and he met divine retribution in being disintegrated by a thunder-flash. She thus became the patron saint of those working with explosives, and her image was often hung up outside a powder room on ships.

SAINT MARY'S ISLAND, ILE SAINTE-MARIE, AMBODIFOTOTRA

Pirate haven until 1722, a 35-mile long island in the Indian Ocean off the north-east of Madagascar. Pirate traders such as Adam Baldridge controlled it as a base for fencing goods looted from shipping in the Indian ocean and Red Sea.

SALAMAGUNDY or SALMAGUNDI

A Crash Test Dummies record refers to Solomon Grundy, who in the old nursery rhyme was *'born on Monday, christened on Tuesday etc. to died on Sunday, That was the end of Solomon Grundy'*. The obscure origin of the name was salamagundy, for which there are many recipes. This was the last dish Black Bart ate before the Royal Navy attacked him. Its origin is the French *'salemine'*, meaning highly salted or seasoned. The basic variety was **'Poor John'** (salt fish) boiled with onions. It could also include chopped meat, eggs and anchovies – whatever was available, in fact. The most luxurious version had meat, turtle, fish and shellfish marinated in spices, herbs, garlic, palm hearts, spiced wine and oil, and served with cabbage, grapes, olives, pickled onions and hard-boiled eggs. The term seems to have come from the French *'salmigondis'*, a communal meat stew to which any available vegetables were added. The dish appealed to the *'Brethren of the Coast'* with its shared contribution to the communal cauldron, and Botting described it as having meats that were *'roasted, chopped into chunks and marinated In spiced wine, then combined with cabbage, anchovies, pickled herring, mangoes, hard-boiled eggs, palm hearts, onions, olives, grapes and any other pickled vegetables which were available. The whole would then be highly seasoned with garlic, salt, pepper and mustard seed, and doused with oil and vinegar - and served with drafts of beer and rum.'*
Reinhardt describes it thus: *'Included might be any or all of the following: turtle meat, fish, pork, chicken, corned beef, ham, duck, and pigeon. The meats would be roasted,*

chopped into pieces and marinated in spied wine, then mixed with cabbage, anchovies, pickled herring, mangoes, hard-boiled eggs, palm hearts, onions, olives, grapes, and any other pickled vegetable available. The entire concoction would then be highly seasoned with garlic, salt, pepper, and mustard seed and soaked with oil and vinegar.' The strong seasonings and vegetables helped suppress scurvy, and Black Bart Roberts was breakfasting on it when surprised by the Royal Navy in 1722.

SALT HORSE, SALT JUNK
Slang for the salt beef carried in casks of brine water. The meat was usually too tough to recognise as beef, so sailors believed that anything had been thrown in the casks. Because it was kept in a barrel called a *'harness cask'* sailors had the idea of a 'horse' in its harness. See Junk.

SALT TORTUGAS
Name for the Isla la Tortuga off Venzuela (see Dry Totugas, Tortuga)

SAND-GLASS
The only way that pirates and buccaneers could tell the time. Like egg-timers, they consisted of two glass globes with a narrow neck, and were turned when the sand ran out of the top globe. They were usually in half-minute, half-hours, hour and four hour sizes. The half-minute was used to judge a ship's speed, by how much line would run out from a ship in a half-minute. The half-hour glass measured time, with a bell or drum being sounded at every turn of
the sand-glass.

SAN JUAN DE ULUA
An island off the Mexican coast, and the port for Vera Cruz, one of the three treasure ports of the Spanish flota. Silver from Mexico was shipped from here, as well as the contents of the Manila galleons which sailed from the Philippines to the Pacific coast and transported across Mexico for shipping to Spain.

SARGASSO SEA
East of the Bahamas, the piece of ocean where an extremely strong eddy causes the Sargasso Weed or Sargassum (*Fucus Natans*) collects in vast quantities on the surface. Columbus mentioned the difficulty of sailing through the waters and the weeds fouled ships. North-east of Bermuda, it lies between 20 degrees North and 35 degrees North latitude and 30 degrees West and 70 degrees West longitude. The sea depth ranges from a mile to four miles. The 'sea' is a large pool of very warm water, rotating clockwise very slowly. Both the Equatorial Current and the Gulf Stream Current push warm water past it, it rarely rains and the weather, like the water, remains very calm, and also very humid and often extremely hot. It has been likened to a desert in the middle of the ocean. The lack of rainfall makes the water very saline.

There are millions of clumps of sargassum, mainly accumulating towards the centre of the sea, and with little current and little wind, sailing ships could be trapped here. Becalmed ships ran out of drinking water. Records show that the Spanish threw their war-horses over the side to conserve precious supplies. Hence the area became known as the *'Horse Latitudes'* , and these latitiudes traverse the sea. The ghosts of these horses and ships and sailors were thought to inhabit the area. Other names for the area were *'The Doldrums'*, *'The Sea of Berries'*, and *'The Dungeon of the Lost Souls'*. In 1492, Columbus was entangled in the 'weed', there were strange effects of light on the water (due to its salinity) and there were extreme compass variations. His sailors implored him to return home. The phenomenon was magnetic variation.

SATCHEL
Before the advent of duffle bags (q.v.), seamen would have leather satchels to keep their belongings in, and took them with them on shore. On Morgan's march to Panama, one of his starving buccaneers wrote that they were forced to eat their satchels – *'slice the leather into pieces then soak, beat and rub between stones to tenderise. Scrape off the hair, then roast or grill. Cut into smaller pieces and served with lots of water.'*

SAWBONES
The ship's surgeon, who was usually not much more knowledgeable than the barber from which his profession stemmed. He was used for bone-setting, dressing wounds and amputation.

SAWDUST
This was kept on board and liberally sprinkled around the gundeck, so that men would not slip on blood in battle.

SCANDALISE (see Cock Up)

SCHOONER

A Schooner

An easily-handled, fast, two-masted ship, with all lower sails rigged fore and aft. With a shallow draft, it could carry up to 75 crew, mounting 8 cannon and 4 swivel guns. Less than 100 tons, it was popular with pirates in the Caribbean and Atlantic in the 18th century, and could reach up to 11 knots. This had all the best features required for a pirate vessel. Its very narrow hull and shallow draft made it ideal for the Caribbean and North American coast, as it was small enough to navigate the shoal waters and hide in remote places. It was small, quick and sturdy – an ideal workhorse for pirateering.

SCOTCH COFFEE
Also known as *'lobscouse'*, this was the ubiquitous salt beef, boiled up with ship's biscuits, potatoes, onions and some vinegar.

SCRAPING THE BOTTOM OF THE BARREL
Removing the last of the hardened pork fat from a cask, to put towards a *slush fund* (q.v.)

SCRATCH
'You scratch my back and I'll scratch yours' - means *'do me a favour and you'll receive one in return'*. This refers to someone who was going to be punished by the *'cat 'o nine tails'*. The victim desperately tried to get a friend to carry out the punishment, or one who might receive the whipping in future. The difference between a *'light'* scratching across the back and a flaying often meant life or death.

SCRUB AROUND IT
When sailors scrubbed (holystoned) the deck, they would *'scrub around'* any obstacle.

SCUPPERED
A term still in use, meaning *'knackered'* or *'finished'*. The *'scuppers'* were the drainage holes in the side of the ship that let sea and rain-water drain off the deck. (From the Dutch *schoepen*, to draw off.) To *'scupper'* a ship meant that your cannons blew holes in it below its water-line, so that the new *'scuppers'* served exactly the opposite purpose and let water in, sinking the ship. A sailor knocked over by a wave, who fell near the scuppers (waterways or gutters), was said to be *'scuppered'*.

SCURVY (1)
In 1593, Captain Richard Hawkins noted that sour oranges and lemons were the best treatment for scurvy, but Not until 1795 did Royal Navy vessels carry lemon juice to combat this disease. Later the far cheaper lime juice replaced lemon, from which the American slang *'limey'* for British immigrants or visitors derived. With no fresh fruit or vegetables, this had been endemic on long voyages, for instance when Black Bart was two months at sea. It also caused shipwrecks, and crews were made so weak by lack of Vitamin C, that they sunk into a dull lethargy from which they could not be shaken. Symptoms began with swollen gums, then loss of teeth, a weakened heart and black blotches beneath the skin, before a sailor sank into a final exhausted torpor with glazed eyes and swollen bodies and legs.
Wounds could not heal. There was the pain of spontaneous haemorrhaging into muscles and joints. Gasping for breath like floundered fish, the blood vessels around the brain eventually ruptures and they died. In 1636, John Woodall wrote in *'The Surgeon's Mate'* that daily orange juice was the antidote. Upon Admiral Anson's round-the-world expedition of 1740-1744, 1051 of his 1955 men died of scurvy. In 1747 Dr James Lind re-established the fact that Vitamin C prevented scurvy. In 1779 2,400 seamen were put into shore hospitals after the Channel fleet had been on a ten-week cruise. Not until 1795 did the Admiralty prescribe citrus juice on all its vessels. This was after an estimated 800,000 British seamen had needlessly died. Merchant vessels only followed the practice from 1854.

SCURVY (2)
This insulting adjective was in use from the 15th century to about 1660, and appeared often in Shakespeare's plays. The origin was the scabby appearance of someone suffering from scurvy.

SCUTTLE
This term is an Anglicised form of the Old French 'escoutilles', and refers to a small hole cut in a hatch cover, or in the side of a ship, to let in light and air. This latter is commonly called a 'porthole' by a landlubber and is apparently referred to as a 'scuttle' by an old seaman. To *scuttle* a ship means to sink her deliberately by opening her seacocks, or by blowing holes in the bottom of the hull, so that she fills with water. In colloquial English, we use the term as synonymous with to abandon or destroy.

SCUTTLEBUTT
This word means gossip. The butt was the cask of fresh drinking water on a ship. The scuttle was the hatch or hole in the water butt, through which sailors reached in to fill a jug of water. This hatch was usually sawn out, about halfway up the barrel, so that the water would be renewed more often and kept fresher. Sailors coming over for a drink used to linger for a short while to exchange the latest news with whoever else was drinking. The term in the USA has been replaced by gossiping '*around the water cooler*'.

SEA
A *heavy sea* is full of large waves. A *great sea* means that the whole ocean is agitated. A *head sea* means that the waves are coming from ahead. A *long sea* has a steady motion of long extensive waves. A *short sea* is when waves are running irregularly, broken and interrupted. A *hollow sea* is where there is shoaling water or a current setting against the waves. The line from crest to trough makes a sharp angle, so the sea is very dangerous.

SEA ARTIST
An excellent navigator, boatswain or respected sailing master. See Artist.

SEA-CARD
A 17th century term for a chart.

SEA CHANGE
A marked change in the state of the sea. In Shakespeare's '*The Tempest*', Ariel sings in Act I, Scene II:
'Full fathom five thy father lies;
Of his bones are coral made;
Those are pearls that were his eyes:
Nothing of him that doth fade
But doth suffer a sea change
Into something rich and strange:
Sea nymphs hourly ring his knell.'

SEA LEGS

Both the ability to resist sea-sickness and to walk steadily on the deck of a pitching ship. Sailors in port took some time to recover their *'land legs'*, and were easily recognisable as seamen by the *'rolling gait'* they had adopted at sea.

(IF A) SEAMAN CARRIES A MILLSTONE HE'LL HAVE A QUAIL OUT OF IT

A saying referring to the ingenuity of ships' cooks in providing food and drink out of meagre resources.

SEA PIE

Ship's biscuits between layers of meat or fish.

SEA ROVERS

Pirates, buccaneers and *'sea-robbers.'* The term was used in Alexander Esquemeling's *'De Americaensche Zee-Roovers'*, published in 1678, and published as 'The Buccaneers of America' in London in 1684. Esquemeling went to Tortuga in 1666 as an indentured servant, but joined Morgan's buccaneers as a *'barber-surgeon'* in 1669, sailing for five years until he settled in Holland. The book was amazingly popular, no doubt because it was rewritten to suit nationalities. In the Spanish version, Henry Morgan was a torturing ogre, but the English and Dutch editions ask the reader to consider how *'God permitted the unrighteousness of the buccaneers to flourish, for the chastisement of the Spaniards.'* Germans referred to a pirate as a *Seerauber*, sea robber.

SEA SHANTY

A song with a definite rhythm, a working song to help men co-ordinate in pulling ropes and lines. They were also known as **chanteys**, so the origin is probably the word chant. Traditional shanties are grouped into the following types. Short Haul Shanties were used for tasks requiring quick pulls over a short period of time. Halyard Shanties were used for heavier work with more set-up time between pulls. Capstan Shanties were used for long, repetitive tasks requiring a sustained rhythm, but not involving working the lines. Often merchantmen were under-manned, and singing shanties helped efficiency. Many have been recorded, including 'Mrs McGraw':

> *'Mrs McGraw', the Captain said,*
> *'Would ye like to make a pirate of your son Ted?*
> *With a scarlet coat and a fine cocked hat,*
> *Mrs McGraw wouldn't ye like that?*

> CHORUS
> *Singing to-ri-yah, fa-la-la-la. To-ri oori orri yah,*
> *With a to-ri-yah, fa-la-la-la, to-ri oori oori yah.*

> *Now Mrs McGraw lived on the sea shore,*
> *For the space of seven long years or more.*

She spied a ship comin' into the bay,
'This is my son Teddy, won't you clear the wat?'
Chorus
'Oh My dear Captain, where hae ye been?
Have ye been out sailing on the Med'ter'ean?
Have ye any news of my son, Ted?
Is the poor boy livin' or is he dead?
Chorus
And up steps Ted, without any legs,
And in their place, there were two wooden pegs.
She kissed him a dozen times or two
Crying 'Holy b'goes, what's become of you?'
Chorus
'Now was ye drunk was ye blind,
When ye left yer two fine legs behind?
Or was ye walkin' out on the seas
That tore yer legs away from yer knees?'
Chorus
'No I wasn't drunk, nor I wasn't blind
When I left my two fine legs behind,
'Twas a big cannonball on the fifth of May
That tore my legs from my knees away!'
Chorus
'Now Teddy, me boy', the old widow cried,
'Your two fine legs were your mummy's pride.
The stumps of a tree won't do at all.
Why didn't ye run from the big cannonball?'
Chorus
'Now foreign wars I do profane
Against Don Juan and the King of Spain.
I'd rather have my Teddy the way he used to be
Than the King of France and the whole Navy.'

SEA SMOKE
A very cold wind can cause vapour to rise from the sea. The phenomenon is also known as *'water smoke'*, *warm water fog'*, *steam-fog'* and *'frost-smoke'*.

SEA TURTLES
These were captured and kept on deck in the Caribbean as a useful source of fresh meat.

SEARCH FROM STEM TO STERN
The stem is the strong piece of timber to which the planks at the front of the ship are fixed, so this implies a thorough search of the whole ship for booty.

SEE HOW THE LAND LIES
To ask for the bill in a tavern.

SELKIRK, ALEXANDER (1676-1721)
The probable prototype for *'Robinson Crusoe'*, marooned at his own request by the Welsh privateer captain Thomas Stradling, on Juan Fernandez Island in 1705. He was rescued by Woodes Rogers, another privateer, in 1709.

SEQUINS, CHEQUEENS
Italian or Venetian gold coins.

SETTING SAIL
In the late 17th century, Smith outlined the procedures necessary for putting out to sea: *'The Master and Company being aboard, he commands them to get the Sails to the Yards, and about your gear, or work on all hands, stretch forwards your main Hailyards, hoist your Sails half mast high. Predy, or make ready to set sail, cross your Yards, bring your cable to the capstern; Boatswain fetch an Anchor aboard, break ground or weigh Anchor. Heave a head, men into the Tops, men upon the Yards; come, is the Anchore, a pike, that is, to heave the Hawse of the Ship right over the Anchor; what is the Anchor away? Yea, Yea. Let your Fore-sail. Cally, that is, hale off the Sheats; who is at the Helm there? Coil your Cables is small fakes, hale the Cat, a Bitter, belay, look fast your Anchor with your Shank-painter, stow the Boat, set the land, how it bears by the Compass, that we may better know thereby to keep our account, and direct our course, let fall your main sail, every man say his private Prayer for a boon voyage, out with your spret-sail, on with your bonnits and drablers, steer ready and keep your course, so, you go well.'*

SEVEN SEAS
The Arctic, Antarctic, North Atlantic, South Atlantic, North Pacific, South Pacific and Indian Oceans. However, from around 1450 to 1650, they were the Atlantic, Pacific, Indian and Pacific Oceans, the Mediterranean Sea, the Caribbean and the Gulf of Mexico, which were the seven navigated seas of the world.

SEWED
When the water level has fallen so that the ship cannot be floated off, she is said to be *'sewed'*. Smith's 1691 *'Seaman's Grammar'* tells us: *'When the water is gone and the ship lies dry, we say she is sewed; if her head but lie dry, she is sewed a head, but if she canot all lie dry, she cannot sew there.'*

SEWN UP
To be *'all sewn up'* means that everything is finished. A sailor who died at sea was sewn inside his hammock with a cannon ball at his feet, before being despatched to the deep. Traditionally, the last stitch was placed through the nose to ensure that the man was dead. The custom is said to have come from a sailmaker accidentally putting his needle through the nose of a *'corpse'*, the shock making the cataleptic victim revive and sit up.

SHAKE A CLOTH IN THE WIND
To be slightly drunk or tipsy, but not helpless.

SHAKES
If a ship altered course to head into the wind, the sails would 'shake'. After a long watch, the helmsman might inadvertently 'nod off' and the ship would naturally start heading into the wind. The head sails would then 'shake' or luff. Sailors came to measure a short period of time before the watch changed as 'a couple of shakes'. Sometimes a sleeping helmsman could lead to the ship being 'taken aback' with the wind on the wrong side of the sails.

SHALLOP
Like a skiff, a smaller boat than the longboat that ships needed to transfer men and supplies on and off the ship when moored. These small boats had a mast, sail and rudder, and often also a tarpaulin to keep goods dry. The term is also loosely applied to a small boat for one or two rowers or a sloop.

SHAPE UP
Today's expression meaning 'to get your act together' stems from the order to get the right 'shape' on the sails for maximum efficiency.

SHARES
In 1691, Smith listed the common apportionment of any prize taken by a privateer as follows:

'The Ship hath one third part, The Victualler the other third. The other third part is for the (ship's) Company, and this is subdivided thus in shares:

The Captain 10 in some but 9 in others; Lieutenant 9 or as he agrees with the Captain; Master 8 in some but 7 in others; Mates 7 (or 5); Chyrugion (Surgeon) 6 (or 3); Gunner 6 (or 5); Boatswain 6 (or 5); Carpenter 6 (or 5), Trumpeter 6 (or 5); the 4 Quarter-Masters 5 (or 4); Cooper 5 (or 4); Chyrugion's mate 5 (or 4); Gunner's mate 5 (or 4); Capenter's Mate 5 (or 4); Corporal 4 (or 3); Quarter-Gunners 4 (or 3); Trumpeter's Mate 3 (or 3 or 1); Steward 4 (or 3); Cook 4 (or 3), Coxwain 4 (or 3), Swabber 4 (or 3).

In English Ships they seldom use any Marshal (see Ship's Officers) whose shares amongst the French is equal with the Boatswains, all the rest of the Younkers, or Fore-mast-Men according to their desers, some 3, some 2 and a half, some one and a half, and the Boys one, which is a single share, or one and a half, as they do deserve. Shares were distributed not by the Captain, but by the Master, his first Mate, the Gunner, Boatswain and four Quartermasters. The Captain, however, could take away a half share, or full share at most from any 'unworthy' crew member and redistribute it.

SHARKS
Shark meat was eaten by pirates and buccaneers, but the purpose of this entry is to introduce a superb old shanty, called 'The Chivalrous Shark':

> The most chivalrous fish in the ocean,
> To the ladies forbearing and mild,
> Tough his record be dark,

The man-eating shark
Will eat neither woman nor child.

He dines upon seamen and skippers,
And tourist his hunger assuage
And a fresh cabin boy
Will inspire him with joy,
If he's past the maturity age.

A doctor, a lawyer, a preacher,
He'll gobble one any fine day.
But the ladies, God bless 'em,
He'll only address 'em
Politely and go on his way.

I can readily cite you an instance
Where a lovely young lady of Bream;
Who was tender and sweet
And delicious to eat,
Fell into the bay with a scream.

She struggled and flounced in the water
And signalled in vain for her bark.
And she'd surely been drowned
If she hadn't been found
By a chivalrous, man-eating shark.

He bowed in a manner most polished,
Thus soothing her impulses wild.
"Don't be frightened," he said,
"I've been properly bred,
And will eat neither woman nor child."

He proffered his fin and she took it,
Such gallantry none can dispute,
While the passengers cheered
As the vessel they neared,
And a broadside was fired in salute.

The soon stood alongside the vessel,
While a lifesaving dinghy was low'r'd.
With the pick of the crew
And her relatives few
And the mate and the skipper aboard.

They hauled her aboard in a jiffy,
While the shark stood attention the while.
Then he raised on his flipper,
And ate up the skipper,
And went on his way with a smile.

Now this shows the prince of the ocean,
To the ladies forbearing and mild,
Though his record be dark,
The man-eating shark
Will eat neither woman nor child.

SHEBEC
Favoured by the Barbary Corsairs as it was fast and manoeuvrable. A narrow ship with one mast with a latten mainsail and a small foresail on the bowsprit. She also carried 15 oars on each side.

SHELLBACK
An old, experienced seaman, who has probably eaten so much turtle meat in his years at sea that he is developing a carapace.

SHE WON'T WEAR IT
In high seas or strong winds, square-riggers changed tack by *wearing ship*, putting the stern through the wind rather than the bow (known in yachting as *gybing*). In seas which were too big, this could not be achieved, the ship *would not wear it*. (See gybe)

THE SHIP HAS SPENT HER MASTS
Her masts have been broken by foul weather. If the damage occurred in action, the saying was '*her masts have been shot by the board.*'

SHIP'S BISCUITS (HARD TACK)
Bread would not keep on long voyages, so biscuits were made with flour and the minimum of water or milk, moulded into flat cakes and packed tightly into canvas bags. The hard tack should last for up to a year after being baked. The biscuits quickly became infested with a type of black-headed weevil (called '*bargemen*' for some reason). As a result, before any pirate ate a biscuit, he tapped it on the table to knock the weevils out of it. Leavened bread was referred to as '*soft tack*'. They were also known as sea biscuits, and a film was recently made about the legendary 1930's race-horse *Seabiscuit*, the son of *Hard Tack*, whose own parents were the famous *Man o' War* and *Tea Biscuit*.

This also became a seaman's expression of apology when he burped in public – any belch could be blamed on the poor quality of '*ship's biscuits*'. My father-in-law always used this expression from his merchant navy days before the war. (Dried peas also kept for a long time at sea, and so were sometimes the only other source of food when boiled.)

SHIP SHAPE AND BRISTOL FASHION

Bristol was the great port for the slave trade, also importing vast quantities of tobacco, sherry and chocolate. Slave ships not only stank, but also could carry disease, so the citizens of the prosperous port would not allow ships to dock until they were cleaned and *'made tidy'* in the way that the Bristol Channel tides are predictable and orderly. Before entering the harbour, the ships were inspected to ensure that they were *'ship shape and Bristol fashion'*. Even when the ship moored, its sailors were not allowed ashore until they had *'slewed'* the yards, swinging them inboard so as not to obstruct other ships or quayside traffic or buildings. Because of the extreme differences between high and low tide in the Bristol Channel (up to 40 feet at Cardiff and Avonmouth), ships entering Bristol had to be of an especially stout construction, as they were left *'high and dry'* at low tide. If not well constructed and properly laden, at low tide they could break their backs or their cargoes could shift and be damaged. The first docks were not constructed until 1804, and the Floating Harbour in the 1830's.

SHIP'S COUSIN

A favoured person aboard ship.

SHIP'S OFFICERS

Smith's *'Sea-Man's Grammar'* of 1691 tells us of a naval ship:

*The **Captain's Charge** is to command all, and tell the Master to what Port he will go, or to what height. In a Fight, he is to give Direction for the managing thereof, and the master is to see the cunning (running?) of the Ship, and, Trimming of the Sails.*

*The **Master** and his Mates are to direct the course, command all the Sailers*, for Steering, Trimming and Sailing the Ship; his Mates are only his Seconds, allowed sometimes for the two Mid-Ships-Men, that ought to take charge of the first prize.*

*The **Pilot** when they make land doth take the charge of the Ship till he brings her to Harbour.*

*The **Chirurgion** (Surgeon) is to be exempted from all duty, but to attend the Sick, and cure the Wounded: and good care would be had he have a Certificate from the Barber-Chirurgions** Hall of his sufficiency, and also that his Chest be well furnish both for Physic and for Chirurgery, and so near as may be proper for that clime you go for, which neglect hath been the loss of many a man's life.*

*The **Cap Merchant** or **Purser** hath the charge of all the Carragasoun (Cargo?) or Merchandise, and doth keep an account of all that is received, or delivered, but a Man of War hath only a Purser.*

*The **Master Gunner** hath the charge of the Ordinance, and Shot, Powder, match, Ladles, Sprunges, Worms, Cartrages, Arms and Fire-Works; and the rest of the Gunners, or Quarter Gunners to receive their Charge from him according to directions, and to give an account of their stores.*

*The **Carpenter** and his Mate, is to have the Nails, Clinches, Roove and Clinch-Nailes, Pikes, Splates, Rudder-Irons, Pumpnails, Skupper nails, and Leather, Sawes, Files, Hatchets and such like, and ever ready for caulking, breaming, stopping leaks, fishing, or splicing the masts or yards as occasion requireth, and to give account of his store.*

*The **Boatswain** is to have the charge of all the Cordage, Tackling, sails, Fids and Marling-*

Spikes, Needles, Twine, sail-Cloth, and Rigging for the Ship, his Mate the Command of the Long-Boat, for the setting forth of Anchors, weighing or fetching home an Anchor, Warping, Towing or Mooring, and to give an account of his Store.

The **Trumpeter** is always to attend the Captain's Command, and to (be) found either at his going ashore, or coming aboard, at the entertainment of Strangers, also when you hale a Ship, when you charge, board or enter; and the Poop is his place to stand or sit upon, if there be a noise they are to attend him, if there be not, everyone he doth teach to bear a part, the Captain is to encourage him, by increasing his Shares, or pay, and give the Master Trumpeter a reward.

The **Marshal** is to punish Offenders, and to see Justice executed according to Directions; As Ducking at the Yard's Arm, Hauling under the keel, Bound to the Capstern (Capstain), or mainmast with a Basket of Shot about his Neck, Setting is the Bilboes, and to pay the Cobty or the Morjoune; but the Boys the Boatswain is to see every Monday at the Chest, to say their compass, and receive their punishment for all their week's offences***, which done, they are to have a quarter can of beer, and a biskit of bread, but if the Boatswain eat or drink before he catch them, they are free.

The **Corporal** is to see the setting and relieving the Watch, and see all the Soldiers ad sailers keep their arms clean, neat and yare, and to teach them their use.

The **Steward** is to deliver out the Victuals according to the captain's direction, and Mess them four, five or six, as there is occasion.

The **Quarter-Masters** have the Charge of the Howle, for Stowing, Romagng and Trimming the Ship in the hold, and of their Squadrons for the watch, and for Fishing to have a Seine, a Fishgig (trident), a Harpon-yron(Harpoon), and Fish-Hooks, for Porgos, Bonitos, Dolphins, or Dorados, and Rayling-lines for Mackerel.

The **Cooper** is to look to the Cask, Hoops and twigs, to Stave or repair the Buckets, Baricos, cans, Steep-tubs, Runlets, Hogsheads, Pipes, Buts, etc. for Wine, Bear, Sider, Beverage, Fresh-water, or any Liquor.

The **Coxwain** is to have a choice Gang to attend the skiffe, to go to and again as occasion commandeth.

The **Cook** is to dress and deliver out the Victual, he hath his Store of Quarter cans, small cans, Platters, Spoons****, Lanthornes, &C. And is to give his Account of the remainder.

The **Swabber** is to wash and keep clean the Ship, and Maps.

The **Liar** is to hold his place but for a week, and he that is first taken with a lie, every Monday is so proclaimed at the main-Mast by a general cry, 'a Liar, a Liar, a Liar', he is under the Swabber, and only to keep clean the Beak-head, and Chains.

The **Sailers** are the ancient men for hoisting the Sails, getting the tacks aboard, haling the Bowling, and Steering the Ship.

The **Younkers** are the young men called fore-Mast-men, to take in the top sails, or Top and Yard, for furling the sails, Bousing or Tricing, and take their turns at the Helm.

The **Lieutenant** is to associate the Captain, and in his absence to execute his place, he is to see the Marshall and Corporal do their duties, assist them in instructing the soldiers, and in a fight the fore-castle is his place to make good, and the Captain doth the half-deck, and the Quarter-master, or Master's Mate, the Mid-ships, and in a Statesman of War, he is also allowed as necessary as a Lieutenant on Shore.

*Of course, the origin of 'sailor' was 'sailer'.

**The first surgeons were barbers, because of their possession of sharp instruments. For bigger operations on board, the ship's carpenter was used for his knowledge and ownership of saws.

***See 'Blue Monday.

****Men ate off square wooden platters, using both sides, and had generally used no knives or forks, using bread to 'clean' their plates.

SHIVER ME TIMBERS !
An exclamation of surprise, probably coming from the feeling when a wooden ship hit any rocks and the ship vibrated and creaked. Possibly only used in books and articles rather than by seafarers.

SHOAL
A bank or reef, an area of shallow water dangerous for navigation. (In Spanish, 'bajo', 'bajio', 'escollo', 'banco' or 'abrojo').

SHOOT AHEAD
We use this phrase today, as in 'you shoot ahead, I'll catch up with you later'. It literally comes from the days of sail, when a vessel moves ahead of another quickly when both are underway.

SHOT
Round shot, or cannon balls were used to destroy masts and rigging, and splinters of timber could incapacitate crew members. However, they were not as destructive to humans as a **'whiff of grapeshot'**, or **'bar and chain shot'**, which maximised the maiming capacity of cannons.

'**Case shot'** was a cylindrical tin full of small shot, stones, musket bullets and small pieces of iron to scatter destruction in as wide an area as possible on the crowded decks. The bits of metal were usually enclosed in a wooden case. Sometimes canvas bags were used, but there was a danger that the canvas might snag inside the gun barrel and damage the bore.

'**Angel shot'** was slang for chain shot, when two halves of a cannon ball were joined by a short length of chain. It rotated, cutting a swathe through a ship's rigging, so it was also used to clear a deck of sailors, sending many to join the angels in heaven with one discharge. In Spanish ships, 'angelotes' or 'fat angels' were 'hemispheres of shot welded to two bars that interlocked so as to slide from one another, thus doubling their nominal length through the action of centrifugal force after leaving the cannon's mouth... these shot were used against another ship's rigging and sails, although they may have been used as anti-personnel on occasion.'

Mainwaring wrote in 1644: 'There are many kinds of shot. That which flies farthest and pierces most is called **round shot**; the next is **cross bar**, which is good for (shredding) ropes and sails and masts; the other **langrel**, which will not fly so far but is very good for the rigging, and the like, and for men; so is **chain shot** and **case shot**, or **burr shot**, which is good to ply against men which stand naked, plying of their small shot.'

156

This description of different types of shot is taken from Smith (1691): 'A *case* is made of two pieces of hollow wood joined together like two half cartrages fit to put into the bore of a piece (cannon), and a case-shot is any kind of small bullets, nails, old iron and the like to put into the case to shoot out of the ordnance or murderers; these will do much mischief when we lie board and board... **Round-shot** is a round built for any piece: **Cross-bar-shot** is also a round-shot, but it has a long spike of iron cast with it, the ends of which are commonly armed for fear of bursting the piece (cannon), which it to bind a little oakum in a little canvas at the end of each pike. **Trundle-shot** is only a bole of iron sixteen or eighteen inches in length; at both ends sharp pointed; and about a handful from each end a round broad bowl of lead according to the bore of the piece cast upon it. **Langrel-shot** runs loose with a shackle to be shortened when you put it in place, and when it flies out it doth spread itself, it hath at the end of either bar a half bullet either of lead or iron. **Chain shot** is two bullets with a chain betwixt them, and some are contrived round as in a ball, yet will spread in flying their full length in breadth; all these are used when you are near a ship to shoot down the masts, yards, shrouds, tear the sails, spoil the men, or anything that is above decks.'

SHOT-PLUG
A cone-shaped piece of wood, which was hammered into holes made by enemy cannon fire, into the side of the ship to temporarily repair leaks.

SHOVE OFF
To move a ship off the dock and get under way.

SHOW A LEG
Not strictly a pirate term, but the origin of this term, meaning 'get out of bed', or 'move yourself', is intriguing. In the Royal Navy, the crew were forbidden to leave the ship when in home port, for fear they would desert the stinking conditions. As a result their women or 'wives', were allowed to come on board in the port, and slept with the men in their hammocks. The boatswain's mates called the men on deck every morning, and if they saw a hammock with a body still in it, shouted 'show a leg!' If the leg was hairy, the offending crewman was chased to his duties. If it was relatively hairless, the mates allowed the 'wife' to sleep on. Not until 1840 were women prohibited from sleeping when His Majesty's ships were in their home harbours. The original phrase was 'show a leg or a purser's stocking'.

SHOW YOUR TRUE COLOURS
A pirate ship might hoist its pirate flag when in firing distance, but not before. Even English warships carried flags from other nations to deceive the enemy, but the 'rules of war' required a ship to show its real colours, or national ensigns, before firing a shot.

SING OUT
The sailor who was swinging the lead to establish the soundings, would chant out the depths as the ship slowly progressed in uncertain waters. He had to be heard clearly, and the expression has come to mean to invite someone to give his opinion.

SHROUDS
The large horizontal ropes fixed to the masts, which latticed with the vertical 'rat lines' that sailors scrambled up to furl and unfurl sails.

SIR CLOUDESLEY
Drink of small beer and brandy, with spices, sweeteners and lemon juice, named after Sir Cloudesley Shovell (1650-1707, see Introduction)

SKILLYGOLEE, SKILLY
When salt meat was boiled to make it edible, the water was then mixed with oatmeal to make a savoury broth or thick soup. It was served to naval prisoners, and prisoners-of-war kept in hulks. Skillygolee, or Skillygallee, later became an oatmeal drink sweetened with sugar (in place of cocoa) for seamen during the Napoleonic Wars (1803-1815).

SKYSCRAPER
The 18th century origin of this building term was a small, triangular sail set above the sky sail on the old square-riggers, to try and catch more wind in areas of calm air - to 'scrape the sky'. It was later used to describe a tall person, then a tall building for the first time in the 1880's. Other names for the very highest sails used on ships were *moonrakers*, *angel's foot stools* and *star gazers*, all used in times of dead calm. They were never used in strong winds as they would rip away. The fifth verse of the shanty 'The Flash Frigate' is:
The next thing we hear is "All hands to make sail!"
"Way aloft!" and "Let out!" and "Let fall!" is the hail,
Oh, your royals and your skysails and your moonsails so high,
At the sound of the call your skyscrapers must fly.

SKYLARKING
This seems to be a term given to sailors among the skysails, perhaps a hundred feet above the deck, playing around and showing off their agility.

SLANT
All ships have an optimum angle of heel, the angle at which it is better to reduce sail, rather than have too much power in the rigging, pulling the boat over. This critical angle is known as the 'slant' and a good sailor will always know when 'to put a new slant on things' as sea and wind conditions change.

SLAVE PROFITS
Around the time that Howell Davis was trading with 'Old Crackers' we have a merchant captain's bill for dealing with him. In 1721, the price for a male slave was 8 guns, a wicker bottle, 2 cases of spirits and 28 sheets of cloth. A woman cost 9 gallons of brandy, 6 iron bars, 2 pistols, a bag of powder and 2 strings of beads. A boy cost 7 large kettles, an iron bar, a length of cotton and 5 lengths of blue and white cloth. The merchant at the same time would have to pay the Royal Africa

Company £15 for a man, and £12 for a woman, so their forts were always potentially full of money to attract pirates. The price was £60 for a man and £48 for a woman in the West Indies, partially because a 25% death rate on the Atlantic crossing was factored in. From this coast, the Royal Africa Company sold around 18000 slaves a year, and the private traders around 75000, but still could not meet demand. By 1820, Guinea slaves could be bought for a few beads, or $30 at the most, and sold in the Americas for $700, and American captains were said to make a million dollars from each voyage.

The hold on slave ships was usually 6-7 feet high, and was divided half-way up by a platform to double the number of slaves that could be transported. Slaves were chained in pairs at the ankle, and allowed a space of around 6 feet in length, 1 foot 6 inches wide and 3 foot six inches high. They could not stand up in the dark, and lay in their own excrement and vomit. They were daily taken to the open air so that the slave decks could be hosed down. The stench was so bad that the ships could be smelled a mile away, and candles could not be lit in the foetid air on the slave decks. Only the strongest Africans survived the Atlantic Crossing.

Note: Much of the investment capital of the wonderful buildings in Bath came from the Bristol slave trade. The town, possibly the first in the world built solely for pleasure, relied on the arms and cloth sent to Africa, the slaves sent from Africa to the colonies, and the tobacco, rum, sugar and raw cotton that came from the colonies. This triangular trade in described in the next book by this author upon Welsh pirates and buccaneers. As a result, Nash himself noted *'Bath is become a mere sink of profligacy and extortion. Every article of house-keeping is raised to an enormous price...I have known a Negro-driver, from Jamaica, pay overnight, to the master of one of the rooms, 65 guineas for tea and coffee to the company, and leave Bath the next morning, in such obscurity, that not one of the guests had the slightest idea of his person, or even made the least enquiry about his name.'* (From the entry upon Beau Nash in '100 Great Welshmen' by T.D. Breverton). Spanish cathedrals likewise were financed by genocide and the rape of the Spanish Main and South American mainland.

SLAVE TRADE

In 1562, John Hawkins removed 300 slaves from a Portuguese vessel, marking the beginning of the English slave trade. It was difficult to get crew for the 'blackbirders' – their life was short and disease-ridden, and they were often treated worse than the slaves they were transporting to the Indies for work on the sugar plantations, and America for the tobacco crops. The Royal African Company, with its monopoly on the slave trade and royal patron, wished to transport healthy slaves who would achieve top prices on the market. However, merchant captains had their profit assessed on the number that arrived alive, and therefore overcrowded their ships, unknown to the Company. Any numbers left over from the official cargo made the captains extra money. Thus the mortality rate on these voyages, often accelerated by disease such as smallpox, made the mortality rate for the Atlantic crossing at least 25% in 1679. This was a Royal Africa Company estimate, but it was not in possession of the full facts.

Robert Falconbridge wrote (*An Account of the Slave Trade*, 1788) that between half and two-thirds perished each year, and around 40,000 a year were being transported

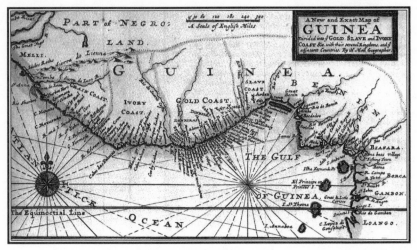

The Guinea Coast in Roberts' time

in the late eighteenth century. Falconbridge describes the disgusting conditions where the slaves were packed on the decks and held in irons by the wrists and legs, lying in their own filth and urine: '*They are frequently stowed so close as to admit of no other disposition than lying on their sides, nor will the height between decks, unless directly under the grating, allow them to stand*'. Brief daily exercise was allowed to keep them mobile, and each morning they were hosed with salt water and the dead thrown overboard. If they did not eat, they were tortured. A Captain Williams used the cat-of-nine tails to keep the slaves fit by making them dance, and '*seemed to find a pleasant sensation in the sight of blood and the sound of their moans.*' His surgeon, James Arnold, gave further evidence to a Parliamentary Committee in 1789 that some of his slaves tried to revolt, and one that could not be removed from the hold had boiling fat poured over him. Two corpses were beheaded, and '*the two gory heads were successively handed to the slaves chained on the deck, and they were obliged to kiss the lips of the bloody heads. Some who refused to obey were unmercifully flogged by the captain and had the bloody part of a head rubbed against their faces.*'

Williams also threw a live slave overboard, and had intercourse with the prettiest of the female slaves. If they refused him, they were flogged until they submitted. Williams also flogged his own crew until they were a '*gory mass of raw flesh*', according to surgeon Arnold. Another captain in 1783 threw 130 sick slaves overboard on the pretext that there was no water for them. This way the underwriters had to pay for the value of the cargo, rather than the owners of the ship lose their profits by the death of the slaves.

Even in the West Indies, the life of a good, strong slave, was reckoned to be no more than 10 years in the brutal conditions of the sugar plantations. Thus, apart from new slaves for new plantations where the land had been cleared by the slaves, and for the tobacco plantations in America, there was also a 10% attrition and replacement rate each year to satisfy. Just to replace dead slaves created a demand in Jamaica for 10,000 slaves a year, and in the Leeward Islands for 6000, and for Barbados 4000 slaves.

The surgeon John Atkins, on board the HMS *Swallow's* expedition to destroy the *'murderous Captain Bart Roberts'*, interestingly noted the differences in the sales of manufactured goods along the slave coast of north-east Africa: *'The windward and leeward parts of the coast are as opposite in their demands as is their distance. Iron bars which are not asked for to leeward are a substantial part of windward cargoes. Crystals, oranges, corals and brass-mounted cutlasses are almost peculiar to the Windward coast; as are brass pans from the Rio Sethos to Applollonia (the Gold Coast) and cowries... at Whydah, copper sheets and iron bars at Calabar; but arms, gunpowder, tallow, old sheets, Indian cottons ... and English spirits (whisky) are everywhere called for. Sealing wax and pipes are necessary in small quantities...'*

SLEWED
To *'Slue'* was *'to turn any cylindrical or conical piece of timber about its own axis without removing it.'* (-William Falconer's *'Dictionary of the Marine'* 1789) The wood might be spun to wind something. A drink twists and spins on his own axis – the 'one-leg syndrome' – so slewed meant to become drunk. (See Half –Slewed)

SLING YOUR HOOK
Unpopular ship mates were told to go and sling their hammocks elsewhere. Space was at a premium on ships, and places to sleep difficult to find.

SLUSH FUND
The grease, or *slush*, from frying salt pork on a long voyage, or from *'scraping the sides of the barrel'* was saved by the cook and sold to tanneries and candle makers. Thus the term *'scraping the barrel'* also comes from the days of sailing ships. In 1866 the US Government applied the term to a contingency fund in one of its operating budgets, and the phrase passed into general knowledge.

SLOOP
A single-masted boat up to 100 tons with a long bowsprit, almost as long as the hull, it was rigged fore and aft. The fastest boat of its day, it was liked by pirates and smugglers because it was easy to handle and had a shallow draught, so could escape in shallow waters. It drew only 8 feet of water and was easy to manoeuvre. From the eighteenth century the term was used for a small vessel with one to three masts carrying four to twelve guns on the upper deck. Capable of around 11 knots speed with the aid of its square topsail, it could take up to 75 crew and mounted 14 cannon. In general, the one-masted sloop was smaller than a 2-masted schooner, then proportionately bigger were a two—masted corvette, a three-masted snow, a three-masted frigate and a three-masted ship of the line. *'A rapier-like bowsprit almost as long as her hull enabled her to mount a parade of canvas that made her even more nimble than the schooner or brigantine.'* (See Naval Sloop).

SLOPPY
A *'sloppe'* was a loose-fitting garment, mentioned by Chaucer. In 1623, because its crews were dressed in tatters, the Royal Navy ordered that *slops* should be carried aboard ships, kept in a *slop chest*, and issued to the men at sea. As they were all one

size, usually damp and musty, the adjective *sloppy* was derived, to mean something untidy or slovenly (as in '*sloppy dresser*'.)

SMACK
A small sloop-rigged boat used for fishing and small coastal trading.

SMALLPOX
This disease exterminated tribes of African, American Indians, and South American Indians when introduced by the white man. A terrible epidemic in Boston in 1721 affected half of its 10,000 population, and the preacher Cotton Mather recounted how the Africans dealt with the disease in their homelands. They said that they cut open a healthy person's skin and put some of the pus from the disease into the wound. On June 26th, 1721, Dr Zabadiel Boylston inoculated his small son and two of his slaves with smallpox, but the city elders were horrified. Around the same time the disease hit London and Lady Mary Wortley Montague convinced the Princess of Wales to support inoculation experiments. She asked the king to pardon six convicts if they would submit to inoculation, and they were treated on August 9th by Dr Charles Maitland. The treatment worked.

SMELLING THE GROUND
When a ship's keel was so close to the seabed that it was almost touching it.

SMOKING LAMP
During the 16th century, sailors began smoking aboard ship. This safety measure was devised to keep the fire hazard away from the combustible tarred woodwork of the vessel. Thus smoking was restricted to a certain area of a vessel, with a lamp located in the forecastle or next to the galley. The smoking lamp was put out whenever smoking was forbidden. Even today the officer of the deck in the Royal Navy says '*the smoking lamp is out*', which is the order to cease smoking before drills, refuelling or taking ammunition.

SNAP ARMS !
Fire! – to fire a pistol was to snap an arm, or firearms.

SNAP DRAGON
An alcoholic punch with raisins that had been soaked in brandy or rum. The raisins were then set alight and floated on the top of the alcohol. Sometimes, for even greater effect, the tops of lighted candles were also included.

SNOTTY (SNOTTER, SNORTER)
Midshipmen were young lads, little more than boys, who carried orders to the guns in the '*midships*' from the officers on deck. Their dream was to become officers and gentlemen. However, being poorly fed and young, they were constantly wiping their noses with the sleeves of their jackets, and became known as '*snotties*'. One admiral decided to put three buttons on their sleeves to prevent this habit. The term '*snotty*'

for someone thinking that they are a gentleman and acting accordingly dates from the midshipmen's running noses. Also a term for a high wind.

SNOW
Like a brigantine, but smaller, with a main and foremast, and a supplementary sail close behind the mainmast.

A SOFT FAREWELL
When two or more crews sailed in consort, one ship was always ready for action, and another carried the stores and captured loot. At night, it was tempting for pirates on the 'treasure ship' to quietly change direction and make off with the booty. This happened to Black Bart Roberts not once, but twice. First Walter Kennedy sailed off with his great Portuguese plunder when Roberts was becalmed, and the disaffected 'Lord' Thomas Anstis did the same in the night during an Atlantic crossing.

SOLDIER'S WIND
A ship which sails across the wind, with her beam (side of the vessel) at a right angle to the wind, is reaching across-wind, or beam-reaching. It requires little nautical skill and no tacking, so is dismissively called a *soldier's wind* by experienced seadogs.

SON OF A GUN
Not a Wild West term used by John Wayne, but a Royal Navy phrase from the days of sail. In the days when the wives and mistresses of sailors were allowed to stay aboard in harbour (and sometimes go to sea), sometimes they gave birth on board ship. Both for procreating and for giving birth, hammocks were useless. There was little room, except the gangways, which had to be kept clear at all time. The only space available was between the guns on the gun decks, and the child was called a 'son of a gun', as often no-one knew its father.
'Begotten in the galley
And born under a gun,
Every hair a rope yarn,
Every tooth a marlin spike,
Every finger a fishhook,
And in his blood right good Stockholm tar'.

SON OF A SEA COOK
Probably a corruption of 'son of a seacock', referring to a bold seaman, it came to be an expression of derision at sea. The other explanation is that the early English settlers could not pronounce the Algonquian Indian name for the skunk, *seganku*, and called it a *segonk*. A term of scorn became 'son of a segonk' and then 'son of a seacook.'

SOUND, SOUND OUT
To try and find the depth of the water. A sound is also a deep bay.

SOUTH SEA BUBBLE

This scandal coincided with Black Bart's years on the high seas. The South Sea Company was founded in 1711, to prosper on the vast trade that could open up with the Spanish New World. In 1713, the Treaty of Utrecht* followed the War of Spanish Succession (1702-1713). The ending of the war gave the Asiento Treaty, whereby Britain held a monopoly on the slave trade, but all other trade was restricted to just one ship a year. Despite this, the king became governor of the company in 1718, and confidence then drove £100 shares to over a £1000 in 1719, before crashing.

*British manufacturers were terrified that the ending of the war would put an end to their lucrative trade into Africa in exchange for Spanish goods, and lobbied hard for the asiento for the slave trade. Alongside the obvious petition from the Birmingham gun makers, we can see one from the makers of Welsh flannel.

SOUTH SEAS

Generally the area around the Caribbean, including the Gulf of Mexico, the Florida Coast, Cuba, Jamaica and Hispaniola.

SPAIN AND SLAVERY

The precious-ore and jewel deposits in Mexico, Peru and Colombia needed slaves to work in the mines. However, war, disease, overwork and suicide caused the native Indian population to plummet, in one of the worst genocides in history. In the Antilles alone the native population dropped from 300,000 in 1492 to 14,000 in 1514, and millions died on the South American mainland. To save the Indians from extinction, a former explorer, Bartolome de Las Casa, proposed that the King of Spain introduced Negroes to save them from extinction, as *'the labour of one Negro is more valuable than that of four Indians'*. Thus in 1517, the first *'asiento'* was agreed, enabling 4000 Negroes to be imported into the West Indies over the following 8 years. By 1540, an estimated 30,000 men, women and children had been transplanted from Africa to Hispaniola alone. From the 1560's, Hawkins, Drake and others were trafficking slaves to Spanish America.

SPANISH

Sack, or Canary wine. Also Spanish gold or coins.

SPANISH FAGGOT

The sun. Any Britons caught by the Spanish were often burnt by the Inquisition as heretics.

SPANISH GOUT, POX or NEEDLE

Syphilis – sometimes Italian or French were the pejorative adjectives. It was fashionable for derogatory terms to be prefaced with the nationality of the enemy of the day - to the French, homosexuality is to this day *'the English disease'* or *'English sickness'*.

SPANISH MAIN

The South American mainland, from Columbia and Venezuela up to the Isthmus of Panama. From the 17th and 18th centuries, the term came to be associated with the buccaneers sailing the Spanish Main, and was more associated with the Caribbean Sea than the mainland. The Spanish called this area '*Tierra Firme*', South America in general but especially the northern coast from Veragua Province in what is now Panama to the delta of the Orinoco in Venezuela.

SPANISH PADLOCK
A kind of chastity belt, Spanish women sometimes were forced to wear when away from their husbands. Pirates, who captured Spanish women en route to or from the Spanish Main, probably invented the term.

SPANISH WALK
To run away.

SPANKING
The brisk and lively movement of a vessel at sea, or the wind. It came to mean 'excellent', as in the following verse from the song '*The Good Ship Calibar*':
The Calibar was a spanking craft it wasn't rigged fore and aft
Her helm it stuck out far behind and her wheel was a great big shaft
With half a gale to fill her sail she do one knot per hour
She's the fastest barge on the Lagan canal and she's only one horsepower.'

SPICK AND SPAN
The origin was '*spick and span new*', meaning that a wooden ship was fresh from the shipyard with all new spikes (nails) and span (wood).

SPIKE
To prevent a gun or cannon being fired by knocking a soft nail into the vent or touch-hole with a spike. Therefore the gunpowder could not be ignited.

SPINDRIFT
The fine mist of water swept from the tops of waves by high winds.

SPITHEAD PHEASANT
The naval seaman's name for a kipper.

SPLICE THE MAINBRACE
The mainbrace is the rope or brace controlling the movement of the ship's mainsail. Hauling on the mainbrace required a great effort from the crew, after which possibly some reward was in order. To splice is to join two strands of rope together. A ship's rigging was always targeted in battle, and it was essential to repair it as quickly as possible in case another ship appeared. The sails and braces (the lines or ropes which passed through the block to hold up the sails) were the priority. After this arduous work was carried out, and everything was '*shipshape*' again,, it became the custom as a reward to give grog to all the crew. Thus to '*splice the mainbrace*' meant to start a drinking session, or give out an extra portion of rum or grog. The term may

come from the Dutch '*splissen*'. *Splissen* means to drink, and Dutch sailors may have confused the terms, and other pirates agreed with their more agreeable interpretation of the order.

SPLICED, TO GET
A seaman's term for getting married, referring to the permanent nature of splicing two pieces of rope together. Two ends of ropes are untwisted, then twisted together and fastened with string to make one continuous length of rope.

SPOILS OF WAR
In Latin, '*spolium*' is '*the hide stripped from an animal*'. Thus in time anything stripped from a country or ship became spoils of war.

SPREAD LIKE WILDFIRE
Wild-fire was a combustible composition, in which were tipped pikes and arrows, to set fire to an opposing ship. These were more often used in times of war or emergency by navies, rather than by pirates, who wanted to keep the 'prize' intact and not risk the fire spreading to their ships. However, they were used by Morgan's men to take forts from the Spanish. (See Fireworks).

SQUARE MEAL
Meals were served on square wooden platters, which could be easily stowed in a rack. When weather conditions were poor, sailors were constantly working, and ate food from their pockets, having to be '*lucky to get a square meal*'. These wooden platters were not often filled, as food ran short, but for those who had been working especially hard, they were given a '*square meal*' filling the dish, as a reward. It seems that '*fair and square*' also had this nautical origin, when all the crew had a fair meal, with the platters being filled to their corners. '*Clean your plate before you have your dessert*' comes from the use of square plates. The stew or whatever was wiped of with bread, and the platter turned over for the sweet, if there was any.

SQUARE UP
Ships in port '*squared*' their yards horizontally to the deck, and at right angles to the fore and aft line. This state of being normal and correct has come to mean to be '*all square*' with someone, to repay debts etc.

STAND OFF
To recede from the shore.

STARBOARD
Until the 13th century in Northern Europe, steering a ship was carried out by means of a huge oar, lashed to the right (steer-board) side of a ship. The boat had always then to be berthed on the left-hand side, i.e. it was secured to the harbour walls of the port. So the left of a boat became known as the port side, and the right as the starboard. The great problem was that a wind blowing on the starboard beam might push the ship away from the vertical, lifting the steer-board out of the water – steering was then impossible. A violent wind on the port side could roll the ship

so badly that the steer-board could be broken off. Only the innovation of the centre-line rudder, brought back by Crusaders, solved the problem and made the steer-board obsolete. *Starboard tack* means sailing with the wind blowing from the starboard side.

START OVER WITH A CLEAN SLATE
A slate tablet was kept near the helm for the watch keeper to record distance, speed, headings and tacks. If there had been no problems, the slate was wiped clean for the next watch keeper.

STAND
A ship will *stand by* in case of trouble, *stand out* to sea, *stand in* the offing, *stand off* a port, stand in with another vessel when they are sailing in consort, stand in towards the land etc. From these terms we get *stand-by*, *stand-off*, *stand-offish*, *stand in favour* and the like.

STAUNCH
Impervious to water, firm, water-tight, from the Old French *'estanche.'*

STAVE OFF
'Fend off' a harbour side or another boat, originally by using the staves used by the ship's cooper.

STAYS
The large ropes coming from the mast heads down before the masts, to prevent them from springing, when the ship is *sending* (*Sending* is the pitching downwards into the hollow between to large waves.)

STAY THE COURSE
The origin of this saying is that if a ship keeps to its course, it will reach its destination.

STEM
The fore-part of the ship. The stern is the after-part. To look for something *'stem to stern'* means that a ship has been searched thoroughly, in all its parts.

STEM THE TIDE
When a ship is sailing against the tide at such a rate that she overcomes its power.

STERN CHASER
A gun fitted on the stern, often a nine-pounder, to deter chasing ships, and aimed at their rigging and masts. From the 19th century it came to mean either a penis, or a homosexual.

STEWS
The raucous area of narrow alleyways, gambling dens, taverns and brothels frequented by sailors in port.

STINKPOTS

Crockery jars filled with sulphur, gunpowder and other combustibles, with a fuse, used to help board ships. They were also sometimes filled with plant gum and rotting fish, and were a crude and early form of tear gas. A popular method was for the pirates to suspend them from their yardarms, and when the ships closed together, light and cut them so they dropped onto the deck of the intended prize. From Falconer's *'Marine Dictionary'* of 1771 we have the following description: *'The fuses of the stinkpot being lighted, they are immediately thrown on the deck of the enemy, where they burst and catch fire, producing an intolerable stench and smoke, and filling the air with tumult and distraction. Amidst the confusion occasioned by this infernal apparatus the (boarding) detachment rush aboard sword in hand, under cover of smoke, on their antagonist.'*

In the early days of steamships, they were known as 'stinkpots' to the men on sailing ships. In return, the last of the commercial sailing ships were called 'windjammers' as an insult.

(AS) STRAIGHT AS THE CROW FLIES

British coastal vessels often carried a cage of crows. They hate large expanses of water, and head straight towards land when released at sea, useful in fogs, or when unsure of one's bearings. The lookout perch on sailing vessels thus became known as the *crow's nest*.

STRANDED (See High and Dry)

STRIKE

To lower or let down anything. Merchant crews would *strike*, or lower the ship's yards in port as a protest, from which we get the modern meaning of an industrial strike. They could not *'strike'* at sea as this was mutiny.

STRIKE COLOURS

Haul down a ship's flag as a mark of surrender. The present term *'to strike'*, i.e. refusing to work for masters (management) in order to look after one's own interests, comes from this nautical expression. The term *'to lay down tools'* and go on strike emphasises this connection, striking being to put something down.

STRUMPET

Harlot, prostitute, bawd, trollop, hussy.

SUCKBOTTLE

A pirate who was always drunk – to *suck* was to drink alcohol. (See the last verse of the Samuel Swipes poem in the entry upon Grog, and the entry on Sucky)

SUCKING THE MONKEY

Not a pirate term, but a tribute to the ingenuity of the poor sailor suffering a disgusting experience in the Royal Navy. In the War of American Independence (1775-1782), England was blockading the United States, and a large fleet was stationed in the West Indies. For years the officers could not understand why their crews of impressed men were often too drunk to stand up. They even stopped the grog supplies for a time, with no change in their condition. Native women boarded the warships, to sell fruit and coconuts. Many men had persuaded the women to replace the coconut milk with rum, and stored and hid up to a dozen coconuts, wherever they could. When 'sucking the monkey' they were secretly drinking rum. When a seaman was sucking rum, the end of the nut resembled a monkey's face*. The term was later applied to illicitly using a straw to suck rum or sprits from a cask, which became known as a *monkey*. The clay pipe-stem or straw used for sucking the cask's contents was known as a 'monkey pump'.

Captain Kidd hanging in chains

*Portuguese sailors first found the nut on Indian Ocean islands. As it was the size and shape of a small head, and the three holes resembled a grinning face, they called it a 'coco', which means 'grinning face' in Portuguese.

SUCKY
Drunk, a 'suck-bottle' was a drunkard. 'Suck' was strong alcohol, and 'rum suck' was very good quality rum. To 'suck one's face' was to drink heavily.

SUIT
Term from the early 1600's meaning the ship's outfit of sails.

SUNDOWNER
Slang for a bullying officer on board ship. The origin was that some captains would only give shore leave up until sunset.

SUN-DRIED
Left hanging in an iron gibbet, after execution, as an example to other pirates. Sometimes the body was tarred to preserve it from falling to pieces, or being pecked to bits by birds, and the grisly remains could be seen at prominent view-points for months or even years.

SUN OVER THE FORE-ARM, SUN OVER THE YARDARM
A reasonable excuse for imbibing alcohol. In the Northern latitudes it was assumed that the sun would show above the foreyard of a ship by 11am, which was approximately the time in many ships for the forenoon 'stand-easy' when many officers would take their first drink of the day.

SUPERSTITIONS

No other calling has so many superstitions as seafaring. We still see a bottle of wine being cracked across the bows of a boat to be launched, which comes down to us from the libation to the gods of the sea by the ancient Greeks and other cultures. Flowers on board have always been unlucky, as they can be made into a wreath for someone who dies on board. Good Friday, the first Monday in April, the second Monday in August and December 31st are unlucky days to start a voyage (being respectively Crucifixion Day, the day Cain killed Abel, the destruction of Sodom and Gomorrah and the hanging of Judas Iscariot). Priests and women are unlucky. The feather of a wren killed on New Year's Day was lucky for a year. Passing a flag between the rungs of a ladder was unlucky. There are hundreds and hundreds of superstitions, which deserve a book to themselves.

SURGEON

These were formerly known as 'barber-surgeons' - barbers became surgeons because they had the sharpest implements for cutting. Surgeons ('sawbones') were in huge demand upon pirate ships, although it was rare for them to be trained as doctors. They were bone-setters, who could extract bullets, treat venereal disease, staunch wounds and amputate to prevent gangrene.

Surgeon's at work

SWAB

From the Dutch 'zwabberen', 'to mop'. The swab was a kind of large mop made of old rope on a four foot handle, used to clean the ship's decks. Someone who was told to clean the decks was referred to as a 'swab'. As it was the lowest form of duty on a ship, to call someone a 'scurvy swab' was to call him a diseased, worthless person.

SWALLOW THE ANCHOR

To leave the sea and settle on land.

SWAMPED
From at least the 17th century, this is when a ship is '*overwhelmed*', filled with water and likely to sink.

SWASHBUCKLER
This is of uncertain origin, but meant a boastful seafaring ruffian originally. The buckler is a smallish round shield worn on the arm to deflect sword blows. It is thought that 'swash' could be the onomatopoeic word sounding like the buccaneer hitting his own shield with his sword, daring someone to fight him.

SWEAR THROUGH A DOUBLE DEAL-BOARD, or TWO-INCH BOARD, or NINE INCH PLANK
Be extremely good at lying. Also to use extremely vigorous foul language.

SWEATING
The ship's band played while one prisoner after another was forced to run between a circle of lighted candles and the mast, while being prodded with knives and swords. It ended when the prisoner collapsed, died or gave information on the whereabouts of treasure.

SWEEP THE BOARD
Win all the money from a gambling table.

SWEET FANNY ADAMS
Not a pirate term, but one dating from 1867, when a little girl named Fanny Adams was found dismembered and mutilated. At this time the Royal Navy was first issued with canned mutton, which became the staple diet aboard its ships. Of poor quality, it came to be known as Fanny Adams, and then mockingly as '*sweet Fanny Adams*'. Her grave can still be seen in Alton, Hampshire. The modern phrase, '*Sweet F.A.*' originally stemmed from this poor young girl.

SWEET TRADE
Piracy or buccaneering.

SWIMMING
William Williams, in his 18th century 'Journal of Penrose, Seaman; wrote of ships '*swimming*' at sea, and the author has corroborated this terminology with a verse from the 1536 song, '*Common Conditions*':
Her flags be new trimmed, set slanting aloft;
Our ship for swift swimming, oh she doth excel.
We fear no enemies, we have escaped them oft;
Of all things that swimmeth, she beareth the bell.

SWING THE LEAD
Slang for '*taking it easy*'. Near land, one job was to lower a lead weight on a line to find the depth near shore, to avoid shallows. It was the easiest and simplest job on

ship, so anyone *'swinging the lead'* was said to be a slacker, not carrying out the normal arduous duties of his shipmates. Also, sometimes the person 'swinging the lead' was pretending to measure the depth, out of sight of officers, especially if he knew the area.

SWIVEL GUN
Small cannon set into sockets on the ship's rail, at whatever point where the pirates were attempting to board.

SWUNG OFF
Hanged on a gallows.

SYLLABUBS
These were drinks or dishes sold in Port Royal taverns, made by curdling cream or milk with a mixture of wine, cider or anything alcoholic, producing a soft curd which was then whipped with gelatine, then sweetened or flavoured - the forerunner of today's alcopops.

TACK
The nautical manoeuvre of bringing a sailing vessel on to another bearing by bringing the wind around the bow, during which the ship is said to be *'coming about'*. Thus *'to tack about'* is to bring the ship's head about to lie the other way. If a ship sails **'too close to the wind'**, it will sail slower, and risk being put about (turned) **'on the wrong tack'** (in the wrong direction) by a small wind shift. The term **'on the same tack'** has the same nautical origin, with two ships heading the same way. **'On the right tack'** means taking the correct direction.

TAKE DOWN A PEG OR TWO
This expression has its origins in post-Spanish Armada Britain when English naval pride was at its highest. Flags and pennants began to play an important role in indicating the official rank and personal status of the ship's commander. Flags hoisted on small halyards were secured to one of a series of pegs arranged vertically on the mast. The higher the flag was flown, the higher the honour. When a commander handed over the ship to a subordinate officer, the new commander's flag would be flown lower down the mast; therefore, the flag had to be taken down a peg or two. Now we use the expression to mean that a person has been humbled.

TAKE DOWN A NOTCH
Warships used to be ranked by the honours that a ship had obtained over the years, and classified by coloured pegs. As other ships earned reputations, perhaps a ship's colours would be taken known a notch.

TAKEN ABACK
When the wind is on the wrong side of the sails and presses them against the mast, forcing the ship astern.

TAKING A CAULK

This means having a short sleep, or nap, on the deck of a ship. The spaces between the deck planks were sealed, or *'caulked'* with tar to help prevent heavy seas penetrating the lower decks. In hot climates like the Caribbean, any sailor lying down usually had stripes of tar along his clothes – he had *'taken a caulk'*.

TAKE THE WIND OUT OF HIS SAILS (see Overbearing)

TAMPA BAY BUCCANEERS

Gasparilla was a Spanish pirate in the Caribbean from 1782, who supposedly attacked an American warship with Jean Lafite in 1822. A former admiral, he allegedly stole an armada's jewels and gold and holed up in western Florida. From the tangled stories about him, a pamphlet describing his exploits was given to visitors to the resort of Boca Grande in the early 20th century. The football team was named in his honour, and Tampa holds an annual Gasparilla Festival.

TAR, JACK TAR

Slang for a sailor. Early sailors wore overalls and hats made of tar-impregnated fabric, which would not rot, and protected the wearer from salt and winds. The hats, as well as the sailors who wore them, became known as *tarpaulins*, shortened to *tars*. Jack is a common name given to men in general, for example *'Jack-of-all-trades'* or *'every man Jack of them'*. It seems to have come from the French synonym for peasant, *Jacques Bonhomme* (Jack the gentleman), which is turn came from *'Jacque'* a leather jerkin. We also see the origin of Jack in the word *'jacket'* today. .It somehow also in England became a slang name for someone christened John. *'Jack the Lad'* means someone who does not care what he does, like a sailor on shore leave.

TARPAULIN, TARPAWLING

Seamen wore canvas hats that had been coated with tar to waterproof them, known as 'tarpaulins'. They also had capes of tarpaulin to cover them in bad weather. Many sailor painted their clothes with tar to keep out the wind and rain, and were known in the North of England as *'tarry-breeks'* (tar covered trousers, or britches). The ship's longboat also often carried a tarpaulin to protect against the ingress of rain-water.

TATTOOS

Like hooped earrings, these were not affected by pirates. The first record of a sailor being tattooed is one of Captain Cook's men in Tahiti in 1764.

TELL IT TO THE MARINES

When King Charles II was told that flying fish existed, he said *'Tell that to my marines.'*

TELL IT TO THE PARROT

Tell everyone, spread gossip. Many ships had parrots as tokens of luck.

TEREDOS WORM
Not a worm, but a soft-shelled mollusc, and the most common and dreaded attacker of ships' hulls in warm water. It could enter planks through tiny holes, and lay a million eggs a year. The young molluscs bored parallel to the surface, honeycombing planks with no outward signs. Ships were double-planked, with a layer of felt and pitch between them, to try to keep the teredos out, as well as other molluscs which attached themselves to the hull and proceeded to devour it layer by layer. If possible, pirates tried to capture brigs and barquentines made from cedar-wood from the Bahamas, which was more resistant to the teredos worm.

THREE MILE LIMIT
This was agreed as the limit of a nation's jurisdiction at sea for reasons of pragmatism. It was able to be enforced because 3 miles was the range limit of the cannon on shore batteries. Not until 1988 with the Territorial Sea Proclamation Act was there a 'high seas' limit of 12 miles established.

THREE SHEETS TO THE WIND
Almost totally drunk. A sheet is a line used for trimming a sail to the wind. There is only one sheet on fore-and aft sails, and there are just two on a square sail set on a yardarm. On a Bermuda-rigged vessel there are two sheets for the jib-foresail and one for the main sail. Thus a drunken man, even if he had three sheets to trim his sails and steer his course, would still be too unsteady to steer a straight course. When all three sheets were allowed to run free, they were said to be 'in the wind', and the ship would lurch and stagger. If the boat is 'three sheets to the wind' the sails are not drawing wind and the ship will not make progress, but drift downwind.

THREE SISTERS
Three rattans bound together with waxed twine, used to hit the backs of seamen to make them 'start' or move more quickly when working. Used by the boatswain's mate in the 17th and 18th centuries, it was used at random, although totally illegal. It was not prohibited until 1809, but still in use long after that in the Royal Navy. The emblem is still seen, as the badge of office on today's master-at-arms.

THROUGH THE HOOP
In the Royal Navy, hammocks were rolled tightly every morning and lashed against the ship's rails to protect against cannon-shot, wood splinters or musket fire. Bosun's mates checked the tightness of each rolled hammock every morning with a regulation-sized hoop. If a hammock could not be 'put through the hoop', the seaman was disciplined.

From the shanty 'The Flash Frigate' the first two verses are:
I sing of a frigate, a frigate of fame,
And in the West Indies she bore a great name,
For cruel, hard treatment of every degree,
Like slaves in the galleys we ploughed the salt sea.

At four in the morning our day's work begun;
"Come, lash up your hammocks, boys, every one."
Seven turns with the lashing so neatly must show,
And all of one size through a hoop they must go.

THUS!
The order to the helmsman to keep the ship *'as she were'*, when sailing with a small wind.

THWARTS
The seats from beam to beam in a small boat where rowers or passengers sit. Thus *'athwart'* means across something.

TIDE OVER
'Alternately sailing and anchoring, depending upon the tide, in order to work a ship in or out of port.' (-Falconer). To 'tide over' was to wait to make progress on the next flowing tide.

TIDY
Derived from 'tide' meaning methodical, well-arranged, just as reliable as the tides.

TIMBER
A wooden leg worn by amputees, or *'peg-legs'*.

TOBACCO
This was the *'cocaine of the 17th century'*. Columbus had noted in 1493 the habit of the (now extinct) Taino Indians of lighting rolls of dried leaves and inhaling the smoke through their nostrils. In the early 17th century, smoking had become so popular that *'many a young nobleman's estate is altogether spent and scattered to nothing in smoke (and) a man's estate runs out through his nose, and he wastes whole days, even years, in drinking of tobacco; men smoke even in bed.'* The leaf's value equalled that of silver. Formerly growing wild in Virginia, it was cultivated by the Virginia Company, which desperately needed people to gather the lucrative crops. After 3 to 4 crops the land was exhausted, and more ground had to be cleared and planted by workers with a short life expectancy.
There were two ways to get labour from Britain - transportation (q.v.) and indentures such as Henry Morgan was supposed to have signed. A new lie in the New World, where one could easily get ownership of one's own land, was an attractive and well-marketed proposition, but people could not afford the crossing. Thus a modified version of apprenticeship, the indenture was devised. Named from the Latin *indentare* or *indentura* (to give a jagged edge, to cut with teeth), it was a contract signed by two or more parties. It was a legal covenant, drawn on parchment and cut into pieces. The fit between the parts signified the agreement between the party of the first part, the master, and the party of the second part, the servant. Typically the indenture bound a person as a servant for a period of 4-7 years, or for a minor until he or she reached 21.

However, life in the plantations was nasty, brutish and short. Governor Thomas Dale of Delaware around 1618 took offence to Richard Barnes uttering *'base and detracting words'* against him. Barnes was ordered to be *'disarmed and have his arms broken and his tongue bored through with an awl and he shall pass through a guard of 40 men and shall be butted by every one of them and at the head of the troop be kicked down and footed out of the fort; and he shall be banished out of James City and the Island, and he shall not be capable of any privilege of freedom in the country.'* This was in effect a death sentence, banishment. Seamstresses who sewed their ladies' skirts too high were whipped. Men who tried to escape were tortured to death. Piracy was a welcome release if the opportunity presented itself.

TOEING THE LINE
When a ship's crew was lined up for inspection or orders, their toes would be along a seam in the deck's planking. The seam was packed with oakum, then sealed with a mixture of pitch and tar, and these lines between planks were about 6 inches apart. There was a punishment for youngsters for any indiscipline, where they had to *'toe the line'* for a designated length of time, in fair or foul weather.

The fourth verse of the shanty, *'The Flash Frigate'* is:
The decks being scrubbed and the rigging coiled down,
It's clean up your bright work which is found all around,
Your gun caps and aprons so neatly must shine,
And in white frocks and trousers you all toe the line.

TOMAHAWKS
These were commonly used by pirates in their heyday – throwing axes.

TON
In the 16th century, the greatest trade was possibly the wine trade. French wine was carried in *'tonneau'*, wooden casks standardised at 2240 lb. Ships were assessed on how many tonneaux (tons, or tuns) they could carry. It is a measure of capacity, not of the weight of a ship.

TOP DRAWER
A naval warship's most important documents and charts were always kept in the top drawer of the chest in the captain's capin.

TOPGALLANT SAIL
The very top sail on a mast – changing this in a Force 9 gale was not a job to volunteer for.

TORTUGA
The most famous pirate island, just off north-west Hispaniola (Haiti and the Dominican Republic). It resembles a great *'sea-tortoise'* or turtle, so was called by the Spanish Tortuga del Mar. The Spanish in Santo Domingo regularly attacked the buccaneers in Western Hispaniola, and Tortuga was more easy to defend and escape

from. Thus the early French settlers and hunters were driven off Hispaniola to settle there. 25 miles long, it has fresh water and excellent defensive positions. The early French governor, Jean le Vasseur, was an engineer who built a 24-gun fort by the harbour to repel Spanish attacks. French governors, like their British counterparts at Port Royal, Jamaica, relied upon buccaneers for local defence. In their turn, buccaneers needed such safe havens and could not let them be taken by the Spanish.

Louis le Golif complained in his 'Memoirs of a Buccaneer' about having to fight two duels on Tortuga to keep suitors at bay. It was reported that its French governor finally imported hundreds of prostitutes to try and wean buccaneers away from *matelotage*, sodomy with their 'mates'. In the early 1670's there was a series of Spanish and French raids, and Petit Goave replaced it as a pirate haven from the late 17th century. Some Tortugans went to French St Dominique and others to Port Royal. The island is now part of Haiti, with a population of 30,000, and is visited by tourists for its beaches, caves, and ruins.

TORTURE
English law in pirate times allowed a child to be hung for stealing a crust of bread. It also allowed torture if one refused to plead at a trial. In 1725, the Scottish pirate Captain Gow was ordered to be pressed to death, (see Pressing) as he would not answer his accusers or make a plea. Upon hearing this sentence at Newgate, he quickly pleaded 'not guilty', but was still hung and displayed in chains at Greenwich. One of the reasons that privateers and pirates of all nations were so cruel to Spanish captives was the nature of the Spanish Inquisition and its practices. Captives were routinely tortured to death. A revolting account from the Venetian Ambassador in Whitehall in 1604 records that 'the Spanish in the West Indies captured two English vessels, cut off the hands, feet, noses and ears of the crews and smeared them with honey and tied them to trees to be tortured by flies and other insects.'

TOUCH AND GO
Yet another old nautical term in common use today – to touch the seabed with the keel for a few moments and then get off again. These were worrying times in shallow waters, or near shoals and reefs.

It also applied to the dangerous practice of bringing two ships together at sea to transfer goods or people. Spars could break or damage done to the ships' sides, so as soon as possible, the ships would leave each other.

TOUCH THE WIND
'Touch the wind', and 'war no more', is no more but to bid him at the Helm to keep her so near to the wind as may be;' no near'. 'Ease the Helm' or 'bear up' is to let her fall to the leeward. 'Steady', that is to keep her right upon that point you steer by; be 'yare' at the Helm, or a fresh man to the Helm. But he that keeps the ship most from yawing, doth commonly use the least motion with the Helm, and those steer the best. – Smith 1691.

TRADE WIND
A regular and steady wind in a certain direction, either perpetual or at a certain

season of the year. The main trade winds are those regular winds due to the earth's motion and the action of the sun, between 30 degrees north and 30 degrees south of the equator. They were invaluable in the days of sail, those south of the equator blowing from the south-east, and those in the northern hemisphere coming from the north-east. The meeting of the Trade Winds just north of the Equator creates the *'Doldrums'* where sailing ships can be becalmed for weeks waiting for a wind to carry them back into the Trades. They were known at the trade winds because their regularity assisted in trade. Thus *'feeling **down in the doldrums'*** meant that sun-baked, listless crews became depressed at a lack of progress. The crews would often take to rowing boats and try to tow the ship towards windier conditions. See Sargasso Sea.

TRANSPORTATION
Because of the need for labour in the colonies, and the country's gaols were full to overflowing, a Royal Proclamation of December 23rd, 1617 allowed any felon except those convicted of murder, witchcraft, burglary or rape, to be transported to Virginia's tobacco plantations or to the West Indies sugar plantations. Women were particularly required as *'breeders'*. Thousands of children were also rounded up off London's streets and sent on the terrible passage. A 1627 letter notes that 1500 children had been sent to Virginia in the last year.
A 17th century word for seizing was *'napping'*, and the napping of children (*kids*) to go as servants to America gave rise to the term **'kidnapping'**. Nearly all of the New World's colonists had a criminal background, or were there against their will. Two London merchants, John Jeffries and Robert Llewellin, had a contract to transport 200 *'passengers'* from Dublin to Virginia in the *Unity*. They could only find 14 suitable *'passengers'* in Irish prisons, so hired a press-gang to comb the city and meet the quota with innocent citizens of the right age and fitness. The *'Black Act'* of 1713 expanded the list of capital offences to over 50, including poaching fish, damaging trees, being caught in a game preserve or stealing a silver spoon. Kidnapping was not an offence. In 1717, an Act as passed allowing courts to sentence offenders directly to transportation, so a huge proportion of offenders were transported for periods of 7 to 14 years. Capital sentences could be transmuted to 14 years or life transportation. From 1720-1769, 70% of the Old Bailey's felons were transported, and 16 acts were passed establishing transportation as the sentence for crimes such as perjury. In the 1730's, 10,000 debtors were released to settle the new colony of Georgia. Conditions were almost as bad as the slave ships.

TREATY OF RATISBONE 1684
An agreement between France and Spain to suppress piracy.

TRENCH MOUTH
Sailors ate off square wooden plates, trenchers, which could be easily stored. They were never washed, and usually became infested with worms, which could give one *'trench mouth'*. The trenchers were cleaned by wiping them with a piece of bread. If there was any type of dessert, the plate was turned over and the flat side used.

TRICING
Tying someone to the rigging to administer '*a taste of the rope's end*', a flogging.

TRIM AND PROPER
The origin of this phrase is maritime – if a ship is 'trim', she will sail at her optimum, when her ballast is correctly stowed, her sails are properly set for the conditions, she handles correctly etc. Then everything is as it should be, in a perfect world.

TRIM THE BOAT/SHIP
Keep her straight, often used when rowing.

TRIPOLI
Barbary Corsair haven in Libya from 1550 until 1835.

TUN
Smith in 1691 wrote: '*If you would have a ship built of 400 tuns, she requires a plank of 4 inches; if 300 tuns, 3 inches, small ships 2 inches, but none less*

TUNIS
Barbary Corsair haven in Tunisia from 1574 to 1830.

TROVE
Everyone has heard of '*treasure-trove*'. The author believes that the origin lies in the French *trouver* (to find), the same word as the Italian *trovare*.

A TRYING SITUATION
The author believes that this term, denoting a spot of difficulty, came from the days of sail. '*Trying*' was the situation in which a ship, in a great storm, lies-to in the trough or hollow of the sea, particularly when she is being blown contrary to her course.

TURN CAT IN THE PAN
This was used by Esquemeling to describe two black pirates who turned into '*villains*' by giving evidence for the Crown against their Captain, Bartholomew Sharp. The saying appears in Heywood's '*Proverbes*' of 1546, meaning to prove perfidious, or to change sides. It may be that cat comes from '*cate*', or cake.

TURNIP-MAN
The Hanoverian George I declared upon his accession to the English throne that he would plant St James' park with turnips and employ a man to hoe them. A popular ballad called '*The Turnip-Hoer*' was written, and his navy was known to Black Bart's crew as '*the Turnip-man's ships.*'

TURTLES
A common part of pirate diet, they could be kept alive on ships for fairly long periods by flipping them over on their backs, and keeping them covered from the heat and doused with water. They were the most common form of meat for ships in port, Governor Molesworth writing in 1684 of Port Royal, that it '*is what masters of ships chiefly feed their men in port, and I believe that nearly 2000 people, black and white,*

Pirates turtling

feed on it daily at Palisadoes Point, to say nothing of what is sent inland.' The extent of the turtle hunting of the time is shown on today's maps, with Turtuguero in Costa Rica, Isla la Tortuga off Venzuela (Salt Tortuga), Dry Tortugas off the Florida Keys (cays), Ile de la Tortue off Haiti (Tortuga) and Green Turtle Cay in the Bahamas, etc.

ULUJ ALI PASHA (1520-1587)
The greatest Barbary Corsair was born Giovani Diongi in Italy and was captured to serve in the galleys. He became a Moslem to survive, and bought a galiot. His bravery made him commander of all the Barbary Corsairs, and he fought brilliantly at the massive naval Battle of Lepanto. His Arabic nickname, *'farta'*, meant *'scurvied'*.

UNDER BARE POLES
When the ship has no sails set.

UP THE CREEK (WITHOUT A PADDLE)
This has obscure origins, but means being in an awkward situation, which would occur if a pirate ship was careening or sheltering and a naval ship came to blockade it.

UNDER THE WEATHER
The seaman standing watch on the weather side of the bow will be subject to rain and spray, and consequently feel *'under the weather'*. This miserable job came to mean felling ill.

UNDER WAY
The origin is *'under weigh'*, when the anchor is raised or weighed and sail is set, and the vessel is getting 'under weigh'.

UPWIND
The direction facing towards where the wind is blowing from. To look downwind is to look in the direction to which the wind is blowing.

URUCANA
The effects of the wind and Gulf Steam flowing north through the Caribbean.

VEA, VEA, VEA
'A fresh spell is to relieve the rowers with another gang. Give the boat more way for a dram of the bottle, who says amends, one and all, 'Vea, vea, vea, vea, vea', that is, they all pull strongly together.' – Smith 1691.

VICE ADMIRAL
From 1525 onwards, these worthies were appointed to stop the 'vice' of smuggling and piracy prevalent in Tudor England, Wales and Ireland, being responsible for law enforcement along portions of the coast. Many vice-admirals, like Peter Carew in Cornwall, and Sir John Perrot in Pembroke, dealt actively with pirates and made great gains from the 'vice'. The first effective laws against piracy date from 1700, with a new system of vice-admiralty courts in all the English colonies, which allowed panels of naval officers and harbour officials to try pirates and summarily sentence them without trial by jury. Allied with the rise in British sea power, piracy was thereafter doomed.

VINEGAR-PISSER
Someone who 'pissed vinegar' was disagreeable and surly.

VIRGIN ISLANDS
In the year 238, the legend is that St Ursula took 11,000 British virgins from Britain and France to Rome to protest against oppression in Britain. On their way home, they were all massacred in a village along the Rhine. It was for these virgins that Columbus named the islands. There is an aphorism that he also named them this, as they reminded him of a 'fat virgin lying on her back'.

WAD
Ball usually made of rope, pressed down the cannon barrel to keep the cannon ball and its charge in place in the rolling seas.

WAGGONER
Old sea atlas, named after Wagaenar, the early Dutch cartographer.

WAKE
The smooth water astern, showing the way a ship has gone. 'If the wake be right astern, we know that she makes good her way forwards; but if to leeward a point or two, we then think to the leeward of her course, but she is a nimble ship, that in turning or tackling about will not fall to the leeward of her wake when she hath weathered it.' – Smith 1691

WALES

The reinforcing pieces of strong timber that go around a ship, a little above her water-line. The gunwale (gunn'l) is mentioned earlier, but the *wales*, or *wailes* are mentioned in Captain Smith's 1691 '*Seaman's Grammar*': '*The half deck is from the main mast to the steerage, and the quarter deck from that to the master's cabin called the round house, which is the utmost of all, but you must understand all those works are brought up together, as near equally as can be from bend to bend, or waile to waile, which are the outmost timbers on the ship's sides, and are the chief strengths of her sides, to which the foot-hooks, beams and knees are bolted, and called the first, second and third bend; but the chain-waile is a broad timber set out amongst them, a little above where the chains and shrouds are fastened together, to spread the shrouds the wider, the better to succour (secure) the mast. Thus the sides and decks are wrought until you come at the gun-waile, which is the upmost waile, (which) goeth about the upmost strake or beam of the upmost deck about the ship's mast, and the ship's quarter is from the main mast aftward*'.

WALKING THE PLANK

There is absolutely no evidence of this ever having occurred with pirates, except in Plutarch's account of Cilician pirates around 100 AD making their Roman captives '*walk home*'. However, the old American sea shanty '*Boston Harbour*' ends with the following verse of interest:

'*Now the old bugger is dead and gone*
And damn his eyes, he's left a son,
And if to us he doesn't prove frank
We'll very soon make him walk the plank –
With a big wow wow, tow row row,
Fal dee rall dee di do day.

WANKER

This increasingly common term of abuse is supposed to date from the 1940's, with an unknown origin, according to all the noted dictionaries the author has consulted. In Esquemeling's '*The Buccaneers of America*', dated 1684-85 (1923 Routledge edition), we find the following description upon page 313 describing Captain Ringrose's shipwreck. Some Indians asked about six men in Ringrose's company who spoke a different language and kept apart from the British pirates. '*We told them they were 'Wankers', which is the name they commonly give to the Spaniards in their own language. Their next question was, if they should kill those Spaniards; but I answered them: "No, by no means; I would not consent to have it done."*' My supposition is, without any philological foundation, that the pirates used to call any Spanish man 'Juan-Carlos', and that the term for a group of Spaniards was 'Juan-Carloses', shortened to 'Wankers'. You heard it here first.

WAR OF JENKINS' EAR

Robert Jenkins (c.1700-1745) was a Welsh merchant captain. The Spanish guarda-costa boarded his brig, the Rebecca, in 1731 in the West Indies, and cut off his ear and sacked his cargo. He complained upon his return to England, and the British commander-in-chief in the West Indies confirmed this event. He then entered the

East India Company as a captain, and was for sometime acting governor of St. Helena, a station on the Eastern trading route. In 1738, Jenkins told a House of Commons committee about his ear, producing it in front of them. There was a public outcry, leading to the 'War of Jenkins' Ear' (1739-1742), which merged with the 'War of the Austrian Succession' (1740-1748) also known as the 'War of Spanish Succession' (1739-48). The latter two wars were also known as 'King George's War'. Everything was inconclusively concluded with the Treaty of Aix-la-Chapelle in 1748. (And who says history is difficult?)

WASHED UP
Something that floats in the sea for a long time generally reaches the shore in a worthless condition. Now, anyone who is 'all washed up' will never be worth anything.

WASTERS (see Bilge)

WATCHES
Throughout recorded history, a 24-hour shipboard day has been divided into 'watches'. Generally, there was a larboard watch and a starboard watch. In English ships, the length of the watch was 4 hours, with the exception of the two dogwatches of 2 hours each.

WATER-LOGGED
When a ship is so filled with water that she is heavy and unmanageable. Possibly the origin is that she would be as easy to control as a log in the open seas.

WAVES
It is important to realise, as with storm forces, the types of seas that pirate ships faced. Small ships in high seas were the most unpleasant places on earth.

Wave Code	Description	Height from trough to crest (feet)
0	Glassy Calm	0
1	Calm, ripples	0-1
2	Smooth, wavelets	1-2
3	Slight	2-4
4	Moderate	4-8
5	Rough	8-13
6	Very Rough	13-20
7	High	20-30
8	Very High	30-45
9	Phenomenal	Over 45, the centre of a hurricane

WEATHER BEATEN
When a ship has been badly damaged by a storm.

WEATHER CONDITIONS
'When there is not a breath of wind stirring, it is **A Calm** or a stark Calm. **A Breeze** is a wind blows out of the Sea, and commonly in fair weather beginning about nine in the

morning, and lasteth till near night; so likewise all night it is from the shore, which is called a **Turnado** or a Sea turn, but this is but upon such coasts where it bloweth most certainly, except it be a storm, or very foul weather, as in Barbary, Egypt and most of the Levant. We have such breezes in most hot countries in Summer, but they are very uncertain. **A Fresh Gale** is that doth presently blow after a calm, when the wind beginneth to quicken or blow. **A Fair Loom Gale** is the best to sail in because the Sea goeth not high, and we bear out all our Sails. A stiffe Gale is so much wind as our Top-sails can endure to bear. An **Eddy-Wind** is checked by the sail, a Mountain, turning, or any such thing that makes it return back again. **It Over Blows** when we can bear no Top-sails. A flaw of wind is **A Gust** which is very violent upon a sudden, but quickly endeth. **A Spout** in the West Indies commonly falleth in those Gusts, which is, , as it were, a small river falling entirely from the clouds, like out of our water Spouts, which make the sea where it falleth rebound in flashes, exceeding high. **Whirle-winds** running round, and bloweth divers ways at once. **A Storm** is known to everyone not to be much less than a tempest, that will blow down Houses, and Trees up by the roots. A **Monsoune** is a constant wind in the East Indies, that bloweth always three Months together one way, and the next three Months the contrary way. A **Hericano** is so violent in the West Indies, it will continue three, four, five weeks, but they have it not past in five, six or seven years; but then it is with such extremity, that the Sea flies like rain, they over-flow the low grounds by the sea, insomuch, that Ships have been driven over tops of high trees there growing, many Leagues into the land, and there left, as was Captain Francis Nelson an Englishman, and an excellent Seaman for one.' – Smith 1691.

WEATHER QUARTER
The quarter of a ship which is on the windward.

WELL RIGGED
Smith (1691) states: 'The rigging (of) a ship as all the ropes or cordage belonging to the mast and yards; and it is proper to say the mast is well rigged, or the yard is well rigged when all the ropes are well sized to a true proportion of her burthen. We say also, when they are too many or too great, that she is over rigged, and doth much wrong a ship in her sailing; for a small weight aloft, is much more in that nature than a much greater below, and the more upright a ship goeth, the better she saileth.'

WELSH CRICKET
A louse, or a tailor. A 'Welsh fiddle' or 'Scotch fiddle' was an itch.

WELSH MILE
'Like a Welsh mile' meant long and narrow. As Max Boyce once famously remarked, Wales would be a massive country, 'bigger than England' if it was ironed out flat.

WET
Liquor, as in 'let's have a wet'. As an adjective it meant that someone was under the influence of alcohol, or prone to drinking too much.

WHIPPING

This was the standard punishment of the times for vagrancy and begging, and could also be ordered by clergymen for *'offences against public decorum'*. The law stated that men. Women or children should be stripped to the waist, tied to a whipping post or run through the streets at the back of a cart, and *'whipped until the body be bloody'.'* Females were publicly whipped until 1817, and men until 1850. The insane were routinely whipped, a *'therapy'* to bring them to their senses. Titus Oates was said to have received 2,000 lashes, being virtually flayed alive. A *'whip-arse'* was a schoolmaster, and to *'lick on the whip'* or *'drink whip'* was to be thrashed severely.

'Ashley's Book of Knots' knot number 508 is a double overhand knot tied in a cat-o'-nine-tails and thence termed a *'blood knot'*: *'it may be double, treble, or even fourfold and is designed to add to the discomforts of whipping'*. The 1801 *'British Mariner's Vocabulary'* tells us that a *'cat-o'-nine-tails'* is *'nine cords about half a yard long fixed upon a piece of thick rope for a handle, having three knots on each at small intervals, nearest one end.'*

WHIP THE CAT

To become intoxicated, or *'whipcat'*. To *'whip'* was to drink extremely quickly. *'Whip-belly'* was weak alcohol. Also, *'whip the cat'* meant to play a practical joke.

WHIPSTAFF

Black Bart used a whipstaff to steer, and captured a ship with a new-fangled steering wheel, but its captain had taken the wheel ashore, much to his disappointment. Captain Henry Mainwaring, in his *'Seaman's Glossary'* of 1623, wrote: *'The Whippe is that Staff which the Steeresman doth hold in his hand, whereby he governed the helme, and doth Port it over from one side to another. It hath a Ring at one end, which is put over the end of the helme, and so comes through the Rowle, up into the Steeridge. In great Ships they are not used: for by reason of the Weight of the Rudder, and the Water which lies upon it in fowle weather they are not able to govern the helme with a Whippe, because conveniently there can stand but one Man at the Whippe.'*

In the earliest days of sailing, the officer gave an order such as *'hard-a-starboard'*, meaning *'push the tiller or steering oar as far as you can to starboard'*, whereby the ship turned hard in the opposite direction, to port. From around 1450, however, a new form of steering was used. Ships had added castles to the main deck, so the steersman had to be lifted to a higher level. The deck had become so high above the rudder that the helmsman needed a remote way of turning the tiller, if he was to be on the deck and see the sails. The answer was the whipstaff, a stout piece of timber which passed through a hole in the deck to a pivot and from there to the end of the tiller. A mechanical advantage of about 4:1 was obtained at the cost of limited rudder movement. The helmsman stood with the whipstaff roughly vertical in front of, or beside, him. The whipstaff was pushed in the direction in which the ship was to turn. By the early 18th century, the ship's wheel was introduced on larger ships. As ship size had continued to increase, ships had become increasingly difficult to control. The steering wheel was connected to the tiller by block and tackle, which provided a considerable increase in mechanical advantage, a smoother rudder operation with less effort.

WHISKY GALORE

This book and film set in Scotland has its origins in fairly recent smuggling in the south-west of Wales, of which the 16th century Sir John Perrot would have undoubtedly approved. *'On the night of the 30th January, 1894, a large merchant ship named the Loch Shiel, laden chiefly with cases of Scotch whisky for Australia, on making the Haven (Milford) for shelter, ran aground on the rocks at the back of Thorn Island, practically the northern boundary of West Angle Bay. On this occasion Mr Mirehouse, of Angle, and the crew of the lifeboat, did some brave work in rescuing the crew of the unfortunate ship, which ultimately became a total wreck. The cargo and wreckage floated about the harbour for weeks after, the Salvage of which did not all find its way to the Receiver of Wrecks.'* (Mason, 1905). Basil Hughes reported on the Pembrokeshire Snippets website that some local cottages walled over cupboards shortly after, and recounts whisky-related wedding festivities in the nearby village of Dale some time after the wreck.

WHISTLE DOWN THE WIND

A very old superstition that whistling at sea will cause the wind to rise. If told you can *'whistle for it'* you are unlikely to receive what you want. Some sailors feared that whistling was the Devil's music, and that one would whistle up a storm. Others did not believe in such superstition, so you could whistle for it (the wind), but a fat lot of good it would do you. *'Not worth a whistle'* means worthless or pointless. *'Wet your whistle'* comes from the days when taverns offered ceramic drinking jugs with a whistle built into the rim or handle. To get a refill, one whistled for service.

WHITE MOUSE

An informer or spy amongst the crew, for the master-at-arms.

WHOLE NINE YARDS

Yards are the timber spars at right angles to the masts, supporting square sails. (Either side of the mast is called a yard-arm). A fully-rigged three-masted ship had three major sails upon each mast. If all nine sails were being used, the *'whole nine yards'* were working.

WHYDAH

Launched in London in 1715, this 100-foot three-masted ship was built as a slave ship for the Triangular Trade. With cloth, alcohol, money, hand tools and weapons, 700 slaves were purchased in Ouidah (Whydah) in West Africa, transported to the Caribbean and exchanged for gold, silver, indigo, dye-woods and cinchona, the source of quinine. However, in February 1717 this profitable trade ended as she was captured by Black Sam Bellamy. The treasure-laden Whydah was wrecked in a north-east gale at Wellfleet, Massachusetts. The ship's bell was recovered in 1985, and altogether over 100,000 artefacts including 2000 coins have been lifted from her.

WILLIAM WILLIAMS 1725-1791

This Welsh privateer was marooned in Nicaragua, and hid from the Spanish with the Rama Indians. His is an amazing story. He lost two sons in the American Civil War, who fought for independence; he built the first theatre in America, at Philadelphia; he was America's first professional scene-painter; he painted America's first known seascape; he taught music and painting; he inspired Benjamin West to paint, and West later became President of the Royal Academy; he wrote a 'Lives of the Great Painters', and he wrote America's first novel, 'The Journal of Penrose, Seaman.' This seaman was formative in the first years of American culture, but is unknown today. The Journal is a wonderful tale of faction, based upon his being marooned among the Rama Indians of the Miskito Coast of Nicaragua, full of detailed descriptions of flora and fauna of the jungle and seas, with a strong anti-slavery message. (See Buried Treasure)

WINDBAG
Originally a nickname for a sailing ship, now a term of abuse for a boastful person, full of wind.

WIND DOG
An incomplete rainbow, signifying the approach of a storm.

WINDFALL
This has come to mean an unexpected bonus, but comes from the days of sail. It was a sudden unexpected rush of wind (falling) from a mountainous shore, which allowed a ship more leeway to move away from it.

WIND OUT OF HIS SAILS
A fast pirate sloop could bear down towards merchant, taking the 'wind out of his sails' thus making him difficult to manoeuvre. This was usually preceded by a warning shot across the bows. The present term 'overbearing' has the same nautical origin, meaning using a position of superiority.

WIND'S EYE
The point from which the wind blows.

WITH PLANKS A FLOAT
The term given to returning ships full of loot, so overloaded with bullion that the waves constantly swept over the deck planking. (This was later the main reason for the Plimsoll Line legislation - unscrupulous owners would deliberately overload ships to claim upon the insurance - men were easy to replace.)

WOODEN HORSE
Described by William Williams, the privateer, in the 18th century, the wooden horse was a form of punishment and torture, used in the military for dereliction of duty and drunkenness. Two planks about 8 feet long were nailed together at a sharp angle to make an uncomfortable 'horse's back'. Four pieces of wood were nailed to make the horses legs, and the horse was places on a stand on truckles, so it could move. A 'head and tail' were added. The miscreant was forced to sit on the horse's

back, his hands tied behind him and sometimes weighted to make the pain worse. Weights, often 8-pound muskets, were attached to each of his legs, to 'stop the horse kicking him off'.

WOODEN SHIPS

'were damp, dark, cheerless places, reeking with the stench of bilge water and rotten meat.' They always leak and are difficult to dry, so pirates often suffered from illnesses brought on by wet damp conditions and no dry attire. Additionally, a pirate ship sometimes needed twice the manning of a merchant ship, with men packed in like sardines. As well as carrying loot and more guns and munitions than the average boat, more people were needed to pose a threat in a fight. Pirates tried to keep the decks clean by washing them down with brandy, and to fumigate below decks by burning pitch and brimstone. The ships were full of disease, cockroaches, fleas and rats. However, rats were often used to supplement the diet of salt beef or pork crawling with maggots, foetid water, and mouldy, slimy bread.

WOOLDING

A particularly nasty piece of torture practised to try to get information from captives. One of Captain Morgan's men, present at the rape of Porto Bello, later wrote to the Secretary of State that 'it is a common thing among the privateers, besides burning with matches and such-like torments, to cut a man to pieces, first some flesh, then a hand, an arm, a leg, sometimes tying a cord about his head and with a stick twisting it till the eyes shoot out, which is called woolding.' It was not invented by the buccaneers, but was a recognised part of the torture called 'cordeles' by the Spanish, used in both secular courts and by the Inquisition to extract confessions.

Bannister hanging from the yardarm

WRACK

To wreck a ship by the action of the waves – see 'Rack and Ruin.'

YARD

Any spar horizontal to a mast, used for suspending sails – the yard-arm was the yard on either side of the mast, which was the easiest place to hang any miscreant from.

YAW

The motion of a ship when it deviates from starboard to port and back again, swinging to either side of its intended course.

YELLOW JACK

Tropical fever or yellow fever, which turned the victims yellow with jaundice and made them spew up black vomit. The 'Yellow Jack' was therefore a flag flown by ships to indicate that there was disease aboard. 'Yellow Jack' was also a particularly nasty term of abuse hurled at someone a pirate did not like. Sometimes a ship might hoist the yellow jack to ward off an attack.

ZEE-ROVERS

Dutch for pirates, copied in the English 'sea-rovers'.